ACCOUNTING & FINANCE

An analytical and evaluative approach to business studies

David Horner

Hodder & Stoughton

A MEMBER OF THE HODDER HEADLINE GROUP

Acknowledgements

Love and thanks to Grahame, Valérie, Morag, Sue, Ian and Karen, and all my Accounts students.

The authors and publisher would like to thank the following for permission to reproduce copyright material:

ASA, p. 38.
Biz/ed, pp. 72, 82.
Cadbury Schweppes, pp. 26, 32, 40, 48, 75, 87.
Dun & Bradstreet UK, pp. 28, 30, 88.
J Sainsbury plc, pp. 33, 49, 50, 52, 78, 90, 157.
Random House UK Ltd. (Century Business Books), p. 35.
The Sunday Times, p. 106.
Times 1000, pp. 42, 71, 75.

Every effort has been made to trace copyright holders but this has not always been possible in all cases; any omissions brought to our attention will be corrected in future printings.

If you have any comments on this book or suggestions for future editions, the Series Editor would be pleased to hear from you on: **gillsp@hotmail.com**

20 00002 078

Orders: please contact Bookpoint Ltd, 78 Milton Park, Abingdon, Oxon OX14 4TD. Telephone: (44) 01235 827720, Fax: (44) 01235 400454. Lines are open from 9.00 – 6.00, Monday to Saturday, with a 24 hour message answering service. Email address: orders@bookpoint.co.uk

A catalogue record for this title is available from The British Library

ISBN 0 340 758376

First published 2000

| Impression number | 10 9 8 7 6 5 4 3 2 1 |
| Year | 2005 2004 2003 2002 2001 2000 |

Copyright © 2000 David Horner

Cover illustration by Jon H. Hamilton
Typeset by Fakenham Photosetting Ltd, Fakenham, Norfolk
Printed in Great Britain for Hodder & Stoughton Educational, a division of Hodder Headline Plc, 338 Euston Road, London NW1 3BH by J. W. Arrowsmith, Bristol.

Contents

Acknowledgements   v

General introduction   1

1: What is accounting?   **8**
Financial and management accounting   8
Users of accounts   9
Links with other topics   12
Art or science?   17

2: Published accounts: the balance sheet and the profit and loss account   **25**
Published accounts   25
The balance sheet   27
Working capital (net current assets)   31
Problems involved in valuing assets   33
Intangible assets   37
Balance sheets   40
Profit and loss accounts   43
Using profit and loss accounts   46
Balance sheet *v.* profit and loss items   53
Window dressing   54
How useful are balance sheet and profit and loss statements?   56

3: Ratio analysis   **66**
What is ratio analysis?   66
Performance ratios   68
Efficiency ratios   72
Liquidity ratios   75
Gearing ratios   79
Shareholder ratios   82
Limitations of ratios   87

4: Cash management and budgeting   **101**
Why is cash flow important?   101
Differences between cash and profit   101
Cash flow forecasts   104
How can a firm avoid cash flow problems?   106
Small firms and cash flow   108
Budgeting   109
Variance analysis   112

5: Costing and break even analysis   **123**
Break even analysis   123

Costing methods 131
Allocating overheads 132
Closing an unprofitable business 136
Why allocate overheads? 139

6: Investment appraisal 145
Capital investment appraisal methods 145
Selecting the best investment appraisal method 148
Issues in investment appraisal 150
Investment and risk 154
Risk aversion and investment appraisal 155
Investment appraisal in the public sector 157

7: Recent issues 168
Shareholder value 168
Company reports 169

8: Numerical data 173
Question 1: Liquidity ratios and working capital management 173
Question 2: Profit and loss accounts 173
Question 3: Costing methods 174
Question 4: Cash flows and window dressing 175
Business reports 176

9: Examining tips 180
Interpreting financial data 180
Applying business theory and knowledge 180
Specific advice on accounting and finance topics 182

Index 185

General introduction

This series of six books is designed specifically to develop the higher levels of skill needed for exam success and at the same time provide you with a critical and detailed insight into the subject as a whole. The books are written by a team of highly experienced examiners and authors and provide you with the information and approach you need for the best results. Whereas a traditional textbook tends to simply provide an explanation of topics, this series concentrates on developing ideas in a more analytical manner. When considering a topic such as cash flow, for example, the book will focus on issues such as: why is cash flow important for firms, why do firms have problems controlling their cash flows, to what extent is it more important than profitability and to what extent can it be forecasted effectively?

The whole approach of the series is intended to develop a questioning and evaluative understanding of business issues. The emphasis is on why certain factors are important rather than merely describing what they are. Reading these books will provide you with new insights into topics and help you to develop a critical view of the issues involved in the different areas of the subject.

In this particular book we cover the following topics:

■ The published accounts: the balance sheet and profit and loss statement.

■ Ratio analysis.

■ Cash flow and budgeting.

■ Costing and break even analysis.

■ Investment appraisal.

We examine the significance of financial issues for firms and examine how managers can interpret and use financial information in their decision making. We also question the value of many accounting techniques and consider their relevance in the modern business world.

Throughout the text we provide up-to-date examples of business behaviour in the form of fact files and numerical investigations. There are also numerous progress checks in each chapter to help you to review your understanding of the topics you have covered so far. Each chapter includes sample exam questions, student answers (including marks and marker's comments) and advice on how to answer specific types of question in the exam. We also provide a chapter that is designed to help you interpret and analyse numerical data from this syllabus area.

Another chapter provides information on how the business concepts covered in the book are usually assessed in examinations and focuses on the key underlying issues in each topic that you are likely to need to answer exam questions; this will be invaluable when it comes to preparing for your exams.

A further chapter in the book focuses on the most recent issues in this area of the syllabus to make sure you are completely up-to-date in your understanding and to provide you with the latest ideas to include in your answers.

Not only will this book provide you with a thorough understanding of the significance of accounting and finance topics, it will also help you develop the approach you need to achieve the top grades. This makes it an invaluable resource for students who want to achieve exam success.

The levels of response approach to marking

In AS and A level Business Studies candidates are assessed by their ability to demonstrate certain key skills. A student's final grade will depend on the extent to which he or she has shown the ability to analyse points, structure their ideas and come to a reasoned conclusion. An A grade candidate is someone who demonstrates these skills consistently whereas a C grade candidate shows them more intermittently. To do well at AS and A level, students not only have to know the issues involved in each topic area; they also have to be able to develop their ideas. It is very important, therefore, that candidates provide some depth to their answers as opposed to leaving many ideas left undeveloped. In most cases students do better by analysing a few key points in their answers rather than by listing many different ideas. Unfortunately, many students find it difficult to expand on their initial points; although they often demonstrate a good knowledge of the issues involved they do not necessarily find it easy to explore these ideas further. The aim of this series of books is specifically to help you develop your ideas in more depth, which will enable you to do better in the exam.

The basic approach to assessment at AS and A Level is the same for all the examination boards and is known as levels of response marking. In its simplest form, the mark you get depends on the skill you have demonstrated. The higher the skill shown in your answer, the higher your final mark.

There are four main levels of skill assessed at A level. These are

- Synthesis and evaluation (the highest level skill).
- Analysis.
- Explanation and application.
- Identification (the lowest level skill).

As you can see, the 'identification' of relevant factors is the lowest level skill. This means that listing ideas will not in itself achieve a high grade. It is important that you explain these points (i.e. show what they mean by them), analyse them (i.e. show why they are significant) and evaluate them (i.e. weigh up their relative importance).

In a typical nine mark question, the mark scheme may look something like this:

Candidate *evaluates* relevant factors – 9–7 marks.

Candidate *analyses* relevant factors – 6–5 marks.

Candidate *explains* relevant factors – 4–3 marks.

Candidate *identifies* relevant factors – 2–1 marks.

A candidate who simply identifies factors can only achieve a maximum score of two out of nine. Regardless of how many different points he or she makes, if all they have done is to list ideas they cannot get more than two marks in total. To move up the levels and gain more marks, candidates need to demonstrate the higher level skills. Unfortunately, most textbooks spend so much time explaining ideas that they cannot do much to help your ability to analyse and evaluate. This series focuses throughout on these higher level skills to help you move up the levels of response in the exam and maximise your grade.

Imagine you were faced with a question that asked you to: 'Discuss the factors that might affect whether a firm went ahead with an investment decision.' A good answer would identify a few relevant factors, explain what is meant by them, analyse their relevance and then discuss their importance. Following is an example:

'A firm's decision to invest will depend on the initial investment, the expected returns, the risk and the opportunity costs. The first thing a firm may consider is whether the firm generates a suitable return – it may do this by calculating the average rate of return; this return will be compared with alternatives elsewhere. If the return is higher than those available elsewhere, taking account of the risk involved the firm is likely to proceed. However, the decision to invest may depend on the timing of the payments and so the payback and net present value methods of investment appraisal may also be considered; the payback will highlight when the initial investment is recovered (particularly important for high risk projects), the net present value will take account of the time value of money. A combination of all three methods is likely to be used and compared against the firm's own investment criterion before a decision is made. The firm must also consider whether it can raise the necessary funds – it may be that a project generates a very high return but the firm may not be able to raise the necessary funds. However, non-financial factors may also be important, for example, the impact on the firm's corporate image or the impact on stakeholders. A decision may be financially attractive but may not be selected because of its effect on the environment, for example. The relative importance of the financial factors compared to the non-financial ones will depend on the managers' and owners' values and attitudes.'

This a strong answer that takes a few points and develops them in some depth. In comparison, consider this answer:

'Risk. Expected returns. The cost of borrowing (will not invest if high). The impact of stakeholders. The payback period (better if shorter). The average rate of return (better if longer). Net present value (better if bigger). Opportunity costs.'

This answer has many ideas, however, all of them are left undeveloped and so it is much weaker than the previous answer.

More recent mark schemes adopt a slightly different approach in which content, analysis and evaluation are each given a mark, as in the example below. As you can see in this case (which is the mark scheme for an essay) you can gain up to eight marks for content, eight for analysis and sixteen for evaluation. Within each category the levels approach is used so that strong evaluation can be awarded up to sixteen marks, whereas more limited evaluation may only get one or two marks. The basic principles of this scheme are similar to the original levels of response; certainly the message to candidates is clear: the higher marks require analysis and evaluation; the best marks require good analysis and evaluation!

A content-laden answer would only get a maximum of eight marks.

Example mark scheme

SKILL	CONTENT	APPLICATION	ANALYSIS	EVALUATION
MAXIMUM NUMBER OF MARKS	8	8	8	16
Level of response	8–5 marks Three or more relevant factors identified	8–6 marks Full explanation of factors	8–6 marks Full analysis using theory appropriately and accurately	16–11 marks Mature judgement shown in arguments and conclusions
	4–3 marks Two relevant factors identified	5–3 marks Some explanation of two or more factors	5–3 marks Analysis with some use of relevant theory	10–5 marks Judgement shown in arguments and/or conclusions
	2–1 marks One relevant factor identified	2–1 marks Some explanation of one factor	2–1 marks Limited analysis of question	4–1 marks Some judgement shown in text or conclusions
	0 marks No knowledge shown	0 marks No application or explanation	0 marks No analysis present	0 marks No judgement shown

The key to success in examinations is to consistently demonstrate the ability to analyse and evaluate – this involves exploring a few of the points you have made. All of the books in this series take an approach that should develop your critical ability and make it easier for you to discuss your ideas in more depth.

The higher level skills

What is analysis?

To analyse a point you need to show why it matters. Why is it relevant to the question? Why is it important? Having made a point and explained what it actually means, you need to discuss its significance either by examining what caused it or by exploring its effect on the business.

Example: 'Analyse the ways in which a firm might reduce its break even level of ouput.'

A firm may reduce its break even level of output by cutting costs (*point made*). Costs are fixed and variable. Firms could cut fixed costs by moving to smaller premises where the rent is lower. It could reduce variable costs by using cheaper materials or paying lower wages. With lower costs the firm would not have to sell as many items to break even (*explanation of how break even could be reduced*). However, these actions could have negative effects on the firm. It may not be possible to produce as much in smaller premises (assuming the firm can move in the first place). Cutting costs on materials may lead to a poor quality product and a loss of sales. Cutting wages may lead to industrial action and a loss of output.

These adverse consequences should be considered before proceeding with any cost cutting exercise. It may be better to try decreasing break even by increasing price (although the firm needs to consider the price sensitivity of its products) (*analysis of the impact of cost cutting*).

Example: 'Analyse the possible reasons for a low return on capital employed.'

A firm's return on capital employed may be low because of low sales (*point made*). Sales may have fallen due to internal or external reasons. Internally the firm may have made production errors (for example, defects in the product) or marketing mistakes (for example, charging too high a price). Externally sales may have fallen due to a change in the economic environment, such as an increase in interest rates or a fall in GDP (*explanation of why sales may have fallen*).

With a fall in sales the return on capital employed will fall assuming that the profit margin has stayed constant. The greater the fall in sales the greater the fall in the return on capital employed. However, if the profit margin is higher (for example, due to lower unit costs or a higher price) it may be that the return on capital employed increases even if sales have gone down. The firm may sell less but make more on each item so the overall return is higher (*analysis of the impact of a fall in sales on the return on capital employed*).

What is synthesis?

Synthesis occurs when an answer is structured effectively. Essentially it involves having a well organised answer rather than leaving it up to the reader to make sense of the argument. In a 'discussion' question this means presenting an argument for, an argument against and then a conclusion.

Synthesis tends to come from planning your answer rather than starting writing immediately. Whenever you face a question, try to determine what each paragraph is intended to do before you actually begin to write the answer out in full. This should lead to a more organised response. A final paragraph to bring together the arguments is also recommended.

What is evaluation?

Evaluation is the highest skill and involves demonstrating some form of judgement. Once you have developed various points, you have to show which one(s) are most important or under what circumstances these issues are most likely to be significant. Evaluation involves some reflection of the arguments you have developed already and some thought as to which aspects are most important. This often involves standing back from your argument to decide what would make your ideas more or less relevant and, under what circumstances would one course of action be chosen rather than another?

Example: 'Discuss the value of ratio analysis in business decision making.'

Ratio analysis places one number in context by comparing it with another. For example, a firm's profits may be compared to its capital employed or its sales. By doing this it is possible to analyse information more effectively *(point made)*. For example, if a firm has made a profit of £50 million this may seem to be a very successful business.

However, this depends on the size of the firm. If the capital employed is £500 million then its return on capital employed is only 10%, which is not particularly high. In comparison, if a firm makes £2,000 profit this may not seem significant. If, however, the capital employed is £4,000 this represents a 50% return, which is impressive *(explains the value of ratios)*.

However, analysts must treat ratio analysis with care. This is because the figures may not be up-to-date. Many ratio calculations are based on figures extracted from the final accounts. The problem with this is that the final accounts are often out of date and only show the firm's financial position on a particular date, which may not be representative.

Ratio analysis also tends to focus on quantitative data and not include qualitative information. Even if a firm has a high ROCE, an investor might be wary if the morale within the firm is poor and the management appears to have failed to invest for the long-term *(analyses the value of ratios)*.

Overall, the value of ratios will depend on the quality of the information used and the skill of the user. The more relevant and up-to-date the data is, the more useful ratio analysis should be. Similarly, the more experienced the analyst and the more that the ratios are placed in the context of past results or other firms in the industry the more valuable this type of analysis should be.

Ratios cannot solve a firm's problems or tell an investor what to buy but they can indicate potential problems or areas that are worth investigating in greater detail *(evaluation of issues involved)*.

To evaluate your arguments you need to think carefully about whether the points you have made earlier in your answer are always true. What makes them more or less true? What makes the impact more or less severe? To what extent can the firm avoid or exploit the situation you have described?

To evaluate effectively you must imagine different organisations and think about what would influence them to act in one way or another? What would make the impact of change greater or smaller? Evaluation, therefore, requires a broad appreciation of the factors that influence a firm's decisions and an awareness of the variety of organisations present in the business world.

We hope you find these books useful; they are designed to be very different from a typical textbook, in that we want to help you to use ideas and think about their importance. We also want to provide you with new insights into topics and convey some of the passion and enthusiasm we have for such a fascinating subject.

What is accounting?

Stakeholder
any group or individual affected by a firm's activities. Stakeholders would include the following groups: workers, managers, directors, shareholders, trade unions, suppliers, customers, local communities, pressure groups, the government (local, central and European) and the media.

KEY TERMS

Financial accounting
the broad range of activities that centres around bookkeeping and the construction and analysis of the final accounts of the business (i.e. the profit and loss account, the balance sheet and the cash flow statement).

Management accounting
involves the numerical techniques, forecasts and systems designed to meet the needs of managers.

Accounting involves the preparation and use of financial data for decision making purposes. This data is vital for firms to assess their progress and the effectiveness of their actions; it is also important in the planning process. For example, managers will assess the value of their business at any time, the profits made over the last trading period and the profitability of different projects. However, this information is not simply of interest to managers – it will also be examined by a variety of stakeholder groups, such as employees, suppliers, potential investors and the government.

There are in fact two types of accounting: **financial accounting** and **management accounting**.

Financial and management accounting

Financial accounting uses historical data to construct the final accounts of the business. In the case of companies these must be audited. This involves an outside agency (a firm or an individual) checking that the final accounts of the firm give a 'true and fair' view of the firm's trading. To do this the auditor will look at the valuation methods used by the firm and also check a sample of the firm's debtors to validate their authenticity. If the auditors are not satisfied with the firm's own accounting systems then they will ask the firm to reconstruct their accounts subject to more stringent rules, until they agree that the accounts do present a 'true and fair view'. Company accounts are publicly available and can be used by both inside and outside parties to interpret and analyse the firm's performance.

PROGRESS CHECK

Given the legal status of companies, why do you think external auditing is necessary for this type of business?

Management accounting is a series of techniques used by managers within a firm to help make decisions. Financial data and information will be used by managers for planning and control purposes and to help them develop policies for the future. Common areas of management accounting will involve costing products, appraisal of investment projects and budgeting for different areas of the business.

PROGRESS CHECK

Classify each of the following financial activities into either management or
financial accounting. Explain your reasoning.
1 Constructing cash flow forecasts.
2 Variance analysis.
3 Writing the director's report.
4 Ratio analysis.
5 Investment appraisal.
6 Break even analysis.

Although both of these branches of accounting use financial data there are major
differences between them. Financial accounting is mainly used externally by those
outside the firm. It involves the presentation of the firm's records and performance
and it is concerned with historical data (usually the previous year in question).
Management accounting is concerned not with the past but with the future and is
used for planning. Financial accounting is governed by externally set rules and regulations known as FRSs and SSAPs. Management accounting does not require rules
to be set out as it is only being used internally by managers.

**Accounting helps managers see where they have been
and decide where they need to go next.**

PROGRESS CHECK

Consider whether financial or management accounting is more useful to
managers.

FACT FILE

The world's largest
accounting firms (1997):

	World fee income ($ million)	UK rank
1 Andersen Worldwide	11300	2
2 Ernst & Young	9100	4
3 KPMG	9000	3
4 Coopers & Lybrand	7541	1
5 Deloitte Touche Tohmatsu	7400	6
6 Price Waterhouse	6520	5
7 BDO	1450	8
8 Grant Thornton	1403	7
9 Moores Rowland	1063	—
10 RSM (Robson Rhodes)	1060	10

(Note: Price Waterhouse and
Coopers & Lybrand merged in
mid 1998)

The value of accounting to a firm is undeniable. It keeps a record of what has
occurred and helps assess future projects. It places a value on the activities of a business and allows managers to measure the return they are generating in financial
terms. Accounting statements also enable various stakeholder groups, including
investors, to assess a firm's performance, to monitor its progress over time and compare it with other organisations. Obviously the value of this comparison is reduced
if the way in which the accounts are produced varies and/or if non-financial factors
are important; nevertheless accounting does provide information that is valuable for
monitoring and for the decision making process.

Users of accounts

In most finance questions you will be asked to interpret financial data and make
recommendations based on this to a party that has a particular interest in the firm's
accounts. This means you will have to look at the information and present your
findings from a certain perspective. Each interested party will have their own objectives and these may well conflict with each other. A significant increase in profit
may be welcomed by shareholders but interpreted by employees as evidence that
they are being underpaid, relative to their contribution to the business. This means
your view of the accounts may vary depending on your perspective. An increase in

the amount of cash held may be desirable if you are risk averse, but greater investment in acquisitions may be more attractive if you are more willing to take a risk. Delaying payment to suppliers may be appealing to the managers as the firm can earn greater interest on the money held, however, may be undesirable from a supplier's viewpoint because it is bad for their cash flow.

PROGRESS CHECK

The following is a list of possible interested parties who wish to use a firm's accounts. For each group, identify two possible reasons why they would be interested in the firm's accounts:

Group	Motives
Example: trade unions	• Look for money for wage claims. • To monitor job security (if a firm is making losses then it may shed labour).
Central government Suppliers Banks Rival firms Customers	

Table 1.1

PROGRESS CHECK

Evaluate the usefulness of accounting data to different stakeholder groups.

Do accounts show the 'true' picture?

As you will discover through reading this book, accounting is not the 'exact science' that you may have thought that it was. It is commonly believed that numbers are factual and objective and show the true position of a business. However, either for honest or for more devious reasons, the numbers presented in accounts can be misleading. This might be done in order to provide an unfair advantage to one group of people within the firm or the business as a whole. For example, particular managers may manipulate the data to create the impression their section of the business has done well or the directors may try to make the business itself look more impressive.

Accounting regulation

With this in mind, it is the role of the Accounting Standards Board (ASB) to control the way in which accounts are drawn up and presented.

Part of this process includes the auditing procedure, which is meant to reassure interested parties that the published accounts do represent a 'true and fair view'. However, despite this regulation there have been a number of high profile cases recently where auditors have seemingly failed to predict or even see suspect financial data. The case against Coopers & Lybrand (before the merger with Price Waterhouse) concerned the lack of vigilance when auditing Robert Maxwell's pub-

FACT FILE

PriceWaterhouse Coopers was fined a record £1.2 million for several shortcomings in the auditing of Robert Maxwell's publishing empire.

lishing empire, including 35 separate complaints. For example, it was not known until after Robert Maxwell's death that the pension funds had been raided of £425 million. A loan of £37.5 million from Maxwell pension funds to another part of the empire had gone unchecked by the auditors.

Regulators were also concerned with Price Waterhouse's earlier auditing of the failed Bank of Credit and Commerce International (BCCI). The bank, at its peak, was supposedly worth more than $20 billion, but when it failed, the bank was, in effect, worthless. The case against Price Waterhouse is an example of how $13 billion could disappear without being noticed by the auditors. These cases highlight that even well-known and well respected auditors cannot completely guarantee that the published figures do present a 'true' picture.

In the last twenty years there has also been a dramatic increase in the amount of window dressing used in company accounts. These are techniques used to make a company's financial position look more appealing. They are perfectly legal but involve interpreting accounting rules in a way that is particularly flattering to the business involved. When it was first set up, one of the priorities of the ASB was to tighten up on established window dressing techniques on the grounds that people were being misled about companies' financial position. Whilst a number of changes have been made to accounting rules since then there is no doubt that window dressing still exists. This means that all analysts of accounts must be careful in their interpretation of the figures.

What are the 'rules' of accounting?

To provide guidelines for businesses the accounting profession has set 'rules' that must be followed when drawing up accounts. These were originally known as Statements of Standard Accounting Practice (SSAPs) but are gradually being replaced by Financial Reporting Standards (FRSs). At present there are 16 different SSAPs and over ten different FRSs. These are wide ranging and cover issues from how to value assets to how to deal with research and development expenditure.

Accounting concepts

Underlying all these rules and regulations are a set of rules known as the accounting concepts. These are used as guidelines for how the final accounts should be drawn up. Although a specific knowledge of these is not required by most examination boards, it is useful to see how these influence the way in which accounts are constructed. The concepts are defined as follows:

- Firms are classed as **going concerns**. This means that they are expected to continue trading into the future. As a result of this, assets would be valued at cost rather than selling price, since the firm is not expecting to sell all of its fixed assets at this moment.

- **Business entity** refers to the fact that a firm and its owner should be considered separate entities. It is crucial that business expenses and personal expenses are kept separate. This will be hard for sole traders, for example, as the business car would be the same car as is used personally by the proprietor. In this case, the expenses should be carefully recorded and kept separate. Any business resources used up as a personal expense would be considered to be drawings.

FACT FILE

Companies are not legally obliged to follow the accounting standards, although they must state whether or not they do. If they adopt very different policies from those set out in the standards, they must state this and give reasons for it. Directors of companies are required by the 1985 Companies Act to prepare accounts that give a 'true and fair view' of the state of affairs of the company and of its financial position at the end of the financial year. Any movement away from using accounting standards may make this difficult to do and the directors may be liable to prosecution. In practice, the standards are, therefore, mandatory except in very unusual circumstances.

- **Prudence,** also known as conservatism, suggests a firm should be cautious when drawing up accounts. This concept influences the recognition of when a sale occurs as well as the valuation of assets (current and fixed). To be prudent in accounts a firm should not anticipate sales (unless the order has been received). Also, we should, where possible, anticipate extra expenses.

- **Historical cost** is the basis for valuation of assets and it means that assets should be valued at their cost, due to this being verifiable and objective.

- **Matching concept** means that items of expenditure should be matched against the period in which the expenses generate revenue. If a firm buys materials that it uses to produce goods for resale, then the firm would only include the materials as an expense if the goods are sold. If a firm produces goods in one year but does not sell the goods until the next year, then the cost of those materials would not appear as an expense until the second year. In other words, we are matching the expense against the period in which they generate revenue. The matching principle is used when we provide for depreciation for fixed assets. A fixed asset is long lasting and therefore the asset will be 'charged' for over its useful life.

- **Consistency** relates to how firms must choose from a variety of methods for valuing assets (both fixed and current) and that once a method has been chosen the same method should be maintained. This will enable comparisons to be made (as we are dealing 'like with like'). Being consistent also makes it harder for firms to distort accounts for the advantage of the directors.

PROGRESS CHECK

If we follow the matching concept, how do you think we should account for research and development expenditure in the accounts? Justify your arguments.

FACT FILE

Under *Financial Reporting Standard 10* covering the cost of intangible assets, which was introduced in 1998, all football clubs have had to write off the value of a transfer fee over the life of the player's contract.

Although there are similarities between the accounting rules of different countries they are not exactly the same and each country has its own set of accounting regulations.

PROGRESS CHECK

Consider the possible value of having internationally agreed accounting standards.

Links with other topics

Although this book is concerned with accounting and finance, it is important to appreciate the close links with other topics. The inter-relationships between finance, the other functions of a business and the external environment are incredibly important.

Lowering interest rates

For example, if interest rates were cut by the Bank of England's Monetary Policy Committee this can have numerous effects on a firm's activities and its financial position (see Figure 1.1):

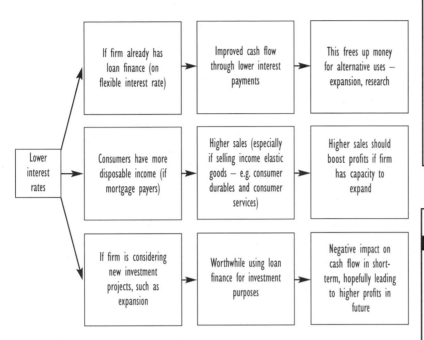

Figure 1.1

Lowering interest rates will usually have a positive impact on a firm's cash flow as less money will be needed to be spent on interest payments. Sales may also increase due to higher consumer demand and this may lead to higher profits. A firm might also undertake more investment projects, as the cost of borrowing is cheaper. It may also decide to hold more cash and stock because the opportunity cost has fallen. Clearly then, the external environment can affect a firm's financial position. The finance function will also be involved in and affected by the decisions of other areas of the business:

- A proposed price cut by the marketing function will have an impact on the firm's profit margins and return on capital employed; the finance function must decide if this is sustainable.

- A plan by marketing and operations to increase capacity and output will require the finance department to consider whether the project is actually profitable, if the capital needed for the project can be raised (and if so how) and to plan the potential impact on cash flow.

- A proposal by the human resources function to increase the salaries of certain staff will have to be costed – can the firm afford this?

FACT FILE

Examples of differences in national standards:

1996 profits compared between firms using domestic rules and US rules

	Dom-ESTIC	USA STANDARDS
Ericsson, Sweden (Skr million)	7,110	7,976
Glaxo-Wellcome (UK £ million)	1,997	979
Alcatel Alsthom (France Fr million)	2,725	(1,198)

KEY POINTS

Differences in international accounting standards means it is more likely that:

- comparisons between firms in different countries will be less meaningful
- firms may not be able to borrow money from foreign bankers or investors
- shareholders will be more likely to invest money in domestic firms
- firms have an accounting system that is more suitable for them.

Reducing marketing expenditure

Changes in the financial position in one area will impact on other functions. For example, imagine that a firm decides to cut its marketing budget in a drive to improve its cash flow position. The possible implications from this change in policy are shown in Figure 1.2.

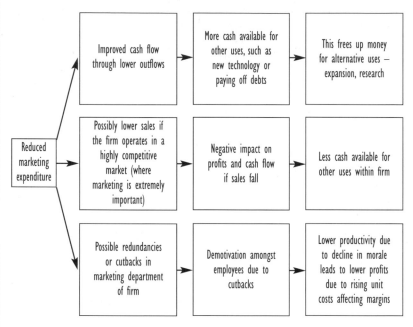

Figure 1.2

The initial cut will have a positive effect on the firm's financial position short-term. However, it could have negative effects on the firm's performance in the future. The cutback may well reduce the level of sales, which will obviously have a negative impact on its cash flow over time. There may also be an effect on the human side of the firm. The cutback in spending may affect the staff of the firm, especially those who would have been responsible for spending this money. It may be the case that the cutback is just seen as a minor inconvenience to the workers. However, it could also be the case that staff are made redundant or that the cutback increases pressures on staff to an unacceptably high level. Either way, this might have an unwelcome effect on the firm's productivity.

The overall effect would depend on how badly sales and morale are affected in relation to the benefits of the cost savings in the marketing department. This in turn will depend on a variety of factors, including the way money is being used and the external competitive environment. If the firm was clearly wasting money on ineffective marketing activities (for example, badly targeted advertising) the effect of the cutback may be broadly positive. If, however, competitors are about to launch a new product it may have been better to increase the marketing budget rather than decrease it.

It is important that you consider how any change in the business environment will affect the different areas of the firm. Copy out the following table and fill in possible effects of the change that will affect the firm. The first two have been partly completed.

	ACCOUNTING	MARKETING	OPERATIONS	HUMAN
UK to enter Euro in two years	Save money in transaction costs	Change pricing policy	?	?
New advanced computer system introduced	High capital expenditure	?	?	?
Move to just-in-time stock policy	?	?	?	?
Trade union pressure for higher wages	?	?	?	?
Cutting out a layer in the hierarchy	?	?	?	?
Take-over of a smaller rival firm	?	?	?	?

Table 1.2

Further issues

The activities of business are clearly interrelated and the finance function forms an integral part of a firm's success. Effective organisation of the firm's finances ensures it remains liquid (and survives) and that it has the funds it needs as and when it needs them; effective financial planning helps ensure that managers choose the right projects and limits the risk of failure.

Consider how financial planning might contribute to a firm's success.

However, it is important to remember that financial analysis can only help managers with decisions – it cannot guarantee success. The effectiveness of management accounting, for example, will depend on the reliability and relevance of the data, the ability of the manager to interpret the data effectively, to select the right plan of action and to ensure the plan is properly implemented. If financial analysis highlights a falling return on capital employed, for example, this is obviously a useful piece of information, however, it does not in itself help solve anything. The managers must identify why this has happened and what to do about it. They must then take appropriate action.

It is also important to remember that numbers will only be useful if the right questions are being asked. Investment appraisal, for example, can help a manager to select between particular projects but it is up to the manager to choose the right projects to assess in the first place. Similarly, if the overall business strategy is wrong, the numbers might highlight this but they will not indicate the 'right' strategy unless the the 'right' questions are asked.

Another point to remember is that management accounting is often based on forecasts of future costs and revenues. It is worth considering how this data has been predicted – has research been used and, if so, how effective is it likely to be? Have past figures simply been extrapolated forward – again is this appropriate for this type of calculation? In the end, the analysis can only be as useful as the underlying data and managers will often need to combine their findings with their own experience and intuition. In the case of financial accounting, the information provided is backward looking – it reports on what has happened. This is useful to assess what has been achieved, however, you cannot necessarily use this to make a decision about the future. Investors who buy shares in a company because it has done well in the past may be unpleasantly surprised by what happens in the next few years.

> **Using financial accounting to make a decision is sometimes compared to driving a car using the rear view mirror. It shows you where you have gone, not where you are going.**

Another key issue when considering the value of a firm's accounts and financial plans, is that they only deal with quantifiable data. As stakeholders focus far more on the social and ethical policies of organisations, traditional accounting procedures seem rather limited. Similarly, given the importance of issues such as effective leadership, an innovative culture and the effective management of knowledge, it is obvious that standard accounting methods will not necessarily highlight or value the key factors in a successful business.

PROGRESS CHECK

The Body Shop Trading Charter

'We aim to achieve commercial success by meeting our customers' needs, the provision of high quality, good value products with exceptional service and relevant information which enables customers to make informed and responsible choices.

Our trading relationships of every kind – with customers, franchisees and suppliers – will be commercially viable and mutually beneficial and based on trust and respect ...

We aim to ensure that human and civil rights, as set out in the Universal Declaration of Human Rights, are respected throughout our business activities ... We will use environmentally sustainable resources wherever technically and economically viable ... We will promote animal protection throughout our business activities ...'

Questions

1 Is profit a relevant measure of business performance for the Body Shop?
2 Discuss how its 'success' might be measured.

Accounting information must, therefore, be placed in context; it provides more data to help managers make decisions but it must be placed alongside other factors, which may even include a manager's gut feeling!

PROGRESS CHECK

Consider the possible limitations of financial planning.

Art or science?

One of the great questions surrounding accounting is whether it is an art or a science. Does it lead to predictable results each time or are accountants artists who are able to paint whatever picture they want? The answer is probably a little of both. The various accounting rules and conventions certainly govern an accountant's behaviour; they determine how items should be treated and how published accounts should be drawn up. Nevertheless there is still room for interpretation – as with all rules people find ways of bending them and redefining them. And as soon as one rule is changed some firms will find another one that can be interpreted differently or a whole new area of accounting which has not really been covered before. This happened with the valuing of brands in the 1980s and 1990s; once one firm valued its brands others were quick to follow. With the rapid growth in this practice the accounting profession had to examine the way this was being done and whether it should or should not be allowed.

In some cases the debate over what figures to include in the accounts is not due to a deliberate attempt by accountants to mislead, but because there is genuine uncertainty about how to apply the rules. Imagine you have to depreciate a newly installed computer system – how would you estimate its useful working life? Is it 5 years, 3 years, 2 years? Given the rate of change in this industry it is genuinely difficult to know how long it will last. What about a newly built runway, or an oil rig? Are these likely to last 10 or 5 years? It is probably not surprising in these cases if accountants have different views about the useful working lives of these assets.

Accounting is therefore a science in the sense that in most cases items will be treated in a similar way. If we repeated the 'experiment' of producing a set of accounts for a firm in most areas we would get the same result, regardless of the accountant. However, there is certainly some room for creativity, which is why analysts need to be careful when examining financial data and make sure they have examined the underlying principles and assumptions.

Summary charts

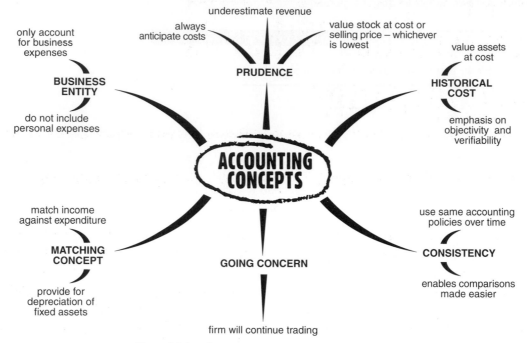

Figure 1.3 Accounting concepts

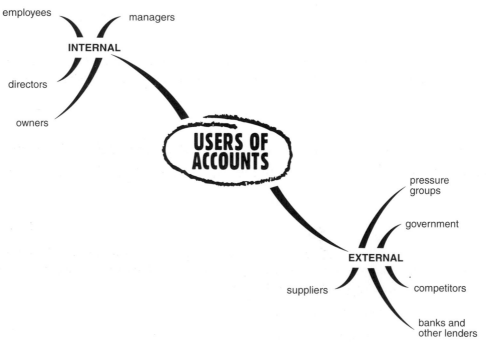

Figure 1.4 Users of accounts

Approaching exam questions: What is accounting?

Analyse the differences between financial and management accounting.

(9 marks)

The temptation in answering this question is to describe the main areas of financial and management accounting and to go into too much detail on the content of these. This is not wanted – it is the differences that are important. Areas to consider could include:

1   The users of each type of accounts – management accounting usually has internal users; financial usually has external. However, these boundaries are not rigid (i.e. employees may also look at final accounts).
2   Time horizon – management is forward looking; financial is historical (backward looking). However, there is not always a clear cut distinction, for example, budgeting can be based on past trends.
3   Regulation – management accounting is not subject to any external 'rules'; financial accounting is subject to FRSs (you might examine why this is the case).
4   However, it is worth stressing there are similarities, for example, both types of accounting are based on financial data.

When answering this question it is important to avoid simply making points. Try to go into more detail and develop your discussion of the differences. For example, why is financial accounting more regulated than management?

To what extent does the increasing number of media reports of firms window dressing their accounts indicate that more regulation of accounts is needed?

(11 marks)

This question can be broken into two sections: the reason why regulations may need to be tightened and the reasons justifying the status quo. A 'to what extent …' question requires evaluation in the answer to score highly. It can be answered by weighing up both sides of the argument.

Possible ideas to include in this answer would be:

1   Does the increase in the reporting of window dressing mean there has been an increase in the incidence of window dressing? It may be the case that it is just more intense media pressure, which makes it seem as if there are more cases. As the media scrutinises firms' accounts, more examples may come to light.

2   Would tightening regulations be desirable? Would it end window dressing or actually create more oppor-
    tunities for it?

Remember, it is a case of weighing up the benefits and problems of tightening regulations that should be
included in this answer. For example, is the number of cases significant or the actual consequences of window
dressing? How would the regulations be altered?

Student answers

To what extent should firms be allowed to regulate themselves when drawing up their final accounts?

(11 marks)

Student answer

One advantage of allowing firms to be self-regulating is that it would save time and money for them by not having to employ auditors to check over their accounts. This money could then be used elsewhere for expansion or for higher dividends. The government would also make savings by not having to spend time in implementing acts of parliament designed to regulate a firm's accounting procedures.

It is likely that if firms were left alone then they would stick to drawing up their accounts in an honest way. If they did not stick to the rules then they would gain a bad reputation and people may stop buying products from them. For example, the misuse of company pension funds by Robert Maxwell led to campaigns to boycott products produced by his firms. Also, there are plenty of financial analysts who may expose firms when they are engaging in creative accounting, which would lead to pressure on the firms to behave.

Marker's comments

This answer shows some knowledge of the topic area and has some valid examples (Maxwell) that are relevant. However, the answer is probably a little naive in that it assumes that firms will not use creative accounting if left to regulate themselves. At present in the UK companies are regulated in that they have to have their accounts audited by an external body. Even with this form of regulation we still have cases whereby firms have attempted to distort their accounts through window dressing their profits and balance sheets to present the firm in a more favorable manner. Would they really change their behaviour if they were self-regulating?

However, the student does consider wider issues about what benefits might occur if firms self-regulated. However, the dangers of self-regulation are not explored. A careful argument would have considered the disadvantages of removing regulation, such as investors being cheated and misled. It could also have considered that it would depend on the type and effectiveness of the existing regulation.

At it stands, this is a one-sided answer that assumes firms would not be creative; to evaluate the other side of the argument must be explored (i.e. that they might mislead analysts, either deliberately or just because of different accounting policies) and judgement needs to be shown (for example, what would make firms more likely to exploit self regulation? What would make them less likely?

A conclusion to this would have probably recognised that, while any regulation might stifle enterprise, some is needed in this area to protect some of the firm's stakeholders (suppliers, investors and creditors). It is more a question of degree of regulation rather than whether any regulation is needed at all.

Mark: Content 2/2, Application & Analysis 2/6, Evaluation 0/3. Total = 4

Evaluate the use of financial accounts to the shareholders of a firm.

(11 marks)

Student answer

The financial accounts of the firm include the balance sheet and the profit and loss account. These will show a shareholder how well a firm has performed over a given period of time (usually one year). The balance sheet would be useful to a shareholder because it shows the assets of the firm and where the money came from to buy these assets. The shareholder can then see if the firm has borrowed too much. For example, if a firm had financed a significant amount of its assets through borrowing, then the firm could be in danger of not being able to meet the interest payments on this debt if interest rates were to rise.

The profit and loss account will show the shareholder how much the firm has earned in the year. The profit can be compared with other firms, or last year's profit in order to see if it is satisfactory. More importantly, the shareholder can look at the profit and compare this with the dividends that have been paid out. It may be the case that the dividends are low when the firm has made a high profit, which may lead the shareholder to sell the shares that they hold.

However, all the information in the final accounts would need to be taken into consideration with other information available. The notes to the accounts would provide useful information of the accounting policy of the firm.

Marker's comments

This answer is generally solid but contains no real evaluation. The student seems to understand what the final accounts will show and highlights that further information is needed to make effective use of them. The idea of using other firms' accounts, or previous years', is valid and perhaps could have been developed further.

The last paragraph could have scored very highly for the student if this had been developed. The notes to the accounts could tell us information such as how the profit had been earned (for example, from continuing or discontinued operations), or whether changes had taken place in depreciation policy, which might distort the profit figure. The answer needs proper evaluation: what would make the financial accounts more or less useful, for example, have they been audited? How effective are accounting regulations? What is the skill or experience of the user? What are the limitations of the financial accounts?

Mark: Content 2/2, Application & Analysis 4/6, Evaluation 0/3. Total = 6

Evaluate the view that financial accounting is not a science.

(11 marks)

Student answer

It is often assumed that accounting is a science. This is because it deals with financial data that is fact and therefore cannot be subject to differing interpretation. The Companies Acts lay down strict guidelines on how accounts should be drawn up and there are various laws that dictate what is and what is not allowed. Therefore, it would appear that accounting is scientific – there are rules to be followed, which means that if firms perform in the same way then their accounts will show the same results.

However, this is not strictly the case. There is plenty of scope for 'creativity' when drawing up the accounts. Firms can distort their profits in various ways. For example, the amount charged as depreciation can be changed by changing the method or lifespan of an asset and this will affect the profit of the firm without any change in the money actually spent or earned by the firm. Secondly, some assets are intangible and do not physically exist. This means that firms can include assets on the balance sheets for brand names or even for research spending, which would normally be classified as an expense. These possibilities mean that firms can spend identical amounts of money but come up with entirely different profit figures.

The scope for changing and distorting these figures means that firms can mislead investors by window dressing their accounts. Recently, the government has tried to tighten the laws that govern how accounts must be drawn up. However, there is still scope for differing interpretations and ways of constructing accounts. As long as these remain, there will always be a non-scientific nature to financial accounting.

Marker's comments

This is a strong answer. The important point to realise is that there are plenty of other ways in which the non-scientific nature of accounting could have been explored – methods such as stock valuation and bringing sales forward. However, this does not matter. When answering a question you only have a limited time to write your answer and this particular answer is almost as good as could be expected in the time allowed.

The answer was well laid out – agreeing with the statement first and then launching the counter-argument in the second paragraph. The answer is evaluative – especially in the last section, whereby the government is trying to make accounting more scientific by closing the loopholes that allow creativity. Good use of examples was made, which made it easier to understand as well.

Mark: Content 2/2, Application & Analysis 6/6, Evaluation 2/3. Total = 10

End of section questions

1 Assess the view that management accounting is more useful than financial accounting.

(11 marks)

2 'The concepts of accounting provide firm rules that clearly indicate what is and is not allowed.' Assess this statement.

(11 marks)

3 Is auditing necessary?

(9 marks)

4 To what extent is management accounting useful?

(11 marks)

5 Evaluate the value of the final accounts to a manager of the firm.

(11 marks)

6 Discuss the view that accounting regulation is a necessary evil.

(11 marks)

7 To what extent can effective financial planning contribute to a firm's success?

(11 marks)

8 'All business functions are subservient to accounting.' Discuss this view.

(11 marks)

9 Analyse why a firm might engage in 'window dressing'.

(9 marks)

10 Consider the possible limitations of using accounts to make decisions.

(11 marks)

Essays

1 To what extent does the accounting function constrain all the other functions of a firm?

(40 marks)

2 To what extent is accounting an art rather than a science?

(40 marks)

3 'Attempts to tighten regulations governing a firm's accounting policies will only increase the red tape that firms face and ultimately harm shareholders.' Critically evaluate this statement.

(40 marks)

4 To what extent do the final accounts of a firm present a 'true and fair' picture of the firm?

(40 marks)

5 Evaluate the view that the recent increase in the number of financial fraud cases in the news represents a failure on the part of the accountancy profession.

(40 marks)

CHAPTER 2

Published accounts: the balance sheet and the profit and loss account

The final accounts of a business include its balance sheet and its profit and loss account. These can be used to analyse a firm's peformance and make decisions such as whether or not to invest in the business. However, interpreting final accounts is not always easy due to differences in the way the figures are calculated and presented. This is especially true when comparing accounts between different countries or over time due to variations in accounting policies or the format of the accounts. However, the general picture of what the final accounts show is the same for each firm – for example, the balance sheet shows the assets of the business and how these are financed whilst the profit and loss shows turnover in relation to costs.

The skill of an analyst is in interpreting the information provided and being able to place this data in context. A good analyst will be able to identify the figures and trends that matter and find the 'true' story no matter what picture the published figures appear to paint. To fully understand the accounts it is important to ask: does a particular figure look high or low? What would we expect this figure to be in this type of industry at this stage of the firm's life cycle? What do competitors' figures look like? What have the figures looked like in the past?

KEY TERMS

Balance sheet
is a statement of a firm's assets and liabilities at a moment in time. It shows what a firm owns (its assets) and how these resources have been financed (capital and liabilities).

Profit and loss account
is a summary of a firm's trading over a period of time (usually one year). It shows the income generated by the firm (called 'sales' or 'turnover') and the costs incurred by the firm in generating that income.

Published accounts

Final accounts can either be for internal use or for external use. If they are for internal usage then it is more likely that a firm will draw the accounts up in a way which is most suitable for the users of accounts, such as managers or directors. This is because internal balance sheets are not for external publication and do not have to meet any legal requirements in their layout.

However, published accounts must meet with the requirements of the Companies Act of 1989. This means that the accounts must be presented in a common format. The presentation can be seen if you obtain a set of company reports. Some of the terms which now have to be used have different titles from the ones that are often used internally or you may be familiar with. For example, the long-term liabilities are replaced with the term 'Creditors: due after more than one year'. The main reason for this common format as set out by law is to help potential investors to see if the firm has used the balance sheet to show a true and fair picture of the firm,

FACT FILE

'Letter to shareowners
1998 was an important year for Cadbury Schweppes for three key reasons:

1 During the year we announced a number of important strategic initiatives. By far the most important was the proposed disposal of our Beverages operations outside the US ... Other developments were: the strengthening of our route to market for our soft drinks brand within the US, the acquisition of the Wedel confectionery business in Poland.

2 1998 was also the first full year in which our Managing for Value programme was adopted throughout Cadbury Schweppes. The impact of this programme has had a major influence on both our operational and strategic decision making processes and on our culture and behavioural characteristics of the company.

3 Finally against a background of substantial economic upheaval, particularly in Asia and Eastern Europe, your business performed strongly in trading terms.'

Source: *Cadbury Schweppes Annual Report 1998*

rather than distorting the image so as to mislead people (a process known as 'window dressing'). By insisting on a common format it should make comparison easier, although it can still be extremely difficult to directly compare figures due to differences in accounting policies.

As a legal obligation, the published accounts of a company must be accompanied by directors' reports and notes to the accounts. These documents are very important and help explain both what has taken place (for example, in the firm's competitive environment) and the policies that a firm follows. For example, explanations will be given on how a firm chooses to value its assets or how it classifies types of expenditure. Analysts of business accounts stress the need to read the directors' reports and the notes to the accounts to get a fuller picture of what is happening. Even then, however, it may not be the full story.

> **To understand a company's reports do not just look at the balance sheet and the profit and loss. Read the notes to the account to see what is really happening. It may even be worth starting at the back of the account where the technical information is, not at the front where the pictures tend to be!**

Internal and external users of accounts

The various internal and external groups that use a firm's accounts include:

The owners of firms – the owners will want to know the value of the business so that they can assess their investment. They will also be interested in profits due to the impact this can have on the future value of the business and on the level of payouts such as dividends.

Managers – will also be interested in the balance sheet and profit and loss statements to assess the progress of the organisation and their own effectiveness. In many cases their own rewards will be linked to the success of the business as a whole.

Financial analysts, such as stockbrokers – will want some idea of the profit and size of the firm to assess its performance. Typically, they will look at the expected and future profitability of the firm in relation to its market value.

Employees – may want to know the value of the business. It may motivate people to know that they are working for the UK's biggest firm; that their business is bigger than their rivals or that it is growing rapidly. Increasing numbers of employees have shares in the business they work for and are naturally interested in its value at any moment in time. Employees and unions will also look at the firm's profits and relative labour costs when it comes to wage bargaining.

Potential investors – will be very interested in the value of a firm so as to know whether it is worth purchasing shares in the company. If the value is perceived to be high, then investors may wish to sell their holdings to make capital gains. A decision to invest will be based on numerous factors including the liquidity of the business and its expected profitability.

Suppliers of a firm (or potential suppliers) – will be interested in the ability of an organisation to pay its bills. They may assess its liquidity position in addition to its profitability.

Buyers of goods and services – may want to be assured the business is a going concern (i.e. will still be here in a year's time) and so may want to assess the firm's liquidity. Buyers may also look at the typical credit given to customers.

Other stakeholders, such as the local community and the media – may also be interested in the performance of the business. They might have specific interests such as the firm's donations to charities or to political parties, or the level of rewards of the directors, details of which must be provided in the final accounts.

However, simply looking at the accounts is of limited value unless the figures are placed in context. Figures need to be compared with similar data in the past (called intra-firm comparison) and with other similar businesses (inter-firm comparison).

PROGRESS CHECK

Analyse the ways in which different stakeholder groups might make use of the final accounts.

The balance sheet

The balance sheet shows the assets owned by a business at a particular moment in time and the sources of finance for these assets (for example, liabilities and shareholders' funds). From the balance sheet alone analysts can identify what the firm owns, what it owes, where the money has been raised and its level of working capital.

	BALANCE SHEET AS AT **31.12.99**
	£
Fixed Assets	1,300
Current Assets	1,900
Current Liabilities (creditors falling due within one year)	1,700
Total assets less current liabilities	*1,500*
Non current liabilities (includes creditors falling due after more than one year and provisions for liabilities and charges)	500
Net assets	*1,000*
Capital and Reserves	*1,000*

Table 2.1 Typical format of a public limited company's balance sheet

Asset structure

The 'asset structure' of a firm refers to the make-up of its assets, i.e. the different combinations of assets that are held. For example, what is the value of the firm's fixed assets in relation to its current assets?

The 'right' combination of assets (if there is one) will depend on the nature of the business. For example, service organisations, such as consultants and advertising agencies, are less likely to hold stocks of finished goods or works in progress than retailers or manufacturers.

FACT FILE

The published accounts of a public limited company will include:

- a profit and loss statement
- a balance sheet
- a cash flow statement
- details of its principal accounting policies
- notes to the accounts
- an auditor's report
- a chairman's statement
- a director's statement.

FACT FILE

During 1998, contributions within the UK to charities or equivalent organisations through corporate giving or as part of the activity of UK operating companies amounted to £1.4 million (1997: £1.3 million).

Source: Cadbury Schweppes Annual Report 1998

KEY POINTS

A balance sheet is more useful to an analyst if:

- it is relatively up-to-date
- the accounting policies used are clear
- the accounting policies have not been changed
- the figures can be compared over time
- the figures can be compared with similar companies.

NUMERICAL INVESTIGATION

	%
Land and buildings	7.5
Fixtures and equipment	19.3
Intangibles	0.9
Other non-current assets	3.7
Stocks/works in progress	13.9
Trade debtors	27.6
Other debtors	2.8
Cash	17.6
Other current assets	6.7
Total current assets	*68.6*
TOTAL ASSETS	**100 %**
Trade creditors	8.3
Bank loans	5.5
Taxation	4.6
Loans payable	10.4
Other current liability	44.3
Total current liabilities	*73.1*
Share capital	8.2
Retained earnings	0.3
Reserves	4.8
Deferred taxation	0.2
Long-term liabilities	13.4
Total liabilities and equity	**100.0**

Table 2.2 Typical proportions of assets and liabilities for UK business.

a What percentage of total assets are fixed assets for an average UK company?
b What percentage of total assets are debtors for an average UK company?
c What percentage of the total funds of a firm are current liabilities for an average UK company?
d What percentage of the total funds of a firm are long-term liabilities for an average UK company?

Source: Dun and Bradstreet 1995 (taken from a sample of 372,871 establishments)

Typical differences in the asset structure of different sectors might include the following.

Service industries

■ Some service firms may not actually own any of the property they use; they may simply rent the land and buildings instead. This may result in a relatively low level of fixed assets, even if the firm is quite large in other ways (for example if measured by the number of employees or turnover). Many of the very successful organisations now providing internet related services, for example, may have very small fixed assets; their only major assets would be the computers and related equipment.

- It is likely that retailers will have a relatively large amount of their assets tied up in working capital, particularly stock. Also their debtors figure is likely to have increased over the years as increasing amount of sales are now made on credit and debit cards.

- Financial firms (such as accountants or insurance companies) are unlikely to have much stock at all. They do not sell a 'product', in the physical sense. Most of their assets, with the exception of the branch buildings, are closely related to money and their main assets will probably be investments in shares and short-term bills.

Manufacturers

Manufacturers are more likely to have expensive fixed assets, such as plant and equipment than firms in the service sector. Stocks are likely to include raw materials or 'work-in-progress', as well as finished goods.

Other factors affecting asset structure

The asset structure of a firm will also depend on the stage of development of a firm. In its early years a business may not be able to afford to buy premises, for example, and therefore, fixed assets are likely to be low. Microsoft and Amazon.com both began in garages, for example. Dell computers began in Michael Dell's bedroom and Richard Branson started Virgin operating from a phone box at his school! Overtime, with expansion, more buildings and equipment are likely to be purchased increasing the fixed asset level.

The asset structure will also depend on trading conditions – if demand is unexpectedly slow, for example, this may lead to increasing stock levels at least in the short-term until the firm cuts back on production.

KEY POINTS

A firm is likely to have less stock on its balance sheet if:

- it has moved to a system of just-in-time stock management.
- it has a rapid rate of stock turnover.
- the balance sheet is produced after a major sales period.
- the firm is a service provider (e.g. an accountant) based on a non-physical product.

PROGRESS CHECK

Under what circumstances might a firm have:
1 High levels of fixed assets.
2 High levels of stocks.
3 High levels of debtors.
4 High levels of cash ?

The 'typical' asset structure of a firm's balance sheet will also be affected by its production techniques. With more firms now using Japanese production methods such as 'just-in-time' or lean production the stock figures held by the firm are likely to have been reduced as more firms become aware of the 'wasted' costs of holding idle stocks. JIT has meant that organisations generally are holding far less stock than in the past and, instead, are ordering smaller quantities more frequently.

The asset structure can also be affected by external change. For example the uncertainty that existed in markets in 1997 and 1998 meant that some firms began to build up their cash holdings. Fears of recession and possible stock market collapse in both the USA and UK, in addition to the collapse of firms in Asian markets, led to firms becoming uncertain over their current and potential future

Proportion of different types of assets held in different UK sectors (%)

	AGRICULTURE (%)	SERVICES (%)	RETAIL (%)	MANUFACTURING (%)
Land and buildings	13.8	5.5	10.2	5.8
Fixtures and equipment	30.1	22.2	20.7	21.5
Intangibles	1.1	1.1	1.9	1
Other non-current assets	4	2.3	2	2.5
Stocks/works in progress	18	5.1	31	16.4
Trade debtors	16	27.7	15.9	34.4
Other debtors	2	3.3	2	1.9
Cash	10.8	25.4	12	11
Other current assets	4.1	7.4	4.3	5.6
Total current assets	51	68.9	65.2	69.3
Total assets	**100**	**100**	**100**	**100**

Table 2.3 Proportion of different types of assets held in different UK sectors (%)

Source: *Dun and Bradstreet* (1995 data)

1 Which sector holds the greatest proportion of its assets in:
a stock
b debtors
c fixtures and equipment
d cash
2 Explain possible reasons for the differences in stocks, debtors, fixtures and equipment and cash between sectors.

investments. Although cash generates little income, it is risk free and this seemed preferable to the risk attached to investments in volatile markets. Stockmarkets in Asia became very volatile (usually falling in value), which meant that firms holding shares in Asian firms would see the value of their portfolios fall. The chance of making capital losses in this way was a major incentive for firms to hold cash instead.

PROGRESS CHECK

Examine ways in which changes in the external environment might affect a firm's balance sheet.

The nature of the balance sheet will also change due to variations and developments in the legal framework or accounting regulations. In the 1980s and early 1990s firms were very keen to include valuations for intangible assets, such as goodwill or brand names; this led to some significant increases in the value of some firms' fixed assets. However, the rules surrounding the valuation of intangible assets have become tighter in recent years which has now restricted the growth of this type of fixed asset on the balance sheet.

PROGRESS CHECK

Discuss the possible effect of a major fall in interest rates on the asset structure of a firm's balance sheet.

Financing the assets

To acquire assets firms may incur a liability, use their owners' capital (for example, issued share capital) or use the retained profits of the business. The mix of finance will depend on the owners' own attitudes – for example, some people are wary of debt and would prefer to rely on the business generating its own funds for expansion. Although this may make growth slower, it avoids interest payments. The sources of finance used will also depend on the availability of different types of funds. For example, if a firm lacks collateral it may not be able to raise much finance through borrowing; if the project is high risk it may be difficult to attract investors.

The financing of assets will also be affected by economic factors such as interest rates. High interest rates are likely to discourage borrowing, for example, because it makes it more expensive, whilst the falling interest rates of the late 1990s is likely to have encouraged firms to use more loans as a source of finance.

KEY POINTS

Firms are more likely to borrow to acquire assets when:

- the interest rate is low
- the firm expects top generate higher returns from the project than the cost of borrowing
- the firm can find a lender
- the firm cannot find willing investors
- the firm has collateral.

Working capital (net current assets)

Part of the balance sheet shows the firm's working capital (also called net current assets). The working capital position of a firm is crucial since it highlights its current assets in relation to its current liabilities. If the current assets are too high in relation to its current liabilities then too much money may be tied up in stocks (which have an opportunity cost in addition to warehousing costs), debtors (which may lead to poor cash flow) or cash (which could be used to earn higher returns elsewhere). If the working capital is too low the firm may have liquidity problems, which could lead to insolvency.

KEY TERM

Working capital = current assets − current liabilities (working capital is also called 'net current assets').

Causes of commercial insolvency (%)

Loss of market – 17
Tax liabilities – 16
Poor management – 16
Lack of working capital/cash flow – 11
VAT liabilities – 8
Bad debts – 8
Other commercial reasons – 6
Personal extravagance – 4
Legal disputes – 4
Personal guarantee given to lenders – 3
Rent review – 2
Falling property values – 2
Loss of long-term finance – 1
Fraud committed by third party – 1
Fraud committed by debtor – 1
Source: Society of Practitioners of Insolvency, 1998

NUMERICAL INVESTIGATION

Working capital of Cadbury Schweppes

	£ MILLION
1989	68
1990	44
1991	(20)
1992	7
1993	(65)
1994	25
1995	(25)
1996	(7)
1997	3
1998	(100)

Table 2.4

Source: *Annual Report (1999)*

    a What is the average working capital of the firm for the period shown?

    b Examine the possible reasons for Cadbury Schweppes' working capital position in 1998.

    c To what extent should a firm be concerned about a negative working capital position?

NUMERICAL INVESTIGATION

	PIZZA EXPRESS PLC 1998 (£000)	MATALAN 1998 (£ MILLION)	UNITED BISCUITS 1998 (£ MILLION)	MFI 1998 (£ MILLION)
Fixed assets	65,751	4.8	648.7	357.8
Current assets	15,965	36	497.9	203
Creditors: amount falling due within 1 year	40,400	5.2	503.6	293.5
Creditors: amount falling due after more than 1 year	3,076	0	207	17.5
Provisions for liabilities and charges	378	0	32	9.7
Shareholders' funds (and minority interests)	37,862	35.6	404.9	240.1

Table 2.5

    a Calculate fixed assets as a percentage of total assets for the firms above, comment on your findings.

    b Calculate 'current assets minus creditors due within one year' (i.e. working capital) for each of the firms in Table 2.5. Comment on your results.

To increase its working capital a firm could:

■ Try to turn short-term liabilities into long-term ones (e.g. turn an overdraft into a loan).

■ Delay payments (e.g. to creditors).

■ Raise more cash (e.g. through a share issue or sale of a fixed asset).

PROGRESS CHECK

Discuss the possible problems for a firm of a sudden fall in its level of working capital.

Analyse how a firm might improve its working capital position.

NUMERICAL INVESTIGATION

J Sainsbury plc

	1999 (£ MILLION)	1998 (£ MILLION)
Current assets	3,600	2,840
Creditors due within one year	4,549	4,001

Table 2.6 Source: 1999 Annual Report

a Calculate J Sainsbury plc's working capital for 1999 and 1998.
b Analyse the possible reasons for the change in its current assets and current liabilities.

Problems involved in valuing assets

Although the accounting process may seem fairly straightforward, there are in fact many difficult decisions calling for professional judgement, which have to be made when deciding how to value particular assets. This means it is possible for different accountants to produce sets of acccounts for the same company that could actually appear to be quite different. In this sense, accounting is an art rather than a science – although there are accounting rules and regulations set out by the Accounting Standards Board these can be interpreted in different ways.

Valuation issues include: stock, debtors and fixed assets.

Stock

According to accounting principles, firms should be prudent when valuing assets (this means they should be conservative in their accounting and, if in doubt, undervalue rather than overvalue). In the case of stock, this means it has to be valued at the lower of its cost or what it could be sold for (called 'net realisable value'). If the stock is damaged or obsolete then its realisable value may actually be lower than its cost and so in this case this would be the figure that is put on the balance sheet.

FACT FILE

Stock valuation
'Finished goods are stated at the lower of cost or net realisable value and raw materials and other stocks at the lower of cost or replacement price. The first in, first out or an average method of valuation is used ... Net realisable value is determined as estimated selling price less costs of disposal.'
Source: Zeneca Annual Report 1998

However, accountants may disagree over the size of the realisable value of the stock – how do you know what it is worth unless you actually sell it?

To make matters more difficult the calculation of cost can in itself be problematic. If you have two components – one worth £10 and one worth £15 – and you use up one of them, which one has been used? If you assume you used the £10 one (because you are not actually sure which one you did use), then the £15 one is left in stock. If you assume you used the other one the costs recorded will be higher (reducing the profits) but the value of the stock left will be lower (increasing the value of assets left).

A firm has three methods it can choose from when deciding on the value for stock (i.e. the cost of it – this then has to be compared with the net realisable value). The three methods are as follows:

1   *First In First Out (FIFO):* assumes that any stock left over is the most recently bought.
2   *Last In First Out (LIFO):* assumes that any stock left over is the oldest stock.
3   *Average Cost (AVCO):* calculates an average based on the different values.

Whatever method is chosen, it is important that the firm is consistent in this method over time, as changing methods may distort profits.

Debtors

The debtors figures may need to have an amount deducted that reflects the likelihood of some of these debtors turning into bad debts; this is known as the provision for bad or doubtful debts. There is clearly room for professional judgement about which debtors are bad and which ones are not. These differences of opinion may alter the value of a firm's assets.

Fixed assets

These must be depreciated to account for the fact they are being used up over time. This will reduce their value on the balance sheet and be entered as a cost on the profit and loss. However, calculating depreciation requires estimates of the expected working life of an asset and its value at the end; different estimates of these figures will alter the annual depreciation and the value of the fixed asset on the balance sheet.

> **PROGRESS CHECK**
>
> Explain how changes in accounting policies could affect a firm's balance sheet.

It is important, therefore, for analysts to look at the notes to the accounts to identify the different policies which have been used. This is particularly important when comparing figures over time (when policies may be altered) and between companies (where policies may differ).

Depreciation

There are various reasons for providing depreciation. Firstly, the accounts should show realistic values for the fixed assets and because assets do lose value over time, it is considered prudent to reduce ('write down') their value. Secondly, the cost of an asset should be charged to the period of time when it generates revenue. This is known as the matching principle. As fixed assets last more than one year it would seem appropriate to spread the cost of the asset over its useful life by charging depreciation for each year we use the assets.

The depreciation is spread over the life of the machine and, therefore, does not reduce the year's profit in the way that charging it all at once would do. It will, however, have an immediate affect on the cash flow position; this is why firms must monitor and budget their cash flow carefully when purchasing fixed assets.

> **Depreciation is a cost on the profit and loss. It is NOT a cash flow. The cash goes out when you purchase the asset, but the costs are spread over the asset's working life.**

Depreciation is based on estimates of the working life of an asset and its value at the end of this period. In reality a firm is unlikely to know exactly how much an asset will be worth at the end of its life (unless there was an agreement with the supplier of the asset for a 'trade-in' value – this is more likely to happen with vehicle purchases) or how long it will last (unless there has been an agreement made to sell the asset back to the supplier prior to purchase). The annual depreciation figure is, therefore, not 'correct' in the sense that we do not necessarily know two of the key elements needed to calculate it. As a result the value of the fixed asset on the balance sheet is unlikely to accurately represent its actual value.

PROGRESS CHECK

Explain the impact of the depreciation of a fixed asset on a firm's balance sheet and its profit and loss.

BAA Reports & Accounts – useful economic life of certain assets

Years to 31 March	1988	1989	1990
Terminal lives (in years)	16	30	50
Runway lives (in years)	23.5	40	100

Table 2.7

Source: *Accounting for Growth*, T. Smith, Century Business

During the period of 1989 to 1991 BAA spent over £500 million on runway and terminal construction or upgrading. Its change in policy meant that the depreciation on the terminal assets was spread over 50 years rather than 16 and the runway depreciation was spread over 100 years instead of 23.5 years. The effect on the profits was that the resulting annual depreciation was significantly reduced and, therefore, profits appeared to be higher. An estimate of the effect is that if the

FACT FILE

According to the 1985 Companies Act, all assets with a finite life should be subject to depreciation, except for land. Land is assumed to hold its value over time. This means that intangible assets, such as goodwill and brand names, are also depreciated (although it is called amortisation). If, however, brands and goodwill are believed to hold their value they do not have to be amortised.

FACT FILE

The supersonic jet, Concorde, was launched in 1969 and has served the company for over 30 years. On the British Airways balance sheet, the entire fleet is valued at zero!

KEY POINTS

The annual depreciation will be lower if:

- the expected working life is longer
- the residual value (value at the end of its working life) is lower
- the initial purchase price is lower.

changes in the policy had not taken place then profits for 1990 would have been over £8 million lower.

Do changes in depreciation policy matter?

The effect of changing depreciation policy is to change the amount charged to the profit and loss account as a cost for any given year. Consider the following example.

A firm has purchased a new computer network system costing £200,000. It was originally expected to last for ten years. It is to be depreciated by the straight line method but with no residual value. Annual depreciation will be £200,000/10 = £20,000 p.a.

The effects of the final accounts are shown in **Table 2.9**

YEAR	Now	1	2		10	TOTAL
Cash flow (£)	(200,000)	0	0	(etc)	0	(200,000)
Profit (£)	0	(20,000)	(20,000)	(etc)	(20,000)	(200,000)
Net book value (£)	200,000	180,000	160,000	(etc)	0	–

Table 2.8

The profit is, therefore, reduced by £20,000 each year for ten years. However, if the firm had used an expected lifespan of 20 years the effects would have been as follows:

YEAR	Now	1	2		20	TOTAL
Cash flow (£)	(200,000)	0	0	(etc)	0	(200,000)
Profit (£)	0	(10,000)	(10,000)	(etc)	(10,000)	(200,000)
Net book value (£)	200,000	190,000	180,000	(etc)	0	–

Table 2.9

After 20 years the effect on the firm's balance sheet and profit and loss are the same. The value of the asset will have been spread over its lifespan. If this lifespan is ten or 20 years is irrelevant, in that the overall cost of £200,000 is eventually charged to the profit and loss accounts. In some ways then, it is simply a matter of choice of whether a firm wishes to charge the overall cost of the asset in larger amounts but quickly, or to take longer and charge smaller amounts. This would appear to suggest that it is irrelevant which method is chosen and which estimate we make for the life of the asset. In terms of cash flow, at least, it makes no difference; in the case detailed in Tables 2.8 and 2.9, £200,000 was spent in year zero, regardless of whether this cost is spread over ten or 20 years.

For the immediate future, however (for example, the present year's accounts and the next year's) this change does matter in terms of profits. In our example, a change in method changes the amount charged for depreciation from £20,000 to £10,000. This would boost the current profits by £10,000 per year. This will have an impact on the published profits for the firm and may affect the ability of the firm to attract shareholders.

Investors are not always going to be so vigilant as to check the depreciation policy to see if the policy has been changed. This again highlights the need to read the notes to the accounts thoroughly and particularly to check if there has been any change in the policies.

KEY POINTS

A firm is more likely to use the straight line method of depreciation if:

- it is less concerned with showing a realistic value for fixed assets
- it places a greater priority on using a method that is easier to calculate
- it is not concerned with the effects on the profit that might arise from charging the same amount over a number of years.

PROGRESS CHECK

Analyse how a change in depreciation policy could affect a firm's profits.

Intangible assets

Fixed assets do not simply consist of tangible fixed assets, such as premises, equipment and vehicles. Many firms also include a section for their intangible assets, such as goodwill, brand names and patents. A fixed asset is usually defined as an income-generating asset, one with a long life, which is not normally acquired for resale. This definition is appropriate to apply to assets such as premises and equipment, however, its application to intangible assets may be more debatable. Do brand names necessarily have a long life, is one question that could be raised. How can we identify the income directly generated through goodwill?

The issue of valuing intangible assets has caused much debate in the accounting profession in the last decade or so. As the UK becomes more service-based, where reputations, contacts and intellectual capital are crucial to the success of a business; the discussions look set to continue. At present, the situation regarding intangible assets is as follows.

KEY TERMS

Intangible assets are those that physically do not exist, however, they will still act as a source of income for the firm. They normally include: goodwill, brand names, research and development or copyrights.

Goodwill is an intangible asset which places a value on the reputation of a firm. It is measured by the difference between the price paid for a firm and the value of the tangible assets acquired. According to FRS 10, goodwill can be defined as: 'The difference between the value of a business as a whole and the aggregate fair values of its separable net assets.'

Goodwill

When a firm acquires another company, it is perfectly permissible for this business to include a value for the goodwill that has, in effect, been purchased. A good reputation can affect a firm for many years, and so goodwill is certainly a long-term asset. Naturally, the enhanced status that goodwill gives the owner will help the firm generate income through sales that are higher than average. In some cases a good reputation and large customer base is far more important for income generation than any amount of fixed, tangible assets – management consultants, advertising agencies and lawyers are some examples.

In comparison, if a firm has been trading for several years successfully and has built up a good customer base, it is not allowed to value this 'internally generated goodwill' (rather than acquired goodwill) on its balance sheet. The reason for this is that goodwill cannot be 'reliably measured', according to the Accounting Standards

FACT FILE

FRS 10: Goodwill and Intangible Assets
The standard requires purchased goodwill and certain intangible assets to be capitalised and, in most circumstances, to be amortised systematically through the profit and loss account (usually over 20 years or less). Impairment reviews must be undertaken, particularly if the goodwill or intangible asset is regarded as having an infinite life and is therefore not being amortised. Internally generated goodwill should not be capitalised and internally developed intangible assets should be capitalised only where they have a readily ascertainable market value.
Source: ASA

Board. The firm may be able to charge a premium price due to the degree of brand loyalty it has acquired, and this could result in profits being higher than a firm without this reputation. Nevertheless, under present rules this cannot be included on the balance sheet.

Example:

A firm purchases a business that has been trading successfully for many years, for £10 million. The book value of the assets was ascertained to be £7 million.

On the original firm's balance sheet it will have paid out (i.e. decreasing its cash) a sum of £10 million. However, the assets of the firm would have only been boosted by £7 million. The remaining £3 million would appear under the firm's fixed assets as goodwill.

ASSETS DECREASE	ASSETS INCREASE
Cash decreases by £10 million	Tangible assets increase by £7 million Goodwill increases by £3 million

Table 2.10

Questions

1 Examine the possible ways in which a firm could create goodwill internally.
2 Outline the arguments for and against including internally generated goodwill as an intangible fixed asset.

FACT FILE

In early 1999 the Coca Cola brand was estimated by Interbrand to be worth $83.8 billion. This represented almost 60% of the company's market value. In other words, the brand was worth more than all the company's offices, manufacturing plants, distribution systems and other assets put together. In July 1999 there was a health scare crisis with Coca Cola products in Europe, which led to their withdrawal in several countries; this may well have affected its brand value, at least in the short-term.

Brand names

Over the last 20 years we have seen the number of mergers and acquisitions that have taken place rise rapidly. In the 1990s alone, the number occurring has almost tripled. These factors have led to a situation in which firms are acquired for values far in excess of their book value (i.e. the value stated in the published accounts). Part of this excess value can be attributed to the skilled marketing of the firms' brands.

Companies such as Coca Cola, Sony and Marlboro are global brands and undoubtedly have a major impact on the success of these firms. For example, they enable the business to charge a price premium for goods sold under their brand, they generate brand loyalty which makes the firm less vulnerable to changes in market conditions and they enable the firm to launch new products more easily. Therefore, there is certainly an argument for including brand names on the balance sheets.

There is a problem, however, in deciding how this value should be estimated. It may be agreed that brands play a role in a firm's success, but how do we actually place a monetary value on this? Also, it is worth considering that brands can lose their value quickly. A problem with a product, a marketing failure or a change in tastes can lead to brands going out of favour quite suddenly (for example, the rise and fall of some music groups). Placing a value on a brand could, therefore, be very risky, as it may soon be out of date.

Due to uncertainty as to the valuation of brand names, the authorities have decided that brands can only be included on the balance sheet of a firm if they have a historical value and its value and effects can be measured separately from other assets. This basically means that, as with goodwill, internally generated brand names cannot be included, however, brand names acquired can be valued on balance sheets if they have an identifiable effect on the firm's earnings.

FACT FILE

The Interbrand group is a consulting company that specialises in measuring the value of brands uses four criteria in order to calculate the brand's value:

- The weight of a brand is measured through the brand's share in the market it operates.
- The breadth of the brand is measured in terms of the range of people who the brand appeals to (age, character, nationality).
- The depth of the brand is measured by the degree of customer loyalty the brand attracts.
- The length of the brand is measured by the range of different products that are marketed through the brand name. The earnings attributable to a specific brand are estimated by comparing the profits earned by own label manufacturers with profits earned by the branded product or service.

PROGRESS CHECK

Questions

1 Analyse the arguments for regarding a brand as an asset.
2 Analyse the factors that may reduce the value of a brand.

PROGRESS CHECK

Consider the factors that might affect the value of a brand.

Research & Development (R&D)

Certain firms will spend heavily on research and development (R&D). This is particularly common in industries such as the pharmaceutical industry, where a firm's success depends on its ability to innovate. R&D expenditure is money spent on developing new products and processes or generating technological advances which can either be used by the firm to improve efficiency or can be sold to other firms for a profit.

It can be argued that R&D expenditure should be treated in the same way as the acquisition of a fixed asset. The money being spent now is for benefits in the future and therefore, the costs of R&D should not be written off in the period in which they are incurred but spread out over several years. This means R&D would be treated as an asset (it is capitalised) and amortized (depreciated) over the number of years that the firm benefits from the development.

If we are, however, being prudent, then we cannot assume that the R&D expenditure will actually generate any future benefits; as a result some countries have disallowed the capitalisation of R&D expenditure. In the UK it is allowed (the rules are laid out in SSAP 13), however, the policy varies between firms. Once again, the real problem occurs when a firm changes its policy or when one is comparing figures between companies. Differences in accounting policy (for example, over what period the research and development is amortised) can have a major effect on a firm's profits in a given period and analysts must take care to find out the particular policy of a company and whether it has been used consistently.

PROGRESS CHECK

Analyse the factors a firm might take into account when deciding on whether to include intangible assets on the balance sheet.

Balance sheets

What is a 'strong' balance sheet?

When assessing the strength of a balance sheet (i.e. how financially strong the business is) it is worth considering:

Working capital

Looking at the working capital position can prove informative. A strong working capital position would usually refer to the firm having an adequate amount of working capital for its own use. The size of the working capital can be measured as a money figure. However, if we are told that a firm had a working capital of £10 million it would not mean much to us unless we had some basis for comparison.

It may be more useful to analyse the working capital using ratios as well as an absolute figure. Analysts would generally look for a positive working capital position; a current ratio of around 1.5 and an acid test ratio of around 0.8 (this is covered in more detail in Chapter 7 on liquidity ratios). If working capital is low, the firm may become illiquid and be unable to finance its daily operations.

Reserves

The retained profit reserve on the balance sheet represents the sum of all the past years' retained profits added together (with any losses also subtracted). This means that one way we can see how strong a firm is, is to look at the size of the retained profit reserve. If it is large and/or rising over time, then this means that the firm is building up reserves by investing profits into the firm. If the reserves figure falls, this means that the firm has made a loss.

Borrowing

If a large proportion of the firm's assets have been acquired through debt the business is 'highly geared'. This may mean it has high interest payments to pay, which might make the business less attractive to investors. In poor trading years the profits of the business might be swallowed up by the interest payments. Also, if the firm is highly geared it may have problems borrowing more money in the future to finance expansion. On a strong balance sheet, therefore, the gearing ratio will not be too high. The right level of gearing will depend on interest rates, the expected profitability of the firm and the managers' attitude to risk.

Asset structure

The financial position of a firm will generally be considered to be more appropriate if its asset structure is matched by the methods of financing the acquisition of those assets. This means that fixed assets should be financed by long-term finance. If fixed assets are purchased with short-term finance, such as overdrafts or trade credit, it may mean that the firm will have to sell the assets to pay these debts when they are due for repayment.

Trends

A balance sheet simply shows the financial state of the firm at a particular moment in time. To assess the strength of a firm it is best to look at changes in the balance sheet over a period of time. Is stock building up? Is working capital growing or shrinking? Is the firm expanding and acquiring more assets? What is happening to its borrowing?

FACT FILE

Brand value June 1999 ($billion as a % of market capitalisation)

Coca Cola	59
Microsoft	21
IBM	28
General Electric	10
Ford	58
Disney	61
Intel	21
McDonald's	64
Marlboro	19

Source: Interbrand

The value of a business

The balance sheet shows what a firm owns and what it owes; from this we can calculate the book value of the business. However, although this is one measure of what the firm is worth, it does not necessarily reflect its market value (i.e. the value of the business if it was sold). The value of a firm can, therefore, either mean its book value or its market value and these can give very different figures!

The advantage of using the book value as a means of measuring the worth of a firm is that it can be instantly verifiable, that is to say, we can check the value of the company's assets simply by looking at the last set of accounts. It is also largely factual, in that the historical cost of the assets actually relates to real values of assets that have been acquired in the past.

A problem with using this method of valuing a business, however, is that although the historical cost of any asset represents an actual amount paid by the firm, it is unlikely that the asset is actually worth this now. For example, property acquired many years ago is likely to be worth much more. Also, the book value of the firm's assets takes no account of the strengths of a firm that are found on a balance sheet.

Many people would value the motivation of staff and the customer service offered by a firm and if these were impressive this would mean that the market value would be likely to exceed the book value. The book value may also ignore the value of brands, internally generated goodwill and the skills of the workforce. On the other hand, the market value may be lower than the book value if, for example, the property market had crashed.

KEY TERMS

Book value
is found by calculating the total of the firm's net assets (fixed and current assets less any liabilities that the firm may have).

Market value
is the value placed on the firm by the stockmarket. This is found by multiplying the number of shares that have been issued by the firm by the current or market price. Also called **market capitalisation**.

The market value of any share will probably change on a daily, if not hourly, basis. The market value is based not only on the valuations of the firm's assets but will also include what investors believe will happen to the firm in the future.

If a firm is expected to declare higher profits in the next few months, then it is likely that there will be a higher market valuation than if the firm was expected to declare a relatively low profit or even a loss. Although the book value of the firm may not be different, the future expected performance of the business (rather than the present performance) can cause the market valuation to differ.

PROGRESS CHECK

Questions

1. How might the market value of a firm be affected by changes in the firm's strategic policy?
2. Analyse the external factors that could in the future increase or decrease the current market value.

NUMERICAL INVESTIGATION

The following table compares the book value of the top ten UK firms at the end of 1997 with their market value 18 months later, in May 1999.

	BOOK VALUE 1997 (£ BILLION)	MARKET VALUE MAY 1999 (£ BILLION)
1 HSBC	26.95	19.46
2 Shell Transport	20.99	46.70
3 BP	20.55	110.17
4 Abbey National	20.14	19.41
5 BT	17.48	65.40
6 Nat West	15.51	24.94
7 Halifax	13.73	20.55
8 Barclays	13.68	27.45
9 Swire & Sons	11.56	N/A
10 British Gas	11.44	14.77

Table 2.11

Source: *Times 1000*, 1998

a. From Table 2.11, calculate the ratio of market value to book value and then rank the firms according to the highest market to book ratio.
b. What reasons may account for differences in the ratio?

PROGRESS CHECK

Examine the factors that might influence the market value of a company.

Profit and loss accounts

The profit and loss account shows the income that a firm has earned during a period of time (usually one year), with the appropriate expenses deducted from this, indicating either the profit or loss for that period of time. The profit and loss account provides important information concerning the firm's performance for the various interested parties of the firm.

	£
Sales	100,000
Cost of sales	65,000
Gross profit	35,000
Expenses	18,000
Operating profit	17,000
Non-operating income	2,000
Profit before interest and tax	19,000
Interest	3,000
Profit before tax	16,000
Corporation tax	4,000
Profit after tax	12,000
Dividends	6,000
Retained profit	6,000

Table 2.12 A typical format for a profit and loss account for a company

PROGRESS CHECK

Questions

1 What groups are likely to be interested in the firm's profit and loss account?
2 For each group explain why they might wish to know the firm's profit or loss.

Different measures of profit

Profit measures the value of what has been sold in relation to the value of inputs used. There are many different types of profit, depending on which costs have been deducted from turnover (for example, gross profit and operating profit, profit before tax and profit after tax). Each of these will highlight a different area of performance of a firm and by analysing profit at different stages rather than just the final figure ('the bottom line'), it is possible to gain more insight into the performance of the business, for example, how much of the profits are paid out in interest payments? How much profit is due to non-operating income rather than typical day to day activities? How much of the costs are due to administrative expenses?

Operating profit

One of the most common measures of the performance of a business is operating

FACT FILE

A report by Business Intelligence, a UK research company, called *Measuring the Value of Knowledge*, highlighted the problems of asset valuation in the 1990s due to the increasing importance of intangible assets, such as knowledge and intellectual capital. 'The widening gap between the market and book value of companies (which is over ten times in many knowledge-intensive companies) raises questions about the relevance of traditional measures and accounting methods.'

FACT FILE

In the mid 1970s, more than half the value of every Fortune 500 company was derived from tangible assets. By the mid 1990s, this had fallen to around 25% as intangible assets had risen in value.

KEY POINTS

A firm with a strong balance sheet is more likely to:

● have adequate working capital to finance daily running and potential expansion
● not be so highly geared that an increase in interest rates would place a drain on the firm's cash flow
● have built up reserves over time, reflecting retained profits.

profit. This shows how much profit a firm is generating from its ordinary day to day activities. However, the relevance of this figure depends on who is examining the data and what they want to find out. Shareholders, for example, are more likely to be interested in profit after tax and after interest, as dividends are only paid once these items have been deducted.

PROGRESS CHECK

Analyse the possible value of different measures of profit for analysts.

NUMERICAL INVESTIGATION

Pizza Express plc

	1998 (£)	1997 (£)
Turnover	99,562	71,055
Cost of sales	(70,166)	(49,454)
Gross profit	29,396	21,061
Distribution costs	(2,341)	(1,789)
Administrative expenses	(4,494)	(4,404)
Operating profit	22,561	15,408
Profit on disposal of fixed assets	689	659
Income from fixed asset investment	21	32
Profit on ordinary activities before taxation 23,271	16,099	
Net interest (payable) receivable	(207)	55
Profit on ordinary activities before taxation 23,001	16,154	
Taxation on ordinary activities	(4,965)	(3,534)
Profit on ordinary activities after taxation	18,036	12,620
Dividends on equity shares	(2,833)	(2,214)
Retained profits for the financial year	15,023	10,406

Source: *Annual Report 1998*, for year ended 30 June 1998

Table 2.13

a Explain the difference between gross and operating profit with reference to the data in Table 2.13.
b How much did the company pay out to shareholders in 1997 and 1998?
c Comment on the firm's change in performance from 1997 to 1998.
d There are several measures of profit identified above. Which one is most useful to an analyst? Explain your answer.

NUMERICAL INVESTIGATION

The following is an extract from the final accounts of Orange plc, the manufacturer of mobile telephones.

	1997 (£ MILLION)	1998 (£ MILLION)
Turnover	913.7	1212.7
Cost of sales	737.3	938.3
Gross profit	176.4	274.4

Table 2.14 Source: *Annual Report 1998*

a Calculate the gross profit as a percentage of sales revenue for both years.
b Analyse the reasons that may explain why the percentage has changed between 1997 and 1998.

Are profits under the control of a firm?

The managers of a business exert a degree of control over the performance of their business. Decisions concerning the marketing, operations, human resources and the financial functions, will all have an impact on a firm's success. If the right product is launched at the right time with the right price, if it is promoted effectively with the support and commitment of the employees, this should help a firm's profits. Effective management should enable the firm to boost revenues and/or control its costs.

Firms do not, however, operate in a vacuum and the profits of a firm will inevitably be affected by the environment in which it operates. Changes in market conditions, developments in technology, the power of suppliers, the economic climate and competitors' strategies can all have a major impact on a firm's profitability. This is not to say that managers should be seen as victims of the external environment, but simply that their decisions are inevitably influenced by trading conditions. The successful managers are those who can anticipate such changes (in some cases bring them about) and react effectively to them.

PROGRESS CHECK

'Overseas, economic turmoil and the consequent worsening trading conditions in the Far East coincided with the continued strength of the pound which affected us particularly in Europe and led to a severe fall in operating profits.'
Source: Chairman's Statement, *Marks and Spencer Annual Report 1998/1999.*

Questions

1 Examine the ways in which the external environment might have reduced Marks and Spencer's profits.
2 To what extent is a fall in profits beyond the control of a firm's managers?

FACT FILE

In 1999, Punch Taverns and Whitbread were engaged in a fierce and very public battle to buy up Allied Domecq. As the battle progressed the companies were offering very different valuations of Allied Domecq showing that, to some extent, the worth of the business depends on who wants it and what they think they can do with it. Finally, Punch Taverns won, agreeing to pay £2.75 billion for the 3,500 pubs and half share in First Quench off licence business. This was £175 million less than Punch's third offer and £75 million less than Whitbread's final £2.85 billion offer, which was withdrawn when the deal was referred to the Competition Commission.

KEY POINTS

The market value of a company is likely to increase if:

- the market is believed to be growing fast
- the firm is expected to have high profits in the future
- a takeover bid is expected.

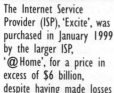

KEY POINTS

The book value is likely to be lower than the market value if:

- investors believe the company has a good future ahead of it
- the company's property has not been revalued for many years
- low interest rates are encouraging investors to borrow and buy shares.

KEY TERMS

Turnover
measures the value of the sales in a given period.

Costs
measure the value of inputs used up to provide the goods or services.

Using profit and loss accounts

What information does the annual profit figure give us? For most firms it is assumed that making a profit is the main aim for the firm. In fact, it is often assumed that the real objective for a firm is not just achieving a profit but maximising profits.

Profits can easily be measured; they are found annually in the final accounts. However, it is impossible to establish if a firm is maximising its profits. The problem with profit maximisation as an objective is that it cannot really be measured. How can you tell if a firm has made the most profit possible?

> **Some firms may aim to maximise profits but we will never know if they have succeeded – how can we tell if they are making the highest profit possible?**

'Satisfactory' profit

With this in mind, some theorists believe that firms do not aim for profit maximisation; they aim for profit satisfaction. This is where the firm aims for a satisfactory level of profit. Again, a 'satisfactory' level of profit is hard to measure, however, there are some ways in which it can be checked. For example, profits could be compared with other firms in the same industry. They could also be compared with previous figures or targets set by managers. This would enable a firm to establish if they are performing better or worse than expected. This still assumes that profit is a good indicator of company performance. This may not always be the case and it is quite possible a firm that is quite successful does not make any profit at all in any given period. For example, a firm may be trying to enter a market and be willing to sacrifice profit or it may be deliberately selling items at a loss to damage a competitor's sales. Alternatively, the firm may have other non-profit making goals, for example, a charity.

Defining profit

It is important when discussing profit to be very precise with the definition – after all you can measure profit before and after tax, profit before and after interest, profit excluding or including extraordinary items, and so on. There is a danger when analysing accounts of focusing purely on the final published figure. However, to gain a real insight into the performance of the business it is necessary to work backwards to see what happened at each level of the profit and loss statement. Profits attributable to shareholders may have risen but it may be worth checking whether this is due to normal trading acitivity. In particular, it is worth considering the quality of the profit – is this year's level of profits likely to be achieved again? Is the firm in a strong position for the future or is this just a 'one-off'?

A firm might, for example, increase its profit in any given period of time by selling some of its fixed assets. This is not a problem in that profit is officially boosted, and so there is nothing illegal taking place. However, it is a problem in that the sale of fixed assets will deprive the firm of potential production or retail facilities. If the fixed assets were plant or equipment, this means that the firm has less capacity left to generate future output and future sales. Therefore, although profits are boosted, in the future they are likely to be lower (unless the firm replaces the assets).

The quality of profit might also depend on the firm's investment in research and development expenditure. By cutting back on research and development, for example, a firm could boost its short-term profits. However, research and development is designed to either save money or to develop new products to increase profits in the future. Less spending in this area may, therefore, lead to a decline in the long-term profitability of the business. The same can be said of marketing spending on brand building; investment in brands may drain short-term profits but lead to long-term loyalty and higher returns. A cutback in this area may help profits look better in the short-term, but it could be potentially damaging in the long-term.

An assessment of profit quality might also involve an examination of the firm's cash flow. If sales take place on credit then a firm will count these sales as turnover even though the money for them is still owed. This could mean the firm has made a profit but has underlying cash flow problems. Clearly, if there are difficulties with liquidity this may threaten a firm's survival and limit its ability to make profits in the future.

When examining the profit and loss account it is important, therefore, to consider whether the firm is likely to be able to sustain its level of profit. Is there evidence that it is investing in the future? Are there signs of a long-term approach? If not, even if it has a high level of profit, you might now be concerned about what will happen in the future.

PROGRESS CHECK

Consider the possible factors involved in assessing the quality of a firm's profits.

The profit figures, therefore, need to be placed in context – what is the firm trying to achieve and what is its strategy? What is the economic and market environment? It is also useful to look at the trend over a longer period of time rather than just one year's figures. Sudden shocks or external change may have caused a one-off change in profits, which does not reflect the underlying position of the firm. The size of the profit must also be compared to the overall size of the firm – Tesco is considerably larger than the average corner shop and so we would expect its profit to be much higher.

When analysing the size of a firm's profits, therefore, it is important to place the number on the context of what is happening internally and externally and the overall nature of the business.

PROGRESS CHECK

Analyse the possible reasons for a fall in profit for a firm.

KEY TERMS

Gross profit
is the profit earned by the firm on its main activity: the buying and selling of goods and services. It is calculated by measuring the difference between the sales revenue and the cost of sales.

Operating profit
is the profit earned by the firm after allowing for all the firm's expenses in running the operations. These will include the overheads incurred in running the firm, such as heating or salaries of sales assistants.

FACT FILE

In 1999 Rank, the leisure giant, announced a £51 million pre-tax loss after a £206 million profit in 1998. The deficit was after taking £306 million of exceptional charges, which included £208 million of losses on the sale of properties and other businesses. Excluding the exceptional costs, profits were £255 million, against £310 million in 1997, on sales 2.2% higher, at £2.06 billion. Note: an exceptional charge is a one-off cost, such as restructuring or redundancy costs.

FACT FILE

'After a strong first six months, progress for the year as a whole was tempered by the crises in emerging markets, particularly Russia, and to a lesser extent, by the consequent slowdown in the world economy. We estimate that the direct impact of the Russian economic collapse on our European confectionery business reduced confectionery stream growth in trading profit from 10 to 6%.'

Source: *Cadbury Schweppes Annual Report 1998*

Utilisation of profit

The utilisation of profits refers to the way in which profits are distributed – they are either given to the owners as a reward for risking their funds or retained within the business itself.

The decision about how much to pay out (for example, as dividends) and how much to retain will depend on a firm's future plans, its present competitive state and the desire of its owners for immediate rewards. If the firm needs to expand and invest heavily, managers will want to retain more of the profit. If, however, the owners want more income in the short-term they are likely to demand a higher pay out. The desire for more dividends will in turn depend on what other firms are paying, how much the business is increasing in value, the investors' view of the future and their willingness to take a long-term view. In the UK the most powerful investors are institutions, such as insurance companies and pension funds; these institutional investors are said to demand very high pay outs because they are unwilling to wait for long-term gains. This may deny some firms the funds they need to invest and sustain their long-term competitiveness.

PROGRESS CHECK

Consider the factors that might influence how a firm uses its profits. To what extent is it more important to invest profits rather than pay out dividends?

NUMERICAL INVESTIGATION

	PIZZA EXPRESS PLC 1998 (£)	MATALAN 1998 (£MILLION)	UNITED BISCUITS 1998 (£MILLION)	MFI 1998 (£MILLION)
Sales	99,562	278.2	1,685.2	894.8
Operating profits	22,561	23.8	92.1	60.3
Profit before tax	23,001	22.7	79.3	60.4
Profit for the financial year	18,036	15.2	58.2	43
Dividends to ordinary shareholders	(2,833)	(4.5)	(51.6)	(29.3)
Retained profits for the financial year	15,203	10.7	6.6	13.7

Table 2.15 Source: *Annual Report 1998*

a Comment on the profits of the firms listed in Table 2.15 in relation to sales.
b Comment on their apparent policies of paying dividends.

NUMERICAL INVESTIGATION

J Sainsbury plc

	1999	1998	1997	1996	1995
Group sales (£billion)	16.3	15.5	14.3	13.5	14.3
Group profit (£million)	756	728	651	764	808
Dividend per share (pence)	14.32	13.9	12.3	12.1	11.7

Table 2.16 Source: Annual Report 1999

  a Calculate the growth in sales, profits and dividends per share over this period.
  b Analyse the company's policy on dividends relative to its sales and profit performance.

FACT FILE

Proposals by the Accounting Standards Board (ASA) recommend that profit and loss statements are rewritten so that the profit that can be fairly attributed to the operations of a company and the managers who run the core activities is kept distinct from the sales of factories or shares trading, for example. Some notorious company collapses have occurred with businesses that appeared to have a healthy operating profit, which was actually overshadowed by losses in areas such as foreign exchange dealings. The ASA recommended three performance categories should be identified:

- Operating or trading activities – the core business.
- Financing and so-called treasury activities, including gains and losses from derivatives.
- Other gains and losses not actively managed by the business, such as pension liabilities and assets and changes in the value of fixed assets.

Reporting of profits:

Segmental analysis

Most firms produce more than one distinct product; they also operate in a variety of geographical areas. In this case, it is useful to break down the information found in the profit and loss account and present what is known as 'segmental analysis'. This is where the sales and profits are listed both as the main overall figure for the company, and are also broken down by either product line or by geographical area.

Segmental reporting of sales and profits enables the users of the accounts to analyse the performance of different areas of the firm. The performance of a particular manager can be identified if the manager is responsible for a certain product or a certain geographical area. For example, a successful multinational firm may make very large profits overall. Although this may appear satisfactory (assuming it represents a relatively high return on capital employed), it could disguise poor performance in certain parts of the firm. Segmental analysis could help identify areas that were performing less well and appropriate action could then be taken.

PROGRESS CHECK

Questions

1 What effect might segmental reporting have on the performance of managers in charge of regional operations?
2 To what extent can a firm calculate the profits made by individual products or regions?
3 You are the managing director of a company retailing personal computers, operating in five European countries. Segmental analysis shows that the sales of one country are growing significantly slower than in the others. Analyse the possible actions you might take.

KEY POINTS

Profit is more likely to be of higher quality if:

- It has been earned through the sales of goods and services
- The firm has not made profits through the sale of capacity
- The profit is sustainable
- There is an upward trend of profits made over time.

KEY POINTS

Profits are likely to be low if:

- the firm is just starting up
- sales are low or falling
- the economy is in recession
- costs are increasing rapidly.

KEY POINTS

Firms are more likely to pay high dividends if:

- their profit figures are high
- their shareholders expect high levels
- they need to boost the share price
- other firms are paying high returns
- shareholders want immediate, not long-term rewards.

NUMERICAL INVESTIGATION

British American Tobacco (BAT, 1998)

	TURNOVER (£MILLION)	OPERATING PROFIT (£MILLION)	OPERATING ASSETS (£MILLION)
America-Pacific	2,665	539	901
Asia-Pacific	1,259	182	706
Latin America	1,603	318	1,121
Europe	1,486	170	948
AMESCA	573	118	345
Imasco	1,662	253	363
BAT Head Office	–	(30)	–

Source: *Annual Report (1999)* IMASCO is an associated company of BAT

Table 2.17

Compare the performance of the different parts of the BAT business.

PROGRESS CHECK

Analyse the possible benefits of segmental reporting to a potential investor.

NUMERICAL INVESTIGATION

	SALES INCLUDING TAXES (£MILLION)	OPERATING PROFIT (£MILLION)	NUMBER OF STORES	SALES AREA (SQUARE FEET)	EMPLOYEES
Sainsbury's supermarkets	12,097	714.1	405	11,425	130
Savacentre	875	28.3	13	1,119	10
Homebase	1,270	66.6	288	10,851	18
Shaw's	$3,047	$85.1	127	4,410	20

Table 2.18 J. Sainsbury *Annual Report 1999*

a Calculate the profit margin for each of J Sainsbury plc's businesses.
b Comment on the performance of each of Sainsbury's business units.

Discontinued operations

The published accounts of public limited companies now distinguish between the turnover and profits of continuing and discontinued operations. This allows analysts to get a fuller picture of how a business is doing. If the overall profit figure is high but this is mainly due to discontinued activities (for example, this part of the business has now been sold off), this may suggest that profits next year will decrease. This distinction is particularly important when firms are restructuring, for example, in the late 1990s Hanson, ICI and Tomkins demerged several of their businesses, and it is important that analysts can identify exactly where any given year's profits are from.

Some segmental analysis must now be provided in a public limited companies' accounts and firms must distinguish between their continuing businesses (including acquisitions) and their discontinued operations. Many analysts, however, demand even more information in the published accounts than is already provided. It would be interesting to know, for example, exactly what proportion of profits are generated from new products compared to old ones or the spending of the firm on training or marketing. In some ways the more information an analyst can have, the better. There is, however, the danger of being swamped by too much information.

NUMERICAL INVESTIGATION

United Biscuits plc, *Annual Report 1999*

TURNOVER	1998 (£MILLION)	1997 (£MILLION)
Existing operations	1,544.4	1,549.4
Acquisitions	140.8	–
Continuing operations	1,685.2	1,549.4
Discontinued operations	–	226.5
	1,685.2	1,775.9
Operating profit	**(£MILLION)**	**(£MILLION)**
Existing operations	100.6	106.8
Acquisitions	(8.5)	–
Continuing operations	92.1	106.8
Discontinued operations	–	5.9
	92.1	112.7

Table 2.19

a What percentage of the firm's turnover and profit in 1997 came from operations that were discountinued?
b What percentage of the firm's turnover and profit was generated by existing operations in 1998?
c What can we deduce about the firm's acquisitions and sales policy in 1997 from the data in Table 2.19?

Is profit a useful measure of a firm's success?

Profit is the most commonly accepted measure of a firm's success and yet it is widely misunderstood. Many people perceive profit as cash – they assume a profitable business must also be rich in cash. The profit figure actually only shows if the value of what has been sold is greater than the value of the inputs used up in the process of providing these goods and services.

This is, therefore, important to measure; it is clearly not worth doing something if the value of the output in the long-term is less than the value of the inputs. However, a major failing of this assessment of a firm's success is that it is only measuring its performance in financial terms. It ignores the quality of life for those involved in the business, the motivation of the workforce, the contribution of the firm towards society and the owners' and managers' own objectives. Who is to say that a firm that makes £120 million profit but has highly stressed, overworked employees and whose activities pollute the environment is actually more successful than another business, which only earns £80 million but focuses on recycling and improving the environment and has a highly motivated and content workforce?

Commentators are increasingly seeing the limitations of profit as a measure of success and one which highlights the importance of issues such as:

- A firm's contribution to society.

- A firm's ethics.

- The extent to which the firm's activities match what its owners and its stakeholders want to achieve.

- The nature of employer/employee relations.

- The firm's long-term profit – even if we do accept profit as an indicator of success, simply examining one year may be misleading; it is the long-term success which matters.

PROGRESS CHECK

'Our Objectives

To provide shareholders with good financial returns by focusing on customers' needs, adding value through our expertise and innovation, and investing for our future growth.

To provide unrivalled value to our customers in the quality of the goods we sell, in the competitiveness of our prices and in the range of choice we offer.

To achieve efficiency of operation, convenience and customer service in our stores, thereby creating as attractive and friendly a shopping environment as possible.

To provide a working environment where there is a concern for the welfare of each member of staff, where all have opportunities to develop their abilities and where each is well rewarded for their contribution to the success of the business.

To fulfil our responsibilities by acting with integrity, maintaining high environmental standards, and contributing to the quality of life in the community.'

Source: J Sainsbury plc Annual Report (1999)

Given the above, to what extent would profit be a good indicator of the success of J Sainsbury plc?

Balance sheet v. profit and loss items

All firms spend money in their operations. However, not all this expenditure will appear immediately in the profit and loss account as a cost. This is because we can classify all expenditure into one of two kinds: capital expenditure and revenue expenditure.

Capital and revenue expenditure

Capital expenditure appears on the balance sheet. For example, the purchase of new equipment would be capitalised and listed as a fixed asset. Over time the asset will be depreciated, its value on the balance sheet will be reduced and the annual depreciation will then be listed as a cost on the profit and loss statement.

Revenue expenditure, by comparison, is placed as an expense on the profit and loss statement in the period in which it occurs. For example, if a firms buys and uses up materials, these would appear immediately as a cost in the profit and loss statement.

The difference between the two types of expenditure is significant as, if a firm classifies an item as 'revenue expenditure' this immediately reduces profits by the full amount (it is entered immediately as a cost on the profit and loss statement). If it is classified as a 'capital expenditure' the impact on profits will be spread over a number of years as it is depreciated; this means that that year's profits will be higher than if the item was treated as revenue expenditure.

> **If an input is regarded as having been 'used up' it is a cost on the profit and loss statement and can be called a revenue expenditure. If it is not used up, it is an asset and is called a capital expenditure.**

Although the distinction between 'revenue' and 'capital' appears straightforward, it is not always easy to classify items as one or the other. The classification will partly depend on whether a firm regards an expenditure as significant. When a firm buys a set of chairs, for example, then technically these should be regarded as an asset, which will provide a benefit over the next few years. In other words, it is a capital expenditure that should be put on the balance sheet and depreciated. However, if the cost of the chairs is only a few hundred pounds the firm may write them off all at once, i.e. treat them as a revenue expenditure and put the total expenditure on the profit and loss this year.

In the case of items such as research and development, some firms will treat this as a revenue expenditure on the basis that the benefits of this have been used up this period; other firms will treat it as capital expenditure on the basis that it provides a benefit over time. This lack of clarity about what is and what is not a capital expenditure gives some firms increased scope for 'window dressing' their accounts so as to present the firm in a particularly flattering way. For example, by deciding to classify an item as a capital expenditure rather than a revenue expenditure a specific year's costs will be reduced and profits increased simply due to a change in accounting policy.

KEY TERMS

Capital expenditure
is money spent on items that are long lasting – beyond the current accounting period. It usually involves spending large amounts of money and is normally for the purchases of fixed assets.

Revenue expenditure
is money spent on items that will be used up within the current period, items that can be assigned to a specific period of time, such as salaries or insurance.

Items of expenditure that are more likely to be classified as:

Revenue expenditure	Capital expenditure	Either type
Wages and salaries	Buildings	Computer software
Marketing costs	New machinery	R&D
Production costs	Vehicles	Footballers
Heating and lighting	Computers	Brand names

Window dressing

Due to the different interepretations of accounting rules and regulations, it is quite possible for two people to use the same financial data and to draw up significantly different final accounts. Over the last twenty years, this 'grey area' has led to the development of 'window dressing' or 'creative accounting'. Window dressing occurs because it permits interpretation of accounting procedures in different ways; this differs from companies who illegally misrepresent their financial situation.

Methods of window dressing

Changing depreciation policy

Fixed assets should be valued at historical cost less accumulated depreciation. This depreciation, however, is based on an estimate of the life of the asset and this could be manipulated in order to make the value of the asset higher than would otherwise be the case. By increasing the estimate of the lifespan of an asset, the amounts provided for each year in the accounts as depreciation will be smaller (increasing this year's profits). This will also mean the book value of the asset is higher for a longer period of time, increasing the firm's asset value on the balance sheet.

Sale and leaseback

If a firm's liquidity ratios appear to be low it can arrange to sell its fixed assets and then lease them back. This brings in liquid funds and boosts its current assets, which improves the current and acid test ratio. By organising a sale and leaseback the firm can therefore temporarily disguise its underlying liquidity problem.

Bringing forward sales

Sales are included in the profit figures when the order is received, rather than when the cash for the sale is received. This allows firms to try to bring forward any sales that are likely to occur in the next few months, especially if this is near the end of a poor year. For example, just as the accounts are due to be published a firm may contact customers to try and get them to place their order slightly earlier than they had planned. This effectively moves sales from the beginning of the next financial year back to the end of the current year's to boost that year's results.

Intangibles

Brand names and goodwill can only be included on the balance sheet if they have been purchased and only if their separate value can easily be identified. This removes the possibility of firms including an estimate of their own internally generated goodwill or brand names on the balance sheet. However, a firm can boost its book value by maintaining the value of the intangible assets that it does include rather than depreciating them. To do this it must be able to argue that these intangibles have held their value over time.

Capitalising expenditure

Through capitalising expenditure, an item is listed as an asset on the balance sheet rather than as a cost on the profit and loss; this has the effect of boosting profits and increasing the value of the firm's assets. Computer software is a good example of this – this could be written off as an expense when the software is purchased. However, as the software will be used for a number of years, it could be argued that it really is the purchase of a fixed asset and therefore should be capitalized.

Extraordinary items

Extraordinary items are items of expenditure in the profit and loss accounts that are unusual, given the firm's main operating activities. An example could be the closure of a product line or the launch costs of a new branch. These items used to be kept separate in the profit and loss accounts. This meant that any items classified as extraordinary would not reduce the operating profits. Hence, a firm could boost profits by classifying expense items as extraordinary. This has now been disallowed under the publication of FRSs.

FACT FILE

In 1990 administrators were called in for the company Polly Peck that owed its bankers over £1 billion. The accounts of Polly Peck were found to have irregularities and the Serious Fraud Squad investigated. Even the board of directors appeared to have been deceived about what had happened to various sums of money.
Within a matter of weeks a company that was supposedly worth over £2 billion was worth almost nothing.

PROGRESS CHECK

Examine the ways in which a firm can window dress its accounts.

Why window dress accounts?

Firms will often window dress their accounts to attract investment into the business. By increasing its published profits it may be able to attract more investors. Given that profit is regarded as the major indicator of the success of a firm, firms clearly want to make this figure as flattering as possible. A firm may also need to borrow money from banks or other lenders. This means the business will have to convince the lender that it is able to repay the money borrowed. It may therefore be in a firm's interests to improve its profit and liquidity figures.

A further reason for window dressing is that there is a certain status assigned to a firm that is perceived as being the biggest, either in absolute terms, or the biggest in a particular field. This will motivate workers, attract media attention and attract future investments. It may also encourage firms to appear as 'big' as possible by increasing their asset values.

The pressure to produce flattering results is mainly exerted on public limited companies (plcs). Analysts and institutional investors are constantly monitoring a plc's performance and demanding ever better performance. As a result companies have to try and produce improved results each year. On occasions this may require window dressing. In comparison, there is less pressure on private limited companies from outside investors. This tends to mean they can plan more for the long-term and worry less about short-term fluctuations in results.

Is window dressing a problem in the UK?

The professional bodies who regulate accounting have tightened the rules surrounding financial reporting over the last five years. This has made it increasingly difficult for firms to window dress their accounts. For example, extraordinary items are no longer permitted and rules on the valuation of goodwill and other intangibles have also been tightened. There is, however, still scope for manipulation of the data.

Window dressing will only be useful if it manages to 'fool' the people who it is trying to impress. As cases of 'creative accounting' become more well known in the media, users of accounts will become more vigilant. The publicity surrounding window dressing has certainly increased in recent years (as highlighted in *Accounting for Growth*, by Terry Smith, which detailed many of the techniques being used by well-known firms) and this has made investors more critical. However, as the regulatory body becomes increasingly vigilant, companies themselves continue to search for ways in which the regulations can be interpreted in a particularly favourable light. Given the pressure of plcs to perform, it is unlikely that window dressing will ever entirely disappear.

PROGRESS CHECK

Consider the factors a firm might consider before window dressing its accounts.

How useful are balance sheet and profit and loss statements?

The balance sheet provides an analyst with one measure of a firm's value in addition to detail on its sources of finance. On its own the balance sheet can identify a firm's gearing and liquidity position. The profit and loss statement provides a measure of a firm's performance over a given period. Using both statements together it is possible to calculate a whole range of ratios, such as the return on capital employed, profit margins, debtor days and stock turnover.

It is therefore important to look at both the balance sheet and the profit and loss to get a more complete picture of a firm's performance. A business may have a high level of assets (shown on the balance sheet) but may have performed very badly in the previous year, which will be shown by the profit and loss. Alternatively, the firm may have relatively few assets (for example, a new business) but still have relatively high profit levels, as shown on the profit and loss.

The value of these statements, however, depends on how up-to-date they are (published accounts are often several months out of date) and the ability of the analyst to identify the key figures and interpret them effectively. It is also important to remember that published acounts are inevitably backward looking and do not necessarily reflect what will happen in the future. High performing companies can suddenly struggle due to changes in the market or economic environment, whilst companies with low profits can suddenly experience a breakthrough.

Another problem with published accounts is that they only show quantative data; qualitative issues such as the culture of the firm, its attitude to risk, its social and environmental policies are not included. In some cases we may regard a firm with a strong ethical policy but with lower profits as more successful than one which makes high profits but has a poor record on environmental issues. Interestingly, a small but growing number of firms such as the Body Shop are voluntarily taking steps towards greater levels of disclosure by producing independently audited social reports alongside their financial statements. These usually assess the company's performance by taking account of the interests of a number of stake-holders – such as suppliers, employees and the wider community – in addition to the shareholders.

A further limitation of published accounts is that the balance sheet does not necessarily reflect the true value of the business. Brands, knowledge, intellectual capital (such as its patents, technologies, skills and distribution systems) and business contacts are increasingly being recognised as crucial assets of a business, yet these are not always included in published accounts. Window dressing can also limit the usefulness of published accounts as analysts often use the data in the form that the firms want them to see, as opposed to in the way in which they might want to see it for themselves.

Data must also be analysed over time. A look at one year's accounts can give a particular impression, but the trends may help to highlight the overall direction of the business. The published accounts, therefore, provide some information for analysts, however, it is important to be critical of the data, to be willing to recognise its limitations and to combine it with information from elsewhere. Data in itself cannot make decisions and the value of the information in the published accounts will depend in part on the experience and good judgement of the user.

Summary chart

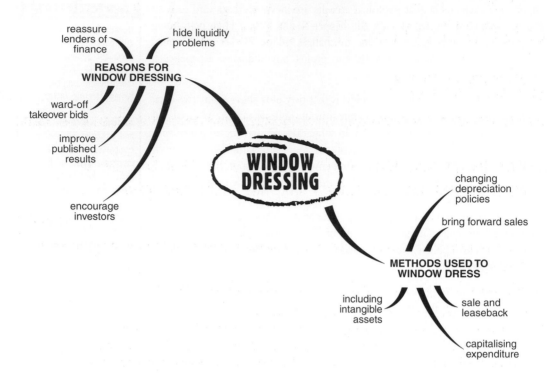

Figure 2.1 Window dressing

Approaching exam questions: Published accounts

Analyse the possible ways in which the accounts of a firm can be 'window dressed' and the reasons why this would take place.

(9 marks)

This question can be broken into two sections: the ways in which accounts can be distorted and the reasons for distorting the accounts.

The ways in which accounts can be window dressed would include the following:

1   Capitalisation of expenditure, such as the expenditure on R&D.
2   Bringing forward sales that were going to be earned next year into this year's accounts.
3   Changing depreciation policy, by either changing methods or extending the life of an asset.
4   Sale and leaseback of a fixed asset to generate cash inflows and hide a poor liquidity position.

When looking at these different ways it is important to go into detail on how these actually work. This will not necessarily involve financial illustrations but will require a good written understanding of some of them (not necessarily all of them!). Try to remember that for the firm to window dress their accounts, there will be a reason for doing so.

Window dressing accounts will usually take place in order to either hide a poor position or to improve the existing position of the firm's financial performance. Firms will not always only window dress their account if they are performing poorly. Sometimes they may reduce the profit figure because they want to reject particular wage or dividend demands. Firms also often aim for stable profit growth and so will smooth out their performance figures; this may involve increasing profits in bad years and reducing profits in good years.

Firms may also window dress their account to avoid a takeover bid being launched. It may do this by boosting profits or assets, to convince existing shareholders that the firm is performing satisfactorily without outside help. To answer this type of question, you should try to link the methods of window dressing and the reason for that particular method. For example, a firm may use sale and leaseback to hide deteriorating liquidity.

Analyse the possible effects of a change in depreciation policy on a firm's performance.

(9 marks)

A change in depreciation policy will probably mean either a change in the method of depreciation, a change in the expected lifespan of the assets being depreciated or the estimate of its residual value. In this question it would be appropriate for you to explore how each of these would affect the firm's financial position.

Depreciation is a provision not an expense and, therefore, although it is charged as if the firm was paying money for the depreciation, no cash actually leaves the firm. The important point here is that a change in depreciation policy will have no effect on the firm's cash flow and a firm's liquidity position will not be affected; cash flow problems cannot be solved by changes in the depreciation policy. However, profit will be affected and this is where the change in a firm's performance can be examined – changing the method will affect the annual amount charged as a cost in the profit and loss account. For example, changing the lifespan of an asset will affect the amount charged per year. Shortening the life of the asset means that the depreciation has to be fitted into 'less years' and, therefore, more will appear each year. Extending the life means that the depreciation can be 'spread' over more years and therefore less will appear each year.

It is important to link these possible changes with the effect on the firm's profit. Obviously, charging less depreciation means higher profits, higher returns on capital and higher profit margins. This will potentially attract more investors. Therefore, the firm's performance may be improved. However, this could be classed as window dressing. The firm has not sold more products and it has not reduced the costs of production; it has purely used an accounting technique to shift today's expenses into future periods and, therefore, is postponing future expenses that will have to be accounted for one day.

A suitable conclusion to this question could look at how short-term (i.e. current) profits can be boosted by changes in policy but how in the long-term (i.e. future years) the effect is cancelled out, through higher depreciation charges and, therefore, in the long-term performance has not changed. The precise effects of a change in depreciation policy will, of course, depend on the nature and extent of the change.

Why is the amount of profit made by a firm of interest to the directors of a company?

(9 marks)

The possible reasons for the importance of profit to the board of directors include:

- influences decisions over level of dividend payments
- may affect any pay awards/pay demands
- may affect investment decisions
- used as a measure of their effectiveness
- likely to affect investors' reactions

To score highly in this question it is important that you not only explain the importance of your points but also go into detail and discuss why they are important. For example, the amount of profit can help show the amount of money available for investment. However, the profit may already be tied up in other assets (such as stock) elsewhere in the firm. Remember, you do not have to include many points, you simply have to analyse the few that you have selected. Three factors would be acceptable, provided they were analysed in sufficient detail.

To what extent are tangible assets irrelevant in determining a firm's success?

(11 marks)

This question is really looking at how important a firm's tangible assets are. It is crucial to realise that there will not be one 'yes' or 'no' answer to this question. It will, as ever, depend on the type of firm – large versus small and manufacturing versus service sector firms. Possible factors to be included in this answer could be:

- Retailers and other service sectors firms' success may be more related to brand names and goodwill.

- Research and development and innovation may be more important for firms in competitive markets.

- New firms may rely more on tangible assets due to lack of developed goodwill and brand names.

- Some tangible assets are likely to be required by any firm.

This question requires evaluation to score full marks. Evaluation of this question would look at how important the tangible assets actually are. For example, for a retailer, it may be the case that it is tangible assets that allow the firm to continue trading and survive, but it may be the intangible assets (e.g. brand names) that give the firm the competitive edge. The answer will depend on what tangible assets the firm has and how they are being used. They are unlikely to be 'irrelevant'; firms generally need premises, transport and equipment, for example. However, success does not just come from tangible assets; it also depends on the skill of the management, the way resources are used, the culture of the firm, the nature of employer/employee relations and the intellectual capital of the business.

Student answers

A firm makes a profit of £2 million from a capital employed of £12 million. Evaluate the usefulness of these figures for potential investors.

(11 marks)

Student answer

The net profit made by the firm is the profit made after all deductions. We can calculate that the firm has made a return on capital employed of £2 million/£12 million = 17%. This is a good figure as it means that the firm is earning a positive return of its shareholders, which is above the return available on other financial assets, such as stocks and shares.

However, we would need other figures for us to make any meaningful conclusions. Last years' profit or the previous few years' profits would be useful as this would help us to identify a trend in the direction of the profit. Making comparisons with other firms would be useful. However, they would need to be similar firms for the comparison to be meaningful. For example, if the firm was making profits above the average for the industry that the firm operates in, then this would be a positive sign for investors.

Looking at the state of the economy would also be useful. If the economy is going through a boom then we would expect the firm to be making high profits. In a recession firms make losses.

It would be also useful to know how the firm made its profit. If a firm has sold any fixed assets then the profits on these sales would be included in the profit figures. This is not necessarily a good sign for investors as it means that the firm is cutting back on its production facilities, for example, if it had sold a machine. A good sign for investors is if the profit was made on its main activities, that is, the buying and selling of goods and services. Profit made this way is sustainable and indicates that the firm is producing products that people wish to buy. So the profit will only be useful if we can examine how it was made.

Marker's comments

This is a fairly good answer. The student obviously understands the basis of accounts and what they do and do not show. The first two paragraphs are fairly basic, but they do understand the need for using more than one isolated figure for making any meaningful conclusion.

The third paragraph is a little simplistic – not all firms make profits in booms or losses in recessions, as it all depends on the product that a firm sells. Also, we would need to look at the market where the firm sells to use the economy as an important factor. For example, if a firm is a large multinational firm then a downturn in one country may not have a large impact. This would be different if a firm sold income elastic products in one country and that country then moved into recession.

The final paragraph moves the student up into the evaluative band. Here we have discussion of what is meant by the 'quality' of a firm's profit. This student understands that profits can be made from sources that do not bode well for the long-term future of the firm.

There is little wrong with this answer. Students will sometimes spend too long on simplistic matters rather than addressing the real issues earlier on in an answer. To score more highly a student would be expected to consider some of the following factors:

- Looking at segmental reporting. A firm can make profits and losses on individual products, or in certain geographical areas. For example, it may be the case that a firm made a higher profit in one area but this was reduced through some external factor affecting another part of the firm. For example, the collapse of the Brazilian currency may have affected profits in the Brazilian markets, but other South American markets may have still yielded profits.

- There are other ways in which a firm can distort the profit figures. A firm may classify some of its expenditure as capital expenditure. This would remove the figure from the profit and loss account, thus boosting profits. The notes to the accounts should illustrate if this had occurred.

- We are, of course, assuming that the potential investor is only interested in profits. It may be the case that the investor would buy shares in order to launch a takeover bid. Although this is not normally the case, it still needs stating.

A candidate could also consider which measure of profit has been used and discuss the implications of this.

Marks: Content 2/2, Application & Analysis 4/6, Evaluation 2/3. Total = 8

Analyse the possible impact on a firm of capitalising its research expenditure.

(9 marks)

Student answer

Capitalising expenditure would mean that it does not appear in the profit and loss account as an expense, but would appear instead on the balance sheet as a fixed asset. This asset of research expenditure could then be depreciated over its life as the firm benefits from the amount spent.

The impact of this is that initially the firm's profits will be boosted, taking expense away from the profit and loss will increase profit and boost ratios such as the ROCE and EPS. This may attract new investors into the company. However, the depreciation of the research will appear every year that the asset appears on the balance sheet. This means that future profit will be lower than it would have been if the expenditure had been written off in the year it occurred.

Overall, the effect will be the same – the amount will pass through the profit and loss account. By capitalising the expenditure it just takes longer for it to pass through. However, in the short-term the boost to profit could significantly affect the performance of the firm and, therefore, benefit the firm from more investment.

In terms of cash flow, the firm should realise that it does not matter whether it is capitalised or not, as depreciation is a provision, and once the expense has been paid it will no longer affect the cash flow of the firm. The impact on the cash flow is always when the expense is incurred and, therefore, the policy on whether to capitalise expenditure is irrelevant. If a firm is running out of money then it does not matter what the profit is, as it will still have problems.

Marker's comments

This is a very strong answer. The student clearly realises that the expense must pass through the profit and loss account eventually but that it may take several years for it to pass through if the expense is capitalised.

The impact of this decision is also explained and considered well. Even though in the long-run the effects will be the same, the short-term results are important and could have a significant impact on the shareholders of the firm through higher profits. The impact on the cash flow is also well considered – solvency is different from the profit and, therefore, the change in the policy on capitalising expenditure will not help hide any problems in the long-term.

The overall impact will depend on whether this is a one-off decision or an ongoing policy, the amount of research the firm does, whether analysts appreciate this change has occurred and the policy of other firms.

Mark: Content 2/2, Application 4/4, Analysis 3/3. Total = 9

End of section questions

1 To what extent does the balance sheet show the strength of a company?

(11 marks)

2 Is the balance sheet more important than the profit and loss statement?

(11 marks)

3 Evaluate the possible arguments for allowing brand names to be included under fixed assets.

(11 marks)

4 Analyse the possible ways in which firms can 'window dress' their own accounts.

(7 marks)

5 Explain why we might need to use a balance sheet and a profit and loss together to assess a firm's financial position.

(9 marks)

6 Discuss the factors that might determine the asset structure of a firm.

(9 marks)

7 What is meant by the 'value' of a company? Discuss the factors which might influence this value.

(11 marks)

8 Discuss the view that the profit figure for a firm is actually meaningless for an analyst.

(11 marks)

9 To what extent can a firm choose what profit figure it puts in the accounts?

(11 marks)

10 Examine the value of the balance sheet and the profit and loss to a potential investor.

(9 marks)

Essays

1 Evaluate the use of the published accounts for making the decision on whether to take over a company or not.

(40 marks)

2 'The bottom line for any firm is whether or not it can increase its profits, if it can then that's good enough'. Evaluate the use of a firm's annual profit in determining the performance of a business.

(40 marks)

3 'Profit is an outdated, misleading measure of business success.' Discuss.

(40 marks)

4 Evaluate the view that the balance sheet is the best source of information in determining the true value of a business.

(40 marks)

5 'Without the notes to the accounts and accounting policies the final accounts of a firm are nothing more than an incomprehensible work of fiction'. Critically assess this view.

(40 marks)

Ratio analysis

What is ratio analysis?

Ratio analysis involves using the data in the final accounts of a business to draw conclusions about its performance. Rather than looking at the size of different figures in isolation, ratio analysis places figures in context by comparing one piece of data with another. For example, we might compare profit to sales or to the capital employed.

Ratios are mainly based on financial data taken from the final accounts of a firm: the balance sheet and the profit and loss accounts. Although each ratio can be used to assess the performance of a firm, each one examines a different area of the firm's overall effectiveness. There are five main areas that financial ratios can be used to examine: profitability, efficiency, liquidity, gearing and shareholder ratios.

Ratio analysis is a useful tool for decision making. It helps place figures in context and identify areas of concern or of particular strength. From this managers can plan and take appropriate action. The question of whether this is the correct action depends on the reliability and usefulness of the data and the ability of the manager to analyse the figures correctly. As with any decision making tool, ratio analysis does not guarantee that the right decison is made or that it is actually implemented. It is one thing to identify that the firm's profits are low; it is another to decide what to do about it and bring about the necessary changes.

> **Ratios do not make decisions but they can help the decision maker decide what to do.**

FACT FILE

Ratio analysis is more likely to be useful when:
- the information is relevant and accurate
- the ratios are placed in the context of other similar firms and past records
- the manager is able to analyse the data correctly

Ratios must be placed in context in order to be useful: what is the precise nature of the firm? What would we expect a particular ratio to be? What figure were the managers aiming for, what has the figure been in the past and what are other firms achieving? Examining just one ratio on its own is probably of limited value; it has to be placed in the overall context of the organisation, its history, its environment and its objectives.

> **Ratios should be placed in context.**

RATIO TYPE	EXPLANATION
Profitability ratios	These ratios examine the profits made by a firm and compare these figures with the size of the firm or its level of sales. Profitability ratios can be used to examine how well the firm is operating or how well current performance compares to past records or to other firms.
Efficiency ratios	These ratios will look at the workings of a firm internally. Although the debtors and creditors of the firm may not seem as important as the profits, it is important that proper control is exerted over these so that the firm can maximise its efficiency. Efficient performance should help maintain profitability.
Liquidity ratios	The purpose of these ratios is to see if a firm is able to pay all its short-term debts. This is known as solvency. It is very important that a firm holds enough liquid assets to meet the demands of its creditors for repayment. Even profitable firms can run into liquidity problems and these ratios will determine a firm's stength or weakness in this area.
Gearing ratios	The gearing position of a firm is measured by examining its financial structure to see if it has borrowed too much money. This is important as the firm may not be able to meet the interest payments if it has borrowed too much.
Shareholders' ratios	These ratios are examined from the perspective of a potential or actual shareholder of a firm. We look at the dividends, share prices, and profits to see if an adequate return is being made for the investor.

Note: the precise categorisation of ratios can vary. Do not worry about this. The important thing to remember is that the ratio should be fit for the purpose, that is, it should be a valuable tool for your analysis.

Table 3.1 Types of ratio

Who uses ratios?

Accounting ratios will be used by different groups of people who are connected with the organisation. Each group will be examining the accounts from a different perspective, each looking for particular information. For example, a bank manager who is considering lending a firm money is likely to be interested in the ability of the firm to pay back the money. In contrast, potential investors will probably be interested in how much they are likely to receive as dividends. The differing objectives mean that the various groups are likely to focus on different accounting ratios:

■ Suppliers may be interested in the firm's liquidity to assess if it will be able to pay its bills; they may focus on the acid test ratio.

■ Customers may be concerned with the firm's debtor days to see how long other customers are given to pay up; they will look at the debtor collection period.

■ Employees may be interested in the firm's profitability as this might affect their pay bargaining; they may consider the firm's return on capital employed.

■ Competitors may be interested in a wide range of ratios to benchmark their performance and because this may determine their strategy; they may look at the stock turnover, profit margins and asset turnover in addition to the overall return on capital employed, for example.

■ Investors and potential investors will be interested in the dividends paid out and the share price. They will typically look at ratios such as the price earnings ratio and the dividend yield.

Examine the possible reasons why competitors might be interested in a firm's ratios.

It is important to select the ratios that are appropriate for the given task and which are relevant to the particular group using them.

Syllabus requirements

Different examination boards will make differing demands on what ratios you are required to know. The ratios marked with an asterisk (*) are **not** required by AQA at A level. However, this does not mean that you cannot use these ratios. Credit would be given to students who used these, if they were appropriate. You will not, however, be asked to calculate these ratios specifically.

Performance ratios

KEY TERMS

Profit
is an absolute figure (e.g. £100 million) measuring revenue minus costs.

Profitability
is a relative figure; it measures the amount of profit in relation to something (e.g. the capital employed) and is measured as a percentage.

Many firms have profit maximisation as their primary objective. It makes sense, therefore, to evaluate the strength of a company's performance on the basis of the size of its profits. Profitability ratios use the profits that a firm makes and compares these to the size of the business (in terms of capital employed) and the sales that it makes over a period of time. Table 3.2 following defines ratio key terms.

RATIO	FORMULA	NOTES
Return on capital employed (ROCE)	$\dfrac{\textit{Operating or net profit} \times 100}{\text{Capital employed}}$	Expresses profits after all operating expenses have been deducted as a percentage of the capital of the firm.
Profit margin	$\dfrac{\textit{Operating or net profit} \times 100}{\text{Sales revenue}}$	Shows the percentage of sales revenue that is made up of profit.
Gross profit margin	$\dfrac{\textit{Gross profit} \times 100}{\text{Sales revenue}}$	Similar to the general profit margin, but tells us what percentage of sales is made up of purely gross profit.

Table 3.2 Key performance ratio terms

ROCE

The return on capital employed (ROCE) is often considered to be the key profitability ratio, as it looks at the most important area of interest to people within and outside of the firm, its profit, in relation to the long-term sources of finance in the business. It therefore shows a rate of return on the money invested in the organisation. In general, the higher the return the better; this is because the greater the return generated the more likely it is that the firm will be able to increase dividends and investment into the business. If a firm has falling returns it may prove unattractive to investors; in the case of a public limited company this could lead to a fall in its share price.

The concept of the return on capital employed is crucial to all businesses. Every project should be considered in terms of the return it generates. At any moment in time managers may have hundreds of possible plans presented to them; they need to consider which ones actually generate a worthwhile return. For example, if a project can earn £100 profit but requires an initial investment of £5 million this is a low rate of return – it generates profit, however, compared to the money needed to undertake the project, this is probably not particularly appealing. Alternatively, if the profit is £100 and the initial investment is £200 this is an attractive return and is much more likely to be considered. Every business action has an opportunity cost and so in order to decide on whether to go ahead with a particular plan it is important to think about its return.

> **If the return is not high enough – do not do it.**

To assess the ROCE effectively it should be compared to other firms in the industry, past figures and other alternative investments.

One basis for comparison is to compare the return on the firm's capital to the return on money placed into high interest bank accounts. For example, a firm may have a ROCE of 5% when the level of interest rates available on high interest accounts is at 6%. Logically, this says the firm is not performing well – investors would probably prefer to put their money in the bank than let the firm's managers have it, especially when we consider that the risk of investing in a firm is probably greater than putting money in a bank.

PROGRESS CHECK

Questions

1 Analyse the possible reasons why a firm's managers might want to increase its return on capital employed.
2 Consider the possible ways in which a firm might increase its return on capital employed.

Increasing ROCE

To increase the ROCE firms could try to improve their profits. This can be done by increasing turnover (focusing on the top line) and/or reducing costs (focusing on the bottom line).

To increase sales, the firm may review its marketing activities, seek new markets or develop new products. In each case it must ensure that the extra revenue generated is sufficient given the costs involved. To reduce costs, the firm may restructure or rationalise. In this case, it must be careful of the impact on the quality of the product or service.

FACT FILE

'We expect to maintain our average of over 60% return on capital after the third year of a restaurant's life. Physical expansion of restaurants running at near capacity will continue. Historically the extra seating created has achieved on average an immediate return on capital of over 40%.'

Source: *Pizza Express Annual Report*, 1998

FACT FILE

In 1999 the government announced that it hoped to save up to £200 million on the National Health Service's annual £3.8 billion drugs budget by limiting the pharmaceutical industry's profits. Since the 1950s, prices have been controlled by voluntary agreement. However, the Health Secretary is determined to put this on a statutory footing. Under the voluntary agreement, drug companies submit their accounts to the Department of Health. When their profits reach a certain level, measured by return on capital employed, they must either cut their prices or repay money to the government. The agreement is being renegotiated, however, the industry wants it to remain voluntary.

Possible reasons for low ROCE

Most firms will experience a low ROCE at some stage in their development. A lot of new firms, for example, make losses in the first few years. This could be because they do not have a wide sales base, or because they have to spend heavily on advertising in order to create consumer awareness.

Many firms will also experience lower than average returns if they are trading in a period of low economic growth or recession. If growth is low then this will probably mean lower consumer spending, which in turn is likely to lead to lower sales for many firms. The precise effect of economic growth on a firm's sales will, however, depend on what the firm produces and what market the products are aimed at. Firms that sell income elastic products will be more affected than firms who sell income inelastic products.

There are other reasons for relatively poor ROCE performance. Thus far, we have assumed that a firm will always be aiming for the most profits possible. However, it is possible that a firm will have other objectives, either as a long-term aim or as a short-term tactical change from their usual goals. For example, a firm may deliberately cut selling prices and lose out on possible profits in order to boost sales. This highlights the need to decide over what period the ROCE should be measured.

In the 1970s, several Japanese firms gained control of consumer electronic markets by sacrificing short-term profits to build up sales volume, knowing that this would lead to greater long-term returns. An analysis of their performance in their early years would have suggested they were underperforming; over the long-term they achieved high rates of return.

The ROCE of a firm may also be low if a business needs to spend heavily on investment. For example, if new technology is introduced into an industry or the potential for a new market is opened up, investment may be needed to remain competitive. It could be the case that a firm that invests first in the new technology will experience a drop in its profits and a fall in its ROCE for that year. However, in the future the firm that has been the first or the largest investor in the new technology could gain a competitive advantage over other firms and experience above industry average ROCE. This further illustrates the need to place ratios in context; a low ROCE in one particular year may be due to heavy investment in the future, which will generate high rewards later on.

Profit margin, sales and profits

The profit margin shows the profit per sale as a percentage of the selling price. The size of the profit margin will depend on the nature of the product, the competitiveness of the market and the firm's pricing policy. If the market is highly competitive, the product is not differentiated and the firm is using penetration pricing, then the profit margin is likely to be low. If, however, the product is heavily branded or patented and/or the firm dominates the industry the profit margin is likely to be higher.

If a firm can increase its sales and maintain its profit margin, then its overall return (its ROCE) will increase. However, higher sales do not guarantee a higher return;

in many cases firms will achieve a boost in sales by cutting prices and so reducing the profit margin. If more is sold but the profit per sale is lower, then overall profits and the ROCE may fall.

It is certainly possible, however, to achieve high overall returns even if the profit margin is relatively small; just look at the main retailers, such as Tesco or J. Sainsbury. Although they have comparatively low profit margins, their high level of sales mean their ROCE is also high. They are known as 'high volume, low margin' producers.

FACT FILE

Top 5 UK firms and their ROCE 1997:
1 HSBC: 16.8%
2 Shell Transport: 20.7%
3 BP: 17.8%
4 Abbey National: 5.8%
5 BT: 20.8%

Source: *The Times 1000*

Questions

PROGRESS CHECK

1 Explain how a firm may experience higher profit margins, but lower profits.
2 Analyse the possible impact of a fall in profit margins on a firm's overall profits.

> **More sales do not necessarily mean a ROCE – it may be that the profit per sale is lower (due to a lower price or higher costs) and so the firm's overall returns may go down.**

NUMERICAL INVESTIGATION

Satellite broadcaster BSkyB's profits have taken a fall as the group prepared for the launch of its digital TV service in 1999. The cost of paving the way for the multi-channel service meant that BSkyB's profits fell by 14% to £270.9 million in 1998. Sky's Premier League football contract also contributed to the decline. Turnover rose on the previous 12 months from £1.25 billion to £1.43 billion. BSkyB is Britain's most profitable television company.

a Calculate BSkyB's turnover in 1997.
b Calculate BSkyB's profit margin in 1997 and 1998.
c Consider the possible impact of this change in the profit margin for the firm.

FACT FILE

In 1999 Marks and Spencer was heavily criticised for its poor performance. The origin of its problems could be traced back to its purchase of US men's wear chain Brooks Brothers for $750 million in 1988. The new chief executive also admitted that Marks and Spencer expanded into Europe too quickly and that the Far East has been disappointing. Domestically, the firm has been attacked for its purchase of the Littlewoods stores and a poor selection of stocks. The Marks & Spencer finance director admitted the company's poor return on capital was an overriding priority. It fell from 22% in 1997 to 9% in 1998. The company has calculated its break even point in 1998 for shareholder value as 9.7% (its cost of capital). If the return on capital is less than this, the capital may be better used in other parts of the business.

NUMERICAL INVESTIGATION

Churchill China plc

	1998 (£000)	1997 (£000)
Turnover	50,767	53,855
Operating profit	1,188	5,720

Table 3.3

a Calculate the operating profit margin for 1997 and 1998.
b Explain possible reasons why the profit margin may have changed in this way.

KEY POINTS

ROCE is likely to be lower if:

- a firm is operating in a recession (assuming it sells income elastic goods)
- a firm has only recently begun trading
- the firm has spent more money on R&D
- the firm is engaging in sales maximisation at the expense of profits

KEY POINTS

Profit margins are more likely to be lower:

- in competitive markets
- in high volume markets
- if unit costs are high and the market is price sensitive
- if the firm is aiming to gain market share
- as part of a penetration pricing policy

NUMERICAL INVESTIGATION

1997	ROCE (%)	PROFIT MARGIN
Manchester Utd.	36.18	29.79
Sheffield Utd.	0.09	0.15
Hi-Tec	25.82	5.91
Glaxo	149.31	35.36
Tate & Lyle	16.71	4.18
Zeneca	49.41	20.85
Cadbury Schweppes	30.78	14.41
Harry Ramsdens	17.69	24.14
Unilever	32.17	8.02
J. Sainsbury plc	18.91	4.86
Tesco	19.89	4.82
Somerfield	13.94	2.99
Kwik Save	11.89	1.44
Psion	37.6	13.88

Table 3.4 Source: Bized

a Identify which firm had the highest and which had the lowest ROCE.
b Identify the firm which had the highest and which had the lowest profit margin.
c Explain possible reasons for the differences in profit margins shown.

Efficiency ratios

This group of ratios measures the efficiency of a firm. Efficiency is measured by how the firm controls its working capital in terms of debtor and creditor control, the firm's stock policy and the level of its sales relative to its assets.

Although these ratios do not indicate the profitability of the firm, they could indicate problems that, if not acted upon, might damage future performance.

RATIO	FORMULA	NOTES
Stock Turnover	$\dfrac{\text{Cost of sales}}{\text{Stock}}$	The stock turnover measures how rapidly a firm sells its stocks. The higher the stock turnover, the more rapidly the stock is being sold.
Stock days (*)	$\dfrac{\text{Cost of sales} \times 365}{\text{Sales}}$	This shows the amount of stock held by a firm in terms of its sales.
Debtor days (or debtor's turnover or debt collection period)	$\dfrac{\text{Debtors} \times 365}{\text{Sales}}$	This ratio shows the average amount of time a firm takes to collect payments from its debtors. The figure will give us the average number of days each of the firm's debtors takes to pay the firm the amount that they owe.
Creditor days (*)	$\dfrac{\text{Creditors} \times 365}{\text{Purchases}}$	This is similar to the debtor turnover ratio. This ratio measures the length of time taken by the firm to pay off its own debts to its creditors.
Asset turnover ratio	$\dfrac{\text{Sales Revenue}}{(\text{Net Assets})}$	This shows how well a firm's assets are being used to generate sales. The greater the asset turnover, the more the assets are being utilised to generate sales.

Table 3.5 Key efficiency ratio terms

Stock turnover

The typical value for a firm's stock turnover will depend on the type of goods that it sells. Firms that sell consumer goods normally have a higher stock turnover than other firms, as they are bought more frequently. Firms that sell goods that are not bought frequently (for example, industrial equipment) are likely to have a lower figure.

Stock turnover is likely to be higher if the goods are perishable (for example, fresh flowers). This is because the goods cannot be held for long in stock. A firm that sells perishable goods is more likely to order small amounts in frequent intervals, giving a higher stock turnover ratio. This argument may also apply to firms selling goods with short product life cycles, such as fashion products (for example, chart records or seasonal clothes); these firms will want to avoid being left with high levels of stock. However, a firm must balance the desire for low stocks with the risk that it will run out of stock and not be able to satisfy all the demands for the product.

Stock turnover will also increase if a firm adopts lean production techniques. Firms that operate a 'just-in-time' policy will have to make many orders for supplies as they are required. This will mean that the average stock held at any one time will be relatively small leading to a high stock turnover ratio.

Debtor days

Most firms offer credit to their customers. The credit period offered varies according to the type of business but is typically 30, 60 or 90 days. Almost inevitably, firms will have outstanding debtors owing the firm money. However, if the amount owed to the firm is viewed as too high then it will want to take steps to correct this, as it can cause liquidity problems.

FACT FILE

British Telecom

	Profit margins	ROCE
	(%)	(%)
1995	17.9	16.3
1996	18.2	17.3
1997	18.4	20.8
1998	18.5	19.7
1999	23.6	21.2

Despite deregulation in the telecommunications market and increasing levels of competition, BT has managed to increase its profit margins and its ROCE. Its profits are the equivalent of £135 per second.

FACT FILE

The chief executive of Ford set the company the twin targets of a 5% return on sales. Volume vehicle manufacturers typically manage 2%, and 7% annual revenue growth. The purchase of Kwik-Fit highlighted the sort of overall performance Ford wanted.

Under that vision, Ford would measure itself against world class consumer businesses, rather than the traditional yardsticks of rival car manufacturers.

Questions

PROGRESS CHECK

1 Would you expect the debtor days to be high or low for the following firms:
a launderettes
b solicitors
c car manufacturers
d restaurants
2 Explain your answers.

The longer a customer takes to settle an outstanding debt, the more likely it is that the debt will never be repaid and will have to be written off as a bad debt. Steps to correct this would include:

■ Offering discounts for cash sales.

■ Offering discounts for prompt payment.

Firms may also have to chase existing debtors for repayment or borrow from a debt factor.

KEY TERM

Debt factor
    lends to a firm using its debtors as collateral. This improves a firm's cash flow, although a charge is involved.

FACT FILE

Average debtor days
UK	78 days
France	104 days
Germany	45 days

Source: *Intrum Justitia Survey*

When analysing debtors it is often important to consider how long the money has been outstanding. This can be done by producing an aged debtors statement. Debtors can then be treated differently according to how old they are. For example, a firm will not necessarily need to chase up debtors who have only been outstanding for one week. A firm will, however, want to avoid having debts that have been outstanding for a long time, due to the negative impact on cash flow. On the other hand, offering credit can be a means of generating sales and attempts to reduce the credit period may lose sales and customer goodwill.

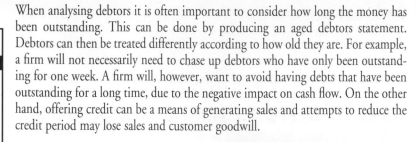

PROGRESS CHECK

Discuss the ways in which a firm might reduce its debtors.

Creditor days

This ratio measures how long a firm takes to pay its creditors. It is interesting to compare this to the debtor days ratio. If a firm is owed 60 days worth of sales but only owes 20 days worth to its creditors, it could cause liquidity problems. If, however, it is owed 50 days and owes 70 days, then once it is paid it can hold on to this money before paying suppliers.

A firm will usually try to negotiate long payment periods so that it can earn interest on the money. However, suppliers will naturally want swift payment, so this can cause conflict. Many smaller firms complain of being bullied by larger firms who delay payment, often for months. Companies now have to publish in their accounts how long they take, on average, to pay their creditors.

What are acceptable times for debtor and creditor days?

There are no ideal figures for the debtors and creditors turnover. Actual figures and time taken to collect and pay their debts will depend on the industry in which they operate. It will also depend on the type of customer that they are selling to. For example, a firm may be more likely to offer generous credit terms to regular customers than to new customers. Firms may have to give longer credit periods than they would have preferred, due to competitors offering a longer credit period. It may also be the case that long credit periods have to be given to encourage consumers to spend in the first place.

Asset turnover ratio

This ratio shows how effective a firm is in utilising its assets, in other words, how much sales revenue is generated from a firm's asset base. A high and/or rising figure would indicate that the firm's assets were being used more successfully to generate sales. However, the right size for this ratio will depend on what industry the firm operates within.

Firms that are highly capital intensive would normally be expected to have a lower asset turnover ratio. This is not due to lower sales but to the high value of assets that this type of firm would have. An example would be a firm selling capital equipment, such as machinery. A retailer, on the other hand, would normally be fairly labour intensive and should, therefore, have lower levels of fixed assets. This would imply a higher asset turnover, assuming sales were high.

NUMERICAL INVESTIGATION

1997	ASSET TURNOVER
Manchester Utd.	1.21
Sheffield Utd.	0.58
Hi-Tec	4.37
Glaxo	4.22
Tate & Lyle	3.99
Zeneca	2.37
Cadbury Schweppes	2.14
Harry Ramsdens	0.73
Unilever	4.01
J. Sainsbury plc	3.89
Tesco	4.13
Somerfield	4.66
Kwik Save	8.25
Psion	2.71

Table 3.6

Identify the firm which has the highest asset turnover and which has the lowest. Explain possible reasons for the differences in asset turnover shown above.

FACT FILE

Top 5 UK Brewers 1997: asset turnover ratio

Grand Metropolitan	1.08
Bass	0.97
Allied Domeq	1.52
Whitbread	0.99
Scottish & Newcastle	1.17

Source: *The Times 1000*

FACT FILE

Utilising our assets
Our focus on creating value requires the optimal utilisation of our assets, be they people, brands or factories. They are all vital components in managing costs and winning customers.

Source: *Cadbury Schweppes Annual Report 1998*

NUMERICAL INVESTIGATION

The following data is from the final accounts of the top 5 banks of 1997 (ranked according to their capital net assets employed).

	NET ASSETS (£000)	SALES (£000)
HSBC	26,947,000	18,481,000
Abbey National	20,143,000	7,044,000
Nat West	15,505,000	14,590,000
Halifax	13,734,100	7,073,782
Barclays	13,681,000	12,523,000

Table 3.7

For each bank, calculate the asset turnover ratio. Comment on your findings.

Liquidity ratios

A good manager will always monitor the firm's cash flow position. This reflects the amount of money available to spend that a firm has at any one time. As we know from earlier work, profit and cash are not the same thing. The profitability ratios will not tell us if a firm will have enough money to trade on a daily basis. Hence the need to use liquidity ratios.

The idea behind liquidity ratios is that a firm will need to have cash or other liquid assets available so that it can settle any debts that will shortly need paying. The liquidity position of a firm can, therefore, be examined by comparing the current assets to the current liabilities from the firm's balance sheet. The ratios used are shown in Table 3.11.

RATIO	FORMULA	NOTES
Current ratio (*)	$\dfrac{\text{Current assets}}{\text{Current liabilities}}$	The current ratio measures relative size of current assets compared with current liabilities. For example, a ratio of two would indicate twice as many current assets as current liabilities. Assumes that all current assets can be quickly converted into cash
Acid test ratio	$\dfrac{\text{Current assets} - \text{stock}}{\text{Current liabilities}}$	The acid test ratio is based on the same principle as current ratio. It assumes that stock cannot be sold and that debtors and cash are the only liquid assets

Table 3.8 Key liquidity ratio terms

Current ratio

Many analysts argue that the current ratio should be between 1.5 and 2, while the acid test ratio should be approximately 1. This means that firms would have no problems in paying off the current liabilities that arise.

In recent years, however, the current ratio has tended to fall as many firms move towards using 'just-in-time' production methods and, therefore, hold little or no stock. The value of the ratios must also be placed in context. Large firms, for example, may survive with relatively low liquidity ratios because they may be able to pressurise suppliers and delay payment.

Acid test ratio

It is also important to consider the nature of the product. A supermarket retailer, for example, will normally have a very high stock turnover, which means stock is an extremely liquid asset. This will allow a supermarket to operate with a very low acid test ratio knowing that stock will be quickly converted into cash through the days. Whereas a firm selling slow moving goods, such as capital equipment, would not be able to rely on selling stock as and when required and might, therefore, need a higher acid test ratio. Other factors that are important to take into account when analysing the liquidity ratios, include credit cards and time of year.

Credit cards

A high proportion of sales are now made on credit cards, especially for retail organisations. Technically, these are debtors, but the firm does not have to worry about chasing these debtors up as the payment is automatically received via the credit card company, who are responsible then for obtaining the money from the customers. This will not apply to industrial firms who still offer trade credit to customers.

Time of year

Some firms sell highly seasonal products. A firm selling fireworks will have its sales peak around November, for example. A balance sheet drawn up just before this point will show excessively high stock figures and possibly a lower than average cash figure. This should not be cause for concern as most of this stock is likely to be sold in the next few weeks and the cash figures will start to rise.

Can a firm hold too many current assets?

It is easy to understand why a firm should always ensure that it has sufficient current assets to remain solvent. However, it is possible for a firm to have too many current assets, in other words to be 'too safe'. There are several reasons for this:

■ Cash balances should not be kept too high. This is because money held in instant access accounts will pay little or no interest on the balance and incurs an opportunity cost. The money could have been invested elsewhere in interest-yielding financial assets, or shares in other companies. However, in the last two years there has been a number of high interest instant access accounts launched, such as the Egg account which pays interest in excess of the Bank of England's base rate, which may make cash balances more acceptable.

■ Debtors should not be allowed to be too high as a certain proportion of debtors will probably fail to pay and be written off as bad debts. The longer debts are allowed to be outstanding, the more likely they are to become bad debts.

■ Stock should be kept to a minimum for a number of reasons. Stock costs money to store, especially stocks of perishable goods that will require refrigeration costs on top of the standard storage costs. Stock held for a long period of time is more likely to end up damaged or could actually become outdated. Stock also has an opportunity cost; the money tied up in stock could be earning a return elsewhere.

However, this is not to say that a firm should never hold relatively large amounts of each of the current assets. It is perfectly logical that a firm may deliberately hold more stock than it would normally hold if it anticipates an increase in sales in the immediate future, for example. Similarly it might make sense for a firm to build up its holdings of cash if it was about to launch a takeover bid.

KEY POINTS

The acid test ratio is less likely to be relevant as a measure of liquidity if:

● the balance sheet date does not provide a typical profile of the firm's working capital (e.g. the day the balance sheet is constructed is unrepresentative)
● if the firm is able to acquire short-term finance without too much trouble
● stock turnover is high and/or stock is considered a liquid asset.

FACT FILE

The most popular toy at Christmas 1998 was Furby, an 'interactive pet' that demanded feeding and affection. It is estimated that two million shoppers were chasing the 350,000 Furbies in Britain. Retailers were sold out and, no doubt, had they predicted such a boom, would willingly have increased their stock levels in advance. Although priced at £29.99 in the shops, some were traded on the black market for as much as £600 as desperate parents tried to buy them for their children. Yo Yos also made a dramatic comeback and demand for Beany Babies also increased rapidly. In 1997 it was the Teletubbies.

PROGRESS CHECK

Questions

For what reasons might a firm deliberately increase its:
1   stock levels
2   debtors
3   cash levels

Does low liquidity equal imminent collapse?

A common misconception is that low liquidity levels will mean that the firm is unlikely to survive for much longer and will be forced to close due to failure to meet its daily running expenses. This is an over simplification. It is true that liquidity is an important area that should be monitored. It is also true that firms that have not survived often failed due to inadequate working capital and cash reserves to continue trading. However, many firms do survive with extremely low levels of liquid assets. Consider the following example:

J. Sainsbury plc:Acid test ratio (Source: *Annual Report 1998*)

1997 0.18
1998 0.52

If we believe that the acid test must be around 0.8 (which is often quoted as the 'ideal' figure) then this firm should not be able to survive for much longer. However, J. Sainsbury plc is one of our most successful retailers in the UK and there are many other firms that operate successfully with seemingly very low liquidity ratios. How is this possible?

■ It is highly unlikely that a firm would receive demands from all the different creditors on the same day that all amounts should be repaid immediately.

■ Any successful firm should be able to arrange temporary facilities for cash, such as arranging a bank overdraft.

■ Most firms, especially larger firms, can stall repayment to creditors for a short period of time until money flows back into the firm from sales.

How useful are liquidity ratios?

Liquidity ratios can highlight whether a firm has enough current assets (with or without stocks) to meet its liabilities. To survive in the long-term, a firm must have enough liquidity to finance its operations and so, a poor liquidity ratio may be a matter for concern. A good ratio, however, only means that the firm is liquid, it does not mean the firm is profitable and, therefore, you would not invest in a business because of the liquidity ratios, although you might avoid a business if the liquidity ratio is a worry.

> **Do not invest simply because a firm has good liquidity, but beware if liquidity is poor.**

As with all ratios, it is important to analyse the liquidity ratios in context. For example, in the short-term some firms may be able to survive with low liquidity levels, as they have the secure knowledge of being able to arrange short-term finance from a bank. However, other organisations, particularly smaller firms, may not have this security or may have already reached the limit of what a bank is willing to lend.

Consider how a firm might improve its liquidity position.

Gearing ratios

Most firms will obtain finance in one of two ways. They will either borrow their money (debt finance) or they will raise finance through issuing shares (equity finance). The proportion of a firm's capital that is raised through borrowing compared with the total capital employed in the business is referred to as the firm's gearing position. It can also be referred to as leverage.

RATIO	FORMULA	NOTES
Gearing ratio	$\dfrac{\text{Long-term liabilities} \times 100}{\text{Capital employed}}$	The gearing ratio measures the proportion of a firm's total capital that is financed through borrowing money. A 50% gearing ratio means that half of the firm's capital is borrowed.
Interest cover (*)	$\dfrac{\text{Operating (or net) profit}}{\text{Interest paid}}$	Interest cover calculates how many times over the firm's interest payments could have been paid out of that year's net profit. For example, an interest cover of 2 means that the firm could have paid the interest payments twice over out of the year's profits.

Table 3.9 Key gearing ratios terms

Effects of high gearing

A firm is said to be highly geared or to have high leverage if it has a high proportion of its capital as borrowed money. This borrowed money can come from any long-term external source of finance. It is hard to give an exact percentage for what a high gearing ratio actually is and this will depend on the industry in which it operates. It may also depend on the type of ownership. For example, many MBOs and MBIs (management buy-outs and management buy-ins) have very high gearing ratios as the managers often have to borrow the money to secure the deal. The general rule is that a higher gearing ratio is potentially more problematic than a lower gearing ratio.

However, high gearing does not necessarily mean the firm is at risk, provided it can cover the interest payments. If a firm can borrow at 7% and earn 8.5% this is a good use of funds. It is also important to remember that borrowing can provide a valuable and in some cases much needed source of finance. By not borrowing, a business may miss out on profitable opportunities.

> **By not borrowing a firm may miss out on profitable projects.**

KEY POINTS

Liquidity is likely to be considered more important than profitability if:

- a firm is experiencing cash flow problems
- a firm has recently set up and finds it hard to acquire short-term finance
- credit periods offered by the firm are increasing
- stock turnover is low.

FACT FILE

In 1999 the parent company of Daewoo, South Korea's second largest conglomerate, had its credit rating from Standard and Poor cut to B- after its debt more than doubled to $18bn last year from $8bn the year before. Daewoo said it had cut its debt equity ratio to 300% at the end of 1998 but commentators said this was mainly due to revaluation of assets; without this analysts believe the debt equity ratio was 500%. *(Note: gearing here is defined as debt/equity * 100)*

When deciding between borrowing or selling more shares to raise finance the firm may consider several factors.

Repayment of money

Most shares are irredeemable (i.e. never paid back). A shareholder can sell their shares on the Stock Exchange but the firm will rarely have to 'buy back' these shares. The shares simply change hands over a period of time. In comparison, loans must be paid back at some point.

PROGRESS CHECK

Why would a firm want to buy back shares it had already issued?

Taxation paid

Firms generally will like to minimise the amount of tax that they pay on their profits. The interest paid on loans is deducted as an expense before tax is calculated. This means that if a firm chooses to raise capital through debt, then it actually reduces the amount it pays for tax (because the interest payments will reduce its taxable profit). If capital is raised through issuing shares then it will probably pay dividends each year. These dividends will, however, be paid out after tax has already been paid. In this sense, equity is more expensive than debt – £1 paid as interest is untaxed, but to pay the equivalent amount in dividends more than £1 has to be generated, because the earnings will have to be taxed first.

Voting rights and control

Ordinary shares carry voting rights. This means that the issue of new shares will give power to the people who hold these newly issued shares. These new owners will, therefore, be able to influence decision making and this may lead to a clash of views with the existing owners. Loans carry no such voting rights, although some loans to small firms (known as venture capital) may carry some conditions on the loans. This is more attractive if the owners are unwilling to lose control of the business.

PROGRESS CHECK

JCB, the manufacturer of industrial equipment and vehicles, used to finance all expansions from internal cash flow. This would mean a gearing ratio of zero. Analyse the merits of only using internal cash flow to finance expansion.

Risk

Borrowing money is riskier than raising equity as interest payments have to be paid, regardless of the level of profits. In the 1980s, for example, many firms were engaged in Management Buy-out (MBOs), whereby a group of managers from the firm got together and actually purchased the firm. This was only possible through the borrowing of large sums of money. The problem was that interest rates rose rapidly and remained at extremely high levels for a number of years – they rose from

7.5% in spring 1988 to 15% in autumn 1989 and remained above 10% for four years. This forced many of these firms into bankruptcy, because the profits were swallowed up by the interest payments on the debt. If the managers are concerned about this risk they will be more likely to try to raise finance through equity.

Existing situation and availability of funds

The ability of a firm to raise finance through shares or borrowing will depend on its existing mix of finance and the availability of funds from the different sources. If the firm is already highly geared it may struggle to raise more money through borrowing. Equally, if it is perceived as high risk it may not be able to attract investors. Companies cannot always choose where they raise money from; they often have to use whichever source is available. Wanting to sell shares, for example, does not guarantee that anyone will want to buy them.

Administration

The decision between debt and equity may also be influenced by how quickly the money is required and the relative ease and cost of raising the money. Issuing shares, for example, is quite expensive in terms of fees for auditors, analysts, lawyers and merchant banks and may take longer to organise than a loan.

FACT FILE

In 1999 BPAmoco, one of the world's largest three oil companies, announced it was to invest over $26 billion (£16.7 billion) over the next three years, cut costs by $4 billion and sell assets worth $10 billion in an attempt to meet new ambitious financial targets. The company's chief executive stated that he aimed to improve the group's return on capital by five or six percentage points to 16% by 2001. BP Amoco, at the time the UK's largest company with a market value of £125 billion, also aimed to keep gearing within a 25–30% band.

PROGRESS CHECK

Consider the following statement by the chairperson of the food and engineering group Tomkins, which owned brand names as diverse as Hovis and Smith & Wesson guns.

'I am sure there will be a recession in the next five years and I don't want to be overstretched. If you go into a recession highly geared, it's tough. I want our capital structure to be effective but not reckless.'

He warned British firms that they were being reckless by pushing up borrowings ahead of a recession. The Tomkins group has refused to follow the 'fashion' of gearing up with extra debt despite the potential benefits for shareholders substituting loans for share capital.

Questions

1 Do you think that the chairperson is right? Explain your reasoning.
2 Why is high gearing likely to be a problem for firms if we enter into a recession?
3 What possible benefits are there to shareholders if a firm borrows money instead of issuing shares?

PROGRESS CHECK

Retailers' gearing ratios 1997

Marks & Spencer	12.0%
Tesco	20.9%
J. Sainsbury plc	16.2%
Somerfield	1.0%
Kwik-Save	2.3%
Source: Bized	

Analyse the possible reasons why the gearing ratios for the retailers above may differ.

NUMERICAL INVESTIGATION

1997	CURRENT RATIO	ACID TEST RATIO	DEBTOR DAYS	STOCK DAYS	GEARING	INTEREST COVER
Manchester Utd.	1.79	1.72	21.09	8.6	7.15	n/a
Sheffield Utd.	0.66	0.64	23.39	4.9	11.47	0.104
Hi-Tec	1.43	0.77	80.57	98.29	0.61	2.39
Glaxo	0.98	0.76	61.43	211.86	97.41	22.94
Tate & Lyle	1.39	0.92	43.16	51.57	76.44	3.18
Zeneca	1.3	0.91	68.09	134.41	23.27	108.3
Cadbury Schweppes	1.03	0.79	59.94	75.08	34.08	9.35
Harry Ramsdens	0.43	0.39	117.67	59.1	20.36	5.19
Unilever	1.77	1.29	31.21	68.92	23.31	32.68
J. Sainsbury plc	0.44	0.17	6.02	21.97	16.19	9.14
Tesco	0.37	0.11	1.77	15.63	15.71	32.25
Somerfield	0.32	0.06	0.05	19.84	0.98	13.99
Kwik Save	0.64	0.18	4.83	25.51	2.33	7.44
Psion	1.77	1.37	55.18	65.66	1.78	n/a

Table 3.10 Source: Bized

Using the ratios given, comment on the financial position of the companies listed above.

Shareholder ratios

The owners of a limited company are the shareholders; each one holds a 'share' of the firm. The reason for holding shares is usually due to the two financial rewards:

■ Dividends – a share of the profit, given out for every share held.

■ Capital gains – from selling shares for a higher price than was originally paid.

Any investor (either current shareholders or potential shareholders) will want to know if the rewards that they receive are adequate compensation for investing in the business and taking a risk. They will judge whether or not this is adequate by comparing the return to other returns made on other investments. The use of investors' ratios will enable this analysis to be made. The ratios that can be used are shown in Table 3.11

Ratio	Formula	Notes
Return on equity (*)	$\dfrac{\text{Profit after tax} \times 100}{\text{Shareholder's funds}}$	The return on equity shows the return made on the funds belonging to the shareholders. Shareholder's funds consist of issued share capital and any reserves built up over time.
Earnings per share (EPS) (*)	$\dfrac{\text{Profit after tax}}{\text{No. of shares issued}}$	The EPS measures how much each individual share earns for the holder in profits. It does not mean that the holder receives this amount, as not all profits are distributed as dividends.
Dividends per share (DPS)	$\dfrac{\text{Dividends}}{\text{No. of shares issued}}$	The DPS is a very similar ratio to the EPS. This ratio differs in that it shows how much that each shareholder actually receives per share as dividends.
Dividend yield	$\dfrac{\text{Dividends per share} \times 100}{\text{Market price per share}}$	The dividend yield relates the dividends received to the amount actually paid for the share. The dividend yield can then be compared to the return available on other financial assets (such as high interest bank accounts).
Dividend cover (*)	$\dfrac{\text{Profit after tax}}{\text{Dividends}}$	The dividend cover measures how many times over the firm could have paid out the dividends from the year's profit after tax. For example, a cover of 2 would mean that the profit after tax is twice as high as the dividend payments.
Price/earnings ratio (*)	$\dfrac{\text{Market price of share}}{\text{Earnings per share}}$	The P/E ratio relates the market price of each share to the amount that each share earns in that year. For example, if the current price of a share is £2 and the earnings per share is 25p, the P/E ratio would be 200p/25p = 8.

Table 3.11 Key shareholder ratio terms

Return on equity (ROE) performance

The return on equity (ROE) will depend on the investment by shareholders and the level of profit the firm generates. This will partly depend on the way in which the firm has raised money.

	Operating profit	Interest	Profit after interest	Tax (33%)	Profit after tax	Return on equity
Company A (£000)						
Year 1	500	50	450	150	300	20%
Year 2	300	50	250	83	167	11.1%
Year 3	100	50	50	17	33	2.3%
Company B (£000)						
Year 1	500	150	350	117	233	46%
Year 2	300	150	150	50	100	20%
Year 3	100	150	(50)	0	0	0%

Table 3.12

Imagine two firms have identical capital employed (£2 million) and identical profits for each of the three years, but company A has 25% gearing and company B has 75% gearing. Also, the loan finance carries a fixed rate of interest of 10% per year. We can see from Table 3.12 that when profits are highest the highly geared company (B) earns a higher ROE; the profit after interest is divided up between relatively few shareholders. As the profit falls away, however, we can see that the ROE declines more rapidly, as the profits are swallowed up by the interest burden. When profits are low the high interest payments mean the returns for shareholders are very poor; by year three the returns are 0%. In comparison, with a low level of gearing interest payments are low, so in poor years investors still get a return. In good years, however, the rewards have to be split up amongst a lot of shareholders, therefore, the return is not much higher. Hence, a firm that is more highly geared will generally see sharper swings in the ROE ratio as profits rise and fall over time. This is significant for potential shareholders who must look at the existing debt:equity mix of a firm's external finance as well as estimating future performance.

Dividend policy

The dividend policy of a firm refers to how much the directors pay out to shareholders. This will depend on the profits the firm has earned, what other firms are paying, the returns available elsewhere and the current share price. Generally, dividends will be a proportion of the company's earnings, although it is possible that a firm could distribute dividends that are actually higher than the profit available. If this is the case, the DPS would be higher than the EPS. This is rare but can occur when a firm needs to boost the share price by paying out more than was actually earned that year. Public companies in the UK have been criticised for paying out too much as dividends and it has been said that, as a result, too little has been left for investment. In their defence, UK directors have criticised institutional investors for being too short-termist and demanding too high a pay out.

NUMERICAL INVESTIGATION

	UNITED BISCUITS (£MILLION)	MATALAN (£MILLION)	PIZZA EXPRESS (£MILLION)	GLAXO WELLCOME (£MILLION)	ROYAL BANK OF SCOTLAND (£MILLION)
Profit attributable to ordinary shareholders	£58.2	£15.2	£18.04	£1,836	£637
Dividends	£51.6	£4.5	£2.8	£1,300	£215

Table 3.13 Dividend payments (1998)

  a Calculate the dividend cover for each of the businesses above.
  b Calculate dividends as a percentage of the profits.
  c Comment on your findings.

Dividend yield

The dividends per share, although useful, does not actually tell shareholders how high or how low their return is. For example, if each shareholder received a dividends per share of 50 pence, then this would appear very high if each share only cost £1 to buy. If each share cost £15 to purchase, then the dividend per share seems very low. Hence, the dividend yield could be a better guide to how 'generous' the dividend payment made by particular firms actually is. However, the yield will change on a daily basis as it is based on the current share price, which usually changes several times in one day.

What leads to a high price/earnings (P/E) ratio?

A high P/E ratio tends to indicate that the shares are in high demand. This is because a high demand for any particular share pushes up the price of the share. What, therefore, causes the high demand for any particular share?

The factors determining the price of a share on any one day are complex. Many firms will spend lots of time and money trying to predict what direction shares will move in. Some of the popular explanations for a rise in the price of a share are as follows.

Predictions

Investors may be expecting that the profits made by the firm in the near future are going to be high, or at least higher than similar firms. This will mean investors would like to buy the share now so that they can receive the, hopefully, higher dividends in the next few years. It is very hard, however, to predict how profitable a firm will be at any time, but the further into the future the predictions are, the less reliable they will be.

Takeovers

If a firm is to be taken over by another firm then the firm launching the takeover bid will usually offer existing shareholders a price for their shares which is higher than the current market price. If there are rumours that a takeover bid is to be launched, then there will be an increase in the demand for the shares of the firm that may be taken over as people will expect to be offered a higher amount for their shares shortly.

Maximising returns

Financial investors will look to maximise their returns on their investments. They will have a wide choice when deciding on investment decisions. The main choices facing investors are whether to hold stocks (i.e. government debentures), equity (shares in companies) or cash. They will base their decision on what is happening in the economy and what they expect to happen to the economy. If investors believed that investing in banks would yield a greater return, then they may sell their shares and invest money elsewhere. The selling of shares would force their

FACT FILE

Over many decades, the overall market dividend yield in the UK has averaged between 4.5% and 5% before tax, although yields have generally been lower in overseas markets. However, dividend yields on individual stocks can be variable and it is usually possible to find yields varying between 10% and 0% within the top UK 100 companies. Usually, the market's expectation of the next or prospective annual total dividend is more important for the share price than the amount actually paid in the past year.

FACT FILE

The largest companies' shares tend to have a price earnings ratio of 40, while the smaller companies have a P/E ratio of around 14. Some commentators believe this is because the major investment fund managers are not interested in researching smaller companies.

price down. However, if returns elsewhere are low, then investors may purchase shares, which forces the prices of shares up. This could happen if interest rates in the economy were reduced suddenly.

As we can see, there are many factors that would push up the price of a share. These factors are not necessarily within the firm's control and may be as a result of external, global factors.

PROGRESS CHECK

Consider why one firm's P/E ratio might be higher than its rivals.

Variable P/E ratios

P/E ratios between firms in different industries will vary considerably. The reason for this is that different industries will be affected in different ways by the stages of the economic cycle and by general trends within the economy. For example, leisure orientated firms will perform strongest in periods of above average economic growth, whereas firms selling necessities will be affected by the economic cycle, albeit less severely.

NUMERICAL INVESTIGATION

The following is taken from the *Financial Times* on 7 April 1998, concerning the share prices of three leading grocery chains.

	ASDA	J. SAINSBURY PLC	TESCO
Share price	203p	519p	578p
Dividend yield (%)	1.9	3.0	2.3
P/E	19.1	21.1	23.0

Table 3.14

a Explain in words what Tesco's P/E ratio of 23 actually means.

b If the average P/E ratio for grocery chains was 15, then what conclusions could you infer about the performance of Asda, J. Sainsbury plc and Tesco?

NUMERICAL INVESTIGATION

Cadbury Schweppes plc

	1998	1997	1996	1995	1994	1993	1992	1991	1990	1989
Interest cover	11.7	10.0	6.4	5.4	12.4	10.4	7.5	6.5	5.8	8.8
Dividend cover	2.1	2.1	2	1.9	2.0	2.0	2.0	2.2	2.2	2.3
Gearing ratio*	27.0	37.0	92.0	102.0	24.0	27.0	37.0	40.0	50.0	63.0
Trading margin (beverages)	18.7	17.5	16.4	15.1	11.6	10.7	9.0	10.1	10.0	9.9
Trading margin (confectionery)	12.9	12.7	11.9	12.2	12.9	12.5	12.7	12.3	12.3	11.4

Table 3.15 Source: *Annual Report 1997*

*Gearing ratio used = net borrowings/(ordinary shareholders' funds + equity minority interests). Trading margin = trading profit/sales

With reference to the data above assess Cadbury Schweppes financial position for the years shown.

Limitations of ratios

It is important to realise that although accounting ratios can be a very useful tool they also have many serious limitations which can render the results meaningless, or worse, can make managers jump to incorrect conclusions.

> **Ratios have limitations – take care when analysing a firm's accounts!**

The best way to avoid falling into these traps is to spend time trying to understand what the ratios actually mean. This is not just a question of learning what they should theoretically show, but also thinking about what lies behind the actual calculation of the ratio. For example, we all know that the current ratio shows us the solvency position of a firm. However, we need to examine various elements of the ratio itself for it to have meaning. A firm may have many current assets, for example, but if these are stocks that are not very liquid then the firm may face problems. If, on the other hand, the stocks are likely to be liquid, this may not be an issue.

It is also important to appreciate the limitations of relying on a set of ratios rather than seeing the whole picture. We need to think about the underlying view, the trends and the market environment. In particular, it is very important that ratios should be considered with the previous years' equivalent figures if any meaningful analysis is to be offered. One-off figures in themselves may be misleading; what we need to know is whether the ratio is increasing or decreasing, by how much and at what rate? Wherever possible, ratios from one firm should also be compared with others in the industry.

FACT FILE

The UK stock market moved to one of its highest valuation in terms of corporate profits in 1998. The price earnings ratio on the FTSE non financials was over 24. The previous high was 23 in 1969. The market stood at 21 just before the crash of 1987. However, the overall market rate does not tell the whole picture: the telecommunications and pharmaceuticals sectors had a P/E of over 50 whilst cyclical construction and paper and packaging sectors had a rating of less than ten, due to fears of recession.

FACT FILE

Until the late 1990s, Tomkins was one of the few remaining UK conglomerates. In 1999 it demerged. Part of the reason for this was that its shares had consistently underperformed since it acquired Rank Hovis McDougall for nearly £1 billion in 1992. Investors did not feel the company could effectively manage a diversified business, which went from Mr Kipling cakes to gravy to bicycles to guns! With the demerger, the price earnings ratio is expected to increase.

FACT FILE

Great Britain Ltd: typical ratios for UK businesses taken from a sample of 372,871 establishments.
Acid test: 0.7 times
Current ratio: 1.1 times
Stock turnover: 12.9 times
Debtors collection period (debtor days): 47.9 days
Profit margin: 3.5%
Return on capital: 11.9%
Sales per employee: £65.6
Profit per employee: £2.2

Source: *Dun and Bradstreet, 1995 median value*

KEY POINTS

Ratios are less likely to be useful if:

- the figures are out-of-date
- they are based on published accounts, which are not representative of the underlying position of a firm
- qualitative factors are ignored
- they are looked at in isolation.

NUMERICAL INVESTIGATION

Key ratios for UK sectors

	AGRICULTURE	SERVICES	RETAIL	MANUFACTURING
acid test (times)	0.5	0.8	0.3	0.8
current ratio (times)	1.1	1.0	1.0	1.1
stock turnover (times)	4.9	35.1	9.5	10.7
debtors collection period (days)	32.6	41.7	11.4	63.8
profit margin (%)	5.3	6.1	1.2	3.5
return on capital (%)	9.1	22.2	7.5	13.3
sales per employee (£)	54.1	42.2	69.8	61.6
profit per employee (£)	2.7	2.0	1.0	2.3

Table 3.16

Source: Dun and Bradstreet (median ratios 1995)

With reference to the data above comment on the financial performance of the different sectors of the UK.

Ratio calculation

It is also important that the ratios are calculated in a similar way (i.e. you are treating 'like with like'). Changes in a firm's accounting policy over the years or differences between firms can make ratio analysis very difficult. To find out about a company's accounting policy it is worth reading the notes that accompany a firm's published accounts. This may give you, for example, information on whether a firm values intangible assets. If it does, it will boost the value of the firm's assets and therefore reduces its ROCE.

Ratio analysis

Ratio analysis should also take into account the external context such as the state of the economy; a ROCE of 12% in a boom may be disappointing, but in a major economic recession it may be impressive. High levels of gearing at a time of low interest rates may be less of a worry than high gearing and high interest rates.

Data quality

The quality of the data should also be considered in ratio analysis. In many cases, external analysts have to use data from the published accounts. These figures may not represent a typical day within the firm (after all, why did the firm choose this particular date to draw up the balance sheet?), they may be window dressed and they may be several months, even years, out-of-date. In this situation their value may be limited.

Whilst ratio analysis can certainly provide some insight into a firm's financial position, a good analyst should also take into account qualitative factors:

- What is the level of motivation within the firm?

- How good is the management?

- What developments are there likely to be in the industry?

A firm's existing profitability ratios may be unimpressive but if an analyst knows of a potential technological breakthrough the firm is developing it may still be worth investing in the business. Good analysis of a firm's position may be based on ratios, but it should be balanced with an analyst's own judgement and experience. In the context of buying shares, success is likely to require a combination of scientific calculation with intuition – if the answer was solely in the numbers all analysts would be able to identify the potential winners, assuming they knew what numbers to look at. In most cases, ratios will be backward looking; this can help guide us in the future, however, we must also be willing to look at other indicators.

KEY POINTS

Ratios are more likely to be useful if:

- compared with past years' figures
- compared with other firms in the industry
- they use up-to-date data
- they are combined with qualitative factors, experience and judgement.

Other ratios

The ratios covered in this section are the main accounting ratios used by analysts when examining a firm's accounts. However, there are many more financial ratios that might be used, depending on exactly what an analyst wants to find out. If you were a union official trying to decide if your members were being paid enough, you might want to examine labour costs as a percentage of turnover. If you were a manager assessing the performance of the workforce you might examine the sales per employee and/or the profits per employee (see Table 3.18).

There are also a host of non-financial ratios that can be used when assessing different issues. For example, a human resources manager is likely to monitor absenteeism rates and labour turnover, whilst an operations manager will probably be interested in productivity rates and the number of defects per thousand items produced.

The ratios used by analysts will also vary from industry to industry. In retailing they might look at sales per square foot; in insurance they might measure the percentage of customers re-insuring with their company each year. There is, therefore, no absolute or fixed number of ratios – managers should identify the variables they are interested in and then compare them. They should be willing to develop their own ratios to analyse specific areas of interest. Ratio analysis is a tool of decision making and as such it should be shaped and adjusted according to the precise needs of the user.

NUMERICAL INVESTIGATION

	1994	1995	1996	1997	1998
Total employees (No.)	21,194	20,210	19,783	18,798	18,637
Total sales per employee (£)	49,769	49,861	53,723	58,357	58,824
Total operating profit per employee	3,860	3,592	3,938	4,963	5,419

Table 3.17 Northern Foods plc

Source: Northern Foods Annual Report (1998)

With reference to the data above, comment on the performance of the workforce of Northern Foods plc.

1998	SALES PER EMPLOYEE (£)	OPERATING PROFIT PER EMPLOYEE (£)	SALES PER SQUARE FOOT
J. Sainsbury plc	144,517.19	7,777.96	567.64
Tesco	143,260.96	6,579.58	1,219.68
Somerfield	75,677.78	2,557.78	573.51
Kwik Save	182,139.05	2,627.59	485.22

Table 3.18 Sales, operating profit and sales per square foot

NUMERICAL INVESTIGATION

	1990	1991	1992	1993	1994	1995	1996	1997	1998	1999
Sales per square foot (incl. VAT) (£)	17.26	18.17	18.51	18.84	18.60	18.53	18.59	18.69	18.87	18.61
No. of stores	420	439	459	486	514	535	781	802	823	833
Sales area (000 sq. ft.)	11,134	12,173	13,065	14,158	15,241	16,046	25,570	26,489	27,299	27,805
Share of national trade in predominantly food stores and pharmaceutical, medical, cosmetics and toilet goods outlets	10.5%	11.1%	11.4%	12.1%	12.1%	12.3%	12.2%	12.3%	12.5%	12.3.%

Table 3.19 Sainsbury's sales intensity

Source: *Annual Report, 1999*

With reference to the table above discuss the sales performance of J. Sainsbury plc.

Summary charts

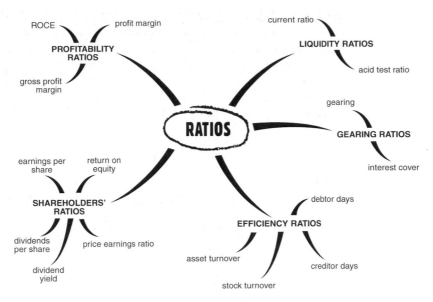

Figure 3.1 Financial ratios

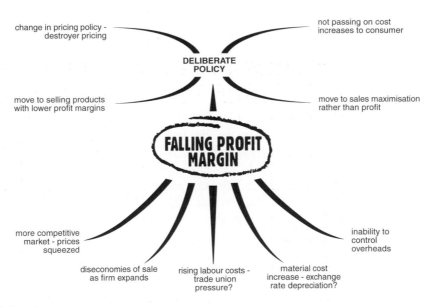

Figure 3.2 Profit margins

Approaching exam questions: Ratio analysis

Saunders Ltd. has an acid test ratio of 0.5. Discuss whether or not specific action should be taken to improve the liquidity position.

(11 marks)

In this question it is important that the answer does not use only theoretical knowledge as the basis for the solution. Standard textbook knowledge would tell us that Saunders Ltd. is in a precarious situation and may face possible closure due to 'running out of cash'. There is a widespread belief that the acid test ratio should always be at least 1 and a ratio of 0.5 would be very worrying. There is some truth in the idea that a low acid test ratio could lead to problems, however, there are other issues that need to be considered first.

One important point to realise is that the acid test ratio is calculated from the balance sheet and, therefore, will only be related to the liquidity position at a specific date. It may be the case that the acid test ratio is low due to special circumstances that are resolved in the next day or week. The firm may, for example, have recently purchased considerable amounts of stock, which leads to lower cash and higher stock values and lowers the acid test ratio. The firm would expect to sell this stock shortly and, therefore, the acid test ratio would increase as debtors and cash increased while stock was sold.

However, even if the acid test ratio of 0.5 is seen as typical for Saunders Ltd. this does not necessarily mean that action should be taken. The following points should be explored first:

1   The size of the firm would be important, as outlined earlier in the chapter. If Saunders Ltd. is a medium or a large firm then cash flow may be less important, due to it being easier for the firm to raise short-term finance. A smaller firm is less likely to have this luxury and, therefore, the acid test ratio could indicate potential liquidity problems in the future.
2   The nature of the product sold would also be important. Stock may or may not be a liquid asset. In general, retailers will sell products which are 'turned over' faster than manufacturers. It follows, therefore, that if Saunders Ltd. is a retailer then it may be the case that stock could be sold quickly and, in effect, turned into cash. It may be useful to also examine the current ratio in this situation.

If these factors are taken into account then it may be the case that Saunders Ltd. can operate quite comfortably with what may be seen as a low acid test ratio.

If the ratio is considered to be low, however, then action would need to be taken to increase the liquid assets available for use within the firm. A low acid test ratio does not mean immediate collapse but could lead to firms having to make decisions that may not normally be considered as efficient. For example, a firm may have to sell off fixed assets and then lease these back, or sell stock at a discount.

Whether or not action will have to be taken depends on factors such as:

■ The figure the managers expected the ratio to be.

■ What the figure has been in the past.

- The ability of the firm to raise cash quickly.
- The manager's attitude to risk.
- The type of firm.
- If this situation is expected to continue for any length of time.

A firm has seen its profit margin fall over successive years. Discuss if this should be seen as a cause for concern.

(11 marks)

A discussion type question will mean that there will be both positive and negative points made in your argument and that these points should be weighed up to assess how important they are.

It may be useful to state what is meant by a falling profit margin, i.e. that the gap between the selling price and the costs incurred by the firm is declining. The cause of the falling profit margin could either be a result of falling selling prices, or that costs are rising disproportionately fast, or a combination of these two factors.

Whether or not this is a concern for the firm will depend on why the profit margin is falling, if it is deliberate or if it is accidental. Reasons for the fall could centre around the following:

1 An attempt to gain market share may mean that the firm reduces the selling price in order to boost sales volumes – this depends on the price elasticity of demand. This may lead to a fall in the profit margin, although if overheads are spread over more units the net profit margin may increase even if the price has been reduced.
2 Other firms entering the market may also mean that selling prices have to be reduced to remain price competitive with other firms.
3 The costs of production may have risen and the firm may have decided not to pass this increase on to consumers in the form of higher prices (perhaps because demand is very price elastic).
4 A growing firm may be becoming less efficient and be facing diseconomies of scale in the form of rising administrative costs or less efficient communication.

The importance of these factors will depend in part on the nature of the products or market. For example, if it is a small firm and it is facing severe price competition from larger firms then it may struggle to survive. Conversely, if the firm is choosing to keep lower profit margins in order to boost sales then this may not be seen as a concern, provided sales increase significantly. Whether a firm should be concerned will depend on the following:

- If the fall has been forced on the firm (e.g. due to higher costs) or it has deliberately cut the price.
- If it is part of a long-term strategy (e.g. to gain control of the market) or because it has had to cut price to survive.
- If the overall return on capital employed has increased.
- The firm's objectives (e.g. how important is profitability?).

Evaluate the possible use of financial ratios for a potential investor.

(40 marks)

An evaluation question will require you to weigh up the evidence that you discuss when answering this question. The main issues in this question are as follows:

Student answers: Ratio analysis

A public limited company that has a gearing ratio of 40% wishes to raise additional long-term finance. Evaluate the sources of finance available.

(11 marks)

Student answer

The gearing ratio of 40% means that the firm has borrowed nearly half of its total capital employed. The other half must, therefore, be made up of reserves and share capital. This is too high and will mean that a firm is probably paying high interest charges on this debt. This will mean that much of the firm's profit is used up in paying the interest.

When deciding on finance a firm must decide on the advantages and disadvantages of each source. For example, if a firm borrows money as a loan then it is committed to paying interest on this each year regardless of the level of the firm's profit. Issuing shares means that the firm can get hold of the money without worrying about paying the money back as share capital is never repaid. However, when issuing shares the firm must realise that the issue of further shares means that the directors may lose control of the firm, because each new share carries a voting right at the firm's Annual General Meeting (AGM).

Marker's comments

This is generally a disappointing answer to begin with as the student automatically assumes that the gearing is too high. We would need to know more about the firm and the industry it operates in. It could be the case that 40% is actually a low gearing ratio for this specific industry or for this firm at this moment in its development, given the plans it has.

Only in the second paragraph, does the student begin to answer the question. However, the merits of debt versus equity is rather simplistic. What is included is true but the student could have considered these factors in much more detail. The student is asked to evaluate the sources of finance and not just to explain what each one entails.

To score more highly a student could have considered some of the following factors:

■ The time taken to actually acquire the finance, focusing on the relative speed of using debt finance compared with the time taken to issue more shares.

■ The current level of interest rates and, more importantly, the expected future levels of interest rates.

- *Profit projections for the next few years to see whether or not the interest burden could be met. This may mean making estimations on future sales and economic growth.*
- *The size of the firm will be an important factor when lenders set interest rates. A smaller firm would expect to pay a higher interest rate on borrowed money due to its being considered a higher risk.*
- *If a share issue would be a success and fully subscribed.*

Mark: Content 2/2, Application & Analysis 3/6, Evaluation 0/3. Total = 5

Consider the possible weaknesses of relying on financial ratio analysis for analysing company performance.

(11 marks)

Student answer

There are several problems when using ratio analysis for examining a company's performance. This answer will need to look at some of these. One of the main problems is that the ratios do not focus on the human side of a firm. If workers are not happy they work badly; this may lead to poor performance and, ultimately, failure for the firm. This is not shown in the company accounts. If workers are happy, they work harder and profits go up.

Also, we need to look at more than one year's accounts. If we are given a set of ratios it does not tell us if the firm is improving or deteriorating in terms of performance. The underlying trends could be more important than just one year's figures. We would also need to consider the plans that the firm has for the future. If the firm is in a growing market then it should be planning to invest for expansion. This is not shown in ratios.

Marker's comments

The weaknesses of ratios included in this answer are correct but the explanations are rather simplistic. The impact of worker motivation is important but will not always affect profits in the exaggerated way that is detailed by the student. For example, 'happy' workers may not be particularly productive if they lack the training and resources required. The importance of non-financial factors is relevant but could have been developed in much greater depth – this could have been used to highlight the danger of relying on ratios.

The idea that one year's figures are not enough is certainly valid and its inclusion will gain the student marks. To develop this point the student could have discussed the idea that a complete set of a number of years' ratios may not be enough if the firm has window dressed their accounts. Also, the point on the strategic planning of the firm could have been developed in greater detail and could possibly have been linked with other external factors (such as the state of the economy) to gain more credit.

Overall, the student needs to consider the weaknesses; this could have been achieved by stating that ratio analysis can have problems. The answer could also have explored when ratio analysis is more or less likely to have been useful.

Mark: Content 2/2, Application & Analysis 3/6, Evaluation 0/3. Total = 5

'Close monitoring of the ratios connected with the liquidity and efficiency is essential if a firm is to maximise profitability.' Discuss this view.

(11 marks)

Student answer

This statement is partly true but does not tell the full story. A firm's profitability ratios are usually seen as the best guide for deciding whether or not the firm is performing well. This can be analysed by comparing the firm's profits with the capital of the firm or the sales generated by the firm. For example, if a firm sells more goods but incurs a disproportionate amount of costs then it would see its profit margins fall.

The other types of ratios, however, are also connected with the firm's overall profitability. For example, if a firm does not monitor its liquidity position, through the acid test ratio, then it may experience cash flow problems. Even if the firm survives these problems, it may have to take action, which would compromise its profitability position. For example, a firm may have to sell stock at a discount in order to generate cash when normally it would sell for a higher price. This would reduce its profits.

A firm should also control the time taken by customers to pay their amounts owing. This can be measured through the debtor days ratio. If the firm allows the debtor days ratio to rise then it may lead to more bad debts occurring and that will also cost the firm money. Control of debtors is not seen as a priority, because it does not directly lead to a firm improving profits. However, as I have just outlined, lack of control of debtors may lead to higher cost, which will be bad for the firm.

Overall, it is important that a firm monitors other ratios, apart from its profitability, as they are all linked together. Therefore, I generally agree with this statement.

Marker's comments

Although the language used in this response is not always business-like, the actual content of the answer is very good. This is a potentially hard question, which is asking a student to see how other ratios can affect the profits made by a firm. Many people would think that only the profitability ratios are worth considering. However, in this answer the student explains fairly well how the control of cash flow and debtors can also affect profitability.

To improve the answer, the student could have discussed the different areas of the firm and how these all affect the profitability, looking at how different firms may be affected. For example, for a smaller firm, it could be more important that debtors, stock and cash are more tightly controlled to ensure survival (if the firm does not survive there will be no profits!). On the other hand, if a firm is overzealous in controlling debtors, it may lead to resentment from customers and, therefore, lower sales in the future.

Ratios are interconnected and although most questions will look at one area (e.g. profitability or gearing) it is possible to consider them holistically. After all if the firm becomes illiquid it may have to cease trading.

Possible areas for discussion in this question include the use of the words 'close' and 'essential' – how close should monitoring be? Can it be 'too close'? How essential is it? Does it guarantee that the firm actually 'maximises' profitability?

Mark: Content 2/2, Application & Analysis 5/6, Evaluation 0/3. Total = 7

'The dividend yield will give the shareholders all the information that they need to know about whether or not to buy shares in a company.' Analyse this statement.

(9 marks)

Student answer

Dividends are the reward given by firms out of their profits to shareholders. They are declared at the AGM. Good dividends should be seen as a sign that the firm is performing really well. However, this does not tell us how much the shareholder has to pay for the share. If the price of a share is cheap and the level of dividends fairly good then the dividends yield would be high. However, even with big dividends, it may not be worth purchasing a share if the current price of the share is really expensive.

The dividends yield is all a shareholder needs to know as the main reason for buying shares is to make money. If the yield is good the investor will buy.

Marker's comments

This answer is of a low standard and is not helped by the rather poor use of language. On the positive side, the student does seem to understand the concept of the dividend yield.

However, this question was looking for an exploration of the problems of relying on this single measure when assessing performance, and this is not examined effectively. For example, the answer might have included the fact that profit can and is manipulated in order to boost measures (such as the earnings per share and the dividend yield) in order to impress shareholders. Other factors will affect a decision to buy shares, such as:

- *The nature of the business and its future plans.*
- *The ethics of the investor and other qualitative factors.*
- *The attitude of the investor to risk.*
- *The expected profits and dividends of the business.*

Mark: Content 2/2, Application 2/4, Analysis 0/3. Total = 4

End of section questions

1 The liquidity ratio of Andrews Ltd. has declined rapidly over the past few years. Analyse the possible implications of this for the firm.

(9 marks)

2 Examine the reasons why a successful firm may experience low profitability ratios.

(9 marks)

3 Discuss the arguments for and against a firm having a high gearing ratio.

(11 marks)

4 Evaluate the usefulness of liquidity ratios to a potential investor examining companies accounts.

(11 marks)

5 Analyse the possible effects of high interest rates on a firm which is highly geared.

(9 marks)

6 Discuss the ways in which potential investors can use ratios to help decide in which company shares should be purchased.

(11 marks)

7 Consider the possible reasons for falling profit margins.

(9 marks)

8 Analsye whether or not the asset turnover provides useful information to analysts.

(9 marks)

9 Evaluate the use of the gearing ratio for a bank manager deciding to grant a loan to a firm.

(11 marks)

10 Analyse whether or not a firm should aim for a high stock turnover.

(9 marks)

Essays

1 'Most firms that fail have cash flow problems and poor liquidity ratio levels, yet many large firms trade successfully with liquidity ratios at levels below those recommended.' Explain and evaluate this apparent contradiction in the sentence.

(40 marks)

2 'The return on capital employed is the best measure of whether a firm is successful'. Discuss whether you agree with this statement.

(40 marks)

3 'Highly geared firms are placing themselves at risk of failure and investors should avoid these firms.' Discuss this statement.

(40 marks)

4 To what extent do profitability ratios provide a useful insight into a firm's financial position?

(40 marks)

5 Evaluate the use of profit margins for determining business efficiency.

(40 marks)

CHAPTER 4
Cash management and budgeting

Why is cash flow important?

Firms usually exist in order to make a profit. This may not always be their prime objective, but it is generally one of their major aims. It is also, however, important for firms to monitor their cash flow position. This is because a firm will need cash to pay for the daily running of the business. Cash will be needed to pay wages, to pay bills, to pay suppliers and for the general upkeep of the firm. If a firm cannot pay one of its creditors, then the firm may ultimately face a bankruptcy order forced on to the firm by those who it cannot pay. If it cannot pay its own workers then industrial action is likely to occur. At the very least, if a firm is unable to pay its own running expenses then there is likely to be some change forced on to the firm by outside agencies, such as reorganisation or removal of the directors. Cash may also be required to finance major projects, such as an acquisition; when firms are significantly building up their cash holdings this is sometimes an indication that they are looking to make a takeover.

Sufficient levels of cash are needed to ensure that a firm is liquid; it is important, therefore, that managers track the cash flow position of the business. This is likely to involve drawing up cash flow forecasts which estimate the likely amounts of cash inflows and cash outflows over the near future. Very short-term cash flow forecasts may be particularly important for small or newly established firms, which often have to target cash flow over a daily or weekly period rather than on a month by month basis .This is because a new or small firm is thought to be more likely to fail than a larger firm. As a result, the sources of cash flow available to a larger firm (such as extended credit periods offered, or extensions to overdrafts) may not be offered to small firms if their cash flow becomes negative.

Differences between cash and profit

The fact that a firm is profitable does not guarantee that it will be solvent. It may seem surprising that a firm that is making a profit or has made profits in the past can run out of cash, but this disbelief stems from a common misunderstanding of what the terms 'cash' and 'profit' actually mean. People often assume that at the end of each year there is an amount of money in the firm's bank account equivalent to its profit and that this can be withdrawn and spent by the owner(s) of the firm. However, this scenario is most unlikely to happen. It is more likely that the profits

KEY TERMS

Insolvency
occurs when a company cannot pay its own debts or when its liabilities exceed its assets.

Bankruptcy
is when an individual or an unincorporated firm is unable to settle its liabilities and may be declared or request to be declared bankrupt and will cease trading.

FACT FILE

The most common reason for business failure:
Poor management – 31%
Lack of demand – 27%
Cash flow problems – 20%
Source: Society of Practitioners of Insolvency

NUMERICAL INVESTIGATION

	CASH AND SHORT-TERM DEPOSITS AT END OF 1998 FINANCIAL YEAR (£)
Tomkins	378.4 million
United Biscuits	60 million
MFI	11.9 million
Liberty	446,000
British American Tobacco	970

Table 4.1 Source: *Annual Report 1998*

Consider why the companies listed above might have held such different levels of cash.

will be tied up in many different areas of the firm. For example, the profit may have been used to acquire new premises, new equipment or stock; if the goods have been sold on credit the revenue may still be in the form of debtors. The profit made by a firm will, therefore, be in the form of a range of assets and not just cash.

> **'Profit' simply records the value of sales compared to the value of inputs used up to produce these goods and services; cash is actual tangible asset.**

It is possible, therefore, for a firm to be profitable but to also be short of cash because:

- Many sales are on credit. These sales will be counted towards that year's profit even though the cash from the sale may actually appear months later.

- The firm may have invested heavily in capital items such as equipment. Although this will involve a cash outflow, the costs of these fixed assets (as entered in the profit and loss account) will be spread out over their working lives. The impact of a major item of capital expenditure on this year's profit, therefore, is far less than the impact on a firm's cash flow.

- The firm may have invested in stocks. These will appear as an asset on the balance sheet but will not appear as a cost until they are used up. The cash outflow will occur when they are bought.

- If a firm has paid for something in advance but not used it up yet (e.g. it has paid for the use of some equipment or property in advance) this will reduce cash flow but will only be recorded as a cost when the service or good is used up next period. Conversely, if the firm has used up something, such as electricity, this will count as a cost even if the bill has not been paid for.

PROGRESS CHECK

Examine the reasons why a firm's profit position might differ from its cash flow position.

Which is more important — cash or profit?

In the long run there is probably little point undertaking an activity if the value of the sale is less than the value of the inputs used up (i.e. if turnover is less than costs). This means that over time a firm will need to make a profit if it is to continue with an activity. Furthermore, the profit must be significant enough to justify all the resources that have been used up; after all, these resources could have been used elsewhere. Firms will, therefore, generally measure not just the absolute size of the profits but their size relative to the capital employed, to decide if an activity is worthwhile.

In the short run, however, the priority is to keep the business going; this means the firm must be liquid and have sufficient cash flow. There is little point in getting involved in a project that is potentially profitable if, in fact, the business will not survive long enough to be able to sell the products it produces. Firms must pay attention to their cash flow as well as their profit. If a bill has to be paid, cash is likely to be regarded as more important than profit; however, when reviewing the firm's activities over a period of time it will usually be expected to achieve a suitable rate of return in terms of profit.

KEY POINTS

Cash flow is more likely to be negative even if the firm is profitable if:

- many of its sales are on long-term credit
- the firm has invested heavily in fixed assets
- the firm has incurred heavy pre-payments
- the firm has high levels of stocks

> **The profit from a project shows if it is worth doing. The cash flow shows if the firm can keep solvent.**

Non-profit organisations

Having said this, some organisations do not even attempt to make a profit. For example, some firms are non-profit organisations such as charities or public sector institutions. These organisations are still subject to financial pressures (for example, having to break even over a number of years) but they are not driven by the motive to make surpluses of income over expenditure, i.e. profit. On the other hand, these organisations will still use cash, and therefore, they would consider it to be more important to have money available for spending than to make a profit.

KEY POINTS

Cash may be considered more important than profit if:

- the firm is a not-for-profit organisation
- problems are experienced when paying bills and creditors
- difficult trading conditions are prevalent or expected.

PROGRESS CHECK

To what extent is cash more important than profit?

Which firms are likely to be affected by cash flow problems?

It is likely that all firms will be affected at some point by cash flow problems. However, certain businesses are more likely to be affected than others:

Production period

Cash flow problems are particularly common when there is a long production period during which bills have to be paid, even though no cash is being generated by sales. In parts of the manufacturing sector, for example, it takes weeks, even

FACT FILE

In 1992 the Canadian developer of Canary Wharf, Olympia & York, went bust. Work on the huge scheme began in 1988, just as the property market in London was reaching its peak. In May 1992, Olympia & York collapsed and Canary Wharf became the largest ever property administration. When the administrators took control of Britain's tallest office tower, with its 4.4m sq. ft. of office and retail space, only 935,000 sq. ft. of it was occupied, a fifth of the total. It is estimated to have cost more than £14 million in administration costs. The banks, led by Lloyds and including Barclays, Credit Lyonnais and Credit Suisse, took the scheme out of administration in 1993 and restored its finances by deferring repayment of £588 million of loans and interest until the year 2007 and putting in an additional £278 million of facilities.

KEY TERM

Overtrading occurs when a firm expands too rapidly without any provision for cash or working capital to finance this expansion.

months to assemble and produce the finished product. During this time employees and suppliers need to be paid, but cash from these sales is not incoming. In some parts of the service sector, by comparison, there is quite a small time gap between the production of the service and payment and so cash flow is less of a problem (e.g. a hairdressing salon).

Overtrading

Firms that are expanding rapidly are particularly likely to experience cash flow problems. This is because the cash outflows associated with producing extra output may be high and that the output cannot be sold quickly enough to generate the cash revenue needed to cover the outflow. The cash flow problems associated with rapid expansion are called overtrading.

Trading on credit

Any firm, which trades on credit, is more likely to be subject to cash flow problems than ones who deal purely in cash, as there is the uncertainty surrounding when and if the payment will arrive. A possible solution to this would be for a firm to only accept cash sales (which require payment on delivery); however, this may mean business is lost because firms often use attractive credit periods to boost their sales.

Lack of planning

Firms that fail to plan ahead are highly likely to experience cash flow problems. Simply being able to produce and sell items at a profit is no guarantee of success. Managers need to identify the timing of inflows and outflows and manage these effectively (for example, by trying to delay payments or bring forward cash inflows). Managers who fail to realise the importance of cash flow and who fail to plan appropriately are more likely to experience cash flow problems than managers who devote sufficient time and resources to this area.

PROGRESS CHECK

Questions

1 Explain possible reasons why a firm might be wise to turn down extra orders.
2 'Many firms experience cash flow problems when they expand.' Analyse the possible reasons for this.

Cash flow forecasts

One way to help avoid a cash flow shortage is to construct a cash flow forecast. Most firms will have attempted to plan ahead for movements in cash at some point in their life. It is highly likely that when the firm was originally set-up its owner(s) had to construct a cash flow forecast to present to a potential investor or lender. Indeed, bank managers would usually expect to see some form of cash flow forecast before granting a loan to the newly created firm. These forecasts need to be regularly updated and maintained for effective financial planning.

A cash flow forecast shows the projections for cash inflows and cash outflows that the firm expects to occur over the near future. The planning horizon for the cash flow forecast can be daily, weekly or monthly. Remember though, it is only a forecast – it does not guarantee these inflows and outflows will happen. An example of a cash flow forecast is shown in Figure 4.1.

In this illustration, D. Clayton is a sole trader who has set up business to begin trading in January 1999, with a balance of £5,000 in the business bank account. He rents the premises but still has had to purchase equipment to be used within the firm.

Normally, items of capital expenditure would not be included in profit and loss accounts, whereas in the cash flow forecast all items are included if they involve money. Provisions, such as depreciation, are excluded because they do not involve money.

Note that D. Clayton is overdrawn significantly from the end of January. This may be typical for new firms due to the heavy set up costs.

ALL IN £	JANUARY	FEBRUARY	MARCH	APRIL	MAY
Opening balance	5,000	(2,050)	(3,700)	(5,250)	(7,500)
Cash inflows					
Cash sales	1,000	1,200	1,300	1,600	2,500
Debtor payments	–	1,000	1,500	1,200	3,000
	1,000	2,200	2,800	2,800	5,500
Cash outflows					
Equipment	4,000				
Rent	600	600	600	600	600
Wages	300	300	300	300	300
Heating and lighting	200			200	
VAT	100	100	100	100	100
Sundries	200	200	200	200	200
Creditors (materials)	2,000	2,000	2,500	3,000	3,000
Insurance	150	150	150	150	150
Drawings	500	500	500	500	500
	8,050	3,850	4,350	5,050	4,850
Net cash flow for month	(7,050)	(1,650)	(1,550)	(2,250)	650
Closing balance	(2,050)	(3,700)	(5,250)	(7,500)	(6,850)

Figure 4.1 Cash flow forecast for January–May 1999 for D. Clayton

The cash flow forecast should help the firm plan ahead and take the necessary action should any shortfall be predicted. It may also highlight periods when the firm will have too much cash and the firm may attempt to arrange for this to be used to generate higher returns by investing it.

However, even with careful planning it is likely that firms will experience periods when their cash flow position is tighter than they had predicted. This could be due to cash inflows being lower than expected or cash outflows being higher than expected.

KEY TERMS

Cash flow forecast
is an estimate of future cash inflows and outflows.

Cash flow statement
is a record of cash inflows and outflows which have already occurred.

KEY POINTS

Cash flow forecasts are more likely to be accurate if:

- the manager has gathered relevant data
- there are few unexpected events
- debtors pay on time
- the cash flow forecast is for the short-term not the long-term.

KEY TERM

The Base Rate
is now set by the Bank of England each month, and it acts as the guide for commercial banks to set their own lending rates.

Cash inflows may be lower than expected due to a fall in sales. This could be due to internal or external factors. Internally, the firm may have adopted an inappropriate marketing mix; external causes for a drop in sales might be changes in the exchange rate, an unexpected fall in GDP or the actions of competitors. Cash outflows may be higher than expected if employees demand higher wages or other inputs increase in price (for example, higher prices from suppliers).

The probability of a cash flow crisis will, therefore, depend on the likelihood of inflows being lower than expected or outflows being greater. This will depend on the extent to which events can be predicted and the ability of the management to foresee such change. If the managers fail to gather relevant data or to research the market and trading conditions effectively, they are unlikely to produce an accurate cash flow forecast. Conversely, if managers spend time on their planning and try to ensure their information is as accurate as possible they are more likely to produce a relevant forecast. This does not guarantee there will be no crisis but limits the risk.

The reliability of the data is more likely to be accurate in the short-term than the long-term. Managers should be able to plan fairly accurately their cash inflows and outflows over the next week. It may be more difficult to forecast accurately over five years. It may also depend on the experience and judgement of the manager. Managers must make decisions about when the cash from particular sales will arrive and when demands for payment by creditors will have to be paid.

PROGRESS CHECK

'Cash flow forecasts are frequently wrong so there is little point producing them.' Discuss.

How can a firm avoid cash flow problems?

A cash flow forecast can identify times when action needs to be taken to avoid a liquidity crisis. However, this does not in itself solve the problem. To actually improve its cash flow position a firm could do any of the following:

- Chase up its debtors (this may lead to a loss of good relations, a poor public image and loss of future business).

- Delay paying suppliers (this may mean the suppliers are less willing to deal with the firm in the future).

- Borrow (this incurs interest charges).

- Sell off fixed assets (these may be needed to produce in the future).

- Sell off fixed assets and lease them back (in the long-term this will tend to cost more).

A cash flow forecast does not solve your cash flow problems. It simply helps you to predict when you will have them.

Late payments

A common cause of cash flow problems is late payments. This tends to be a major problem for small firms who are often reliant on one or two major customers so that any delay in cash coming in from one of these customers can cause real problems. In 1998 the Labour Party government introduced an Act of Parliament to help smaller firms collect their debts more quickly.

The 'Late Payment of Commercial Debts (Interest) Act 1998' is to be phased into practice in three stages. The first stage is already in practice and means that any firm with 50 or fewer employees (the government definition of a small firm) can claim interest from the larger firm over any late payment period. Firms are able to collect interest set at the Base Rate + 8%.

However, small firms have been reluctant to actually pursue their right to claim this interest from larger firms who delay payment. This is because the smaller firms are worried about antagonising larger organisations and losing future orders from them. In effect, the larger firms are informally bullying the smaller firms into accepting late payment. A smaller firm, therefore, has to weigh up the pros and cons of charging interest on late payment. In periods of economic growth or stability, the smaller firms are more likely to accept late payments, because the pressures on cash flow are less likely to be a problem. If a firm is uncertain, however, about the future direction of its sales then it may be more likely to claim its SRI (Statutory Right to charge Interest).

PROGRESS CHECK

Should large firms be made to pay small firms on time?

Can a firm avoid bad debts?

Every firm wants to avoid bad debts. If a bad debt occurs, then the firm will not only lose the costs of production but also the profit margin. It would have been better for the firm not to have accepted the sale in the first place, rather than to accept it, produce the product or service and then not be paid. It is tempting, however, for a firm, especially if facing problems generating sales, to take on as many orders as it can. This may mean that a firm is making itself more likely to incur bad debts by accepting high risk customers. Although no one can predict what will happen to its customers in the near future, there are certain ways in which a firm can protect itself from a bad debt:

■ Firms that trade on credit can employ credit checks before granting a firm the right to delay their payment. This can involve checking out the past records of the firm or examining its public accounts. This could prove difficult if the business has only just been set up and the final accounts may not be particularly helpful as they could have been window dressed. A firm could give the impression that it has sufficient amounts of cash to repay by selling a fixed asset shortly before the balance sheet date. This may hide the true picture of its finances. An alternative is to ask for bank references from the prospective cus-

FACT FILE

Tony Blair, speaking as the leader of the then opposition Labour Party, stated his intentions to help firms collect debts back in 1996:
'We should take steps to generate embarrassment amongst those who wilfully and continually pay late.'

FACT FILE

UK businesses have one of the worst payment habits in Europe. Natwest Bank estimated that at any one time £20 billion worth of trade debts are owed to small and medium companies, costing them more than £3 million per day in additional interest burden.

FACT FILE

Following the introduction of The Late Payment of Commercial Debts Act, Rentokil Initial allegedly sent small companies letters informing them that it would pay interest at only 1% above the base rate for unpaid bills after 65 days, and that it would not do business with companies who did not accept these terms. Following protests from small business groups and criticism from the media, Rentokil is said to have withdrawn its initial conditions.

tomer's bank, however, these may not provide enough information as they tend to be stated in general terms.

■ The firm could chase up outstanding debts but this will cost time and money. Alternatively, a firm could use debt factors to collect the money it is owed. A factoring agency will 'buy' outstanding debt of firms but will charge a fee for doing this.

■ One way to check up on the likelihood of debts being paid would be to analyse the outstanding debt in terms of an aged debtors schedule. This involves analysing each debt in relation to how long the debt has been outstanding. The longer a debt is outstanding, the less likely the firm is to receive this debt. Once analysed, the firm can than devote more time to chasing up these debts.

PROGRESS CHECK

Analyse the possible implications of using a tight credit policy (i.e. offering only limited credit).

NUMERICAL INVESTIGATION

Below is an example of an aged debtors schedule. Action can be taken on debts based on their age. For example, a firm will not worry too much about a debt that has been outstanding by less than one month.

AGE OF DEBT (£)	DEBTORS OUTSTANDING
0 – 1 month	4500
1 – 3 months	3400
3 – 6 months	2500
6 – 12 months	1200
Over 1 year	500
Total debtors	12,100

Table 4.2

a From the above data, how much of the outstanding debt do you believe is likely to be a problem to collect? Explain your answer.
b What different policies would you employ for the differently 'aged' debtors?

Small firms and cash flow

Smaller firms in particular tend to have problems with managing cash flow. There are a number of reasons for this. Firstly, a smaller firm is perceived to be a greater risk than a larger firm. Firms are more likely to fail in the first few years of their life due to a small customer base or lack of knowledge and experience. This will mean that they are less likely to be able to obtain funds from a bank. Even if money is borrowed from a bank, then it is more likely that a smaller firm will be charged a higher interest rate than a larger firm, which is a further drain on its cash flow. As a result of this, many small firms will only obtain funds by securing the value of the loan with their personal property.

Smaller firms also suffer because they are less likely to benefit from economies of scale in the way that larger firms do. For example, they might not gain discounts for bulk ordering or be able to employ specialists with specific responsibilities within a firm. This means their outgoings are likely to be higher as they cannot gain preferential rates from suppliers. Also, the lack of specialist financial skills means that a small business is more likely to plan its cash flow requirements incorrectly.

PROGRESS CHECK

Analyse the possible reasons why small firms may have cash flow problems.

Can a firm hold too much cash?

Firms are advised to have sufficient liquid assets so that they can survive on a daily basis; conversely, too much cash may involve a high opportunity cost. The reason for this is that if a firm holds too much cash then it may be missing out on profitable investment opportunities. Even though a firm can earn interest on its cash holdings at the bank, it is usually possible to earn higher returns by being more active with this money (for example, by investing in either fixed capital or in financial investments). From a shareholder's perspective, if a firm has too much cash, this could have been distributed in the form of higher dividends.

PROGRESS CHECK

Examine the factors that might determine how much cash a firm should hold.

The 'right' amount of cash for a firm to hold will depend on factors such as its short-term liabilities, the timing of payments, the opportunity cost, its objectives and the manager's attitude to risk. When interest rates are high and the firm has few bills outstanding, cash levels may be low. When investments seem to pose a high risk or the firm wants to build cash prior to a takeover bid it is likely to hold more.

Budgeting

The effect of budgeting on an organisation

Most firms will budget for the various different functions of the organisation, for example, there is likely to be a marketing budget, a production budget and a sales budget. The different budgets will be co-ordinated to produce the overall cash budget and the projected final accounts of the forthcoming period (known as the master budget). The budgets will involve financial planning by the different departments; these will be largely based on the expected sales for the next period. This places marketing at the centre of the budgeting process; if sales are

KEY POINTS

A cash flow crisis is more likely to be avoided if:

- stand-by finance has previously been arranged (e.g. an overdraft facility)
- customers are checked carefully before granting credit
- assets can be sold and then leased back if necessary
- cash sales can be generated via discounts
- the managers planned their cash flow requirements carefully.

KEY POINTS

A cash flow crisis is more likely to occur if:

- budgeting has not taken place
- market conditions are deteriorating or uncertain
- other firms are experiencing cash flow problems
- credit policy is not tight enough
- expansion of output has taken place without adequate resources.

KEY TERM

Budget
is a forward financial plan; the master budget will usually include a cash flow forecast, forecast sales and forecast costs.

> **Budgets should be forward looking and not simply based on the past.**

What sorts of firm are likely to set budgets?

Many firms will undertake budgeting of some form. It would be very hard for any entrepreneur to acquire and set-up finance from banks if there was no evidence that cash budgeting had taken place. Also, some form of budgeting is likely to take place for capital expenditure. If new machinery or premises are required, then there is likely to be some form of planning involved to see if the firm can afford this expenditure.

For sole traders and small firms, budgeting is more likely to be restricted to the creation of an overall cash budget for the forthcoming period. There will be no real need of the construction of separate budgets for the different areas of the firm because the whole operation is so small. In a larger, more complex structure, several different budgets may be needed.

> **PROGRESS CHECK**
>
> Are there any hidden costs in delegating tasks down the hierarchy?

Variance analysis

The variance measures the difference between budgeted performance and actual performance. What action is taken when a variance occurs depends on the source of the variance.

It may be that no action is needed. For example, whilst it would be tempting to assume that an adverse cost variance was undesirable, it may in fact be the natural result of higher sales. The firm may have sold more, and so it also spent more on its inputs than it originally expected. In this case, it would not be logical to 'punish' managers or take further action – the higher costs are not due to any inefficiency but to the extra costs required to produce the extra units that have been sold. Not surprisingly, the change in the level of activity altered the costs.

Flexible budgeting

One way to build such changes into the budgeting process is to introduce a system of flexible budgeting. Flexible budgeting means redrafting the budget and targets for the various production costs according to the level of output. For example, if sales are expected to rise by 25% then the budgeted production cost would be increased by 25% to take into account of this extra output. However, one problem with this method may be that if labour resources are close to full utilisation, then output may not be able to be increased without incurring a disproportionate rise in labour costs (either due to overtime rates or the recruitment costs). This would mean that the labour costs would rise by more than was normally predicted. Managers would have to take this into account when analysing the variance figures.

Why do adverse variances occur?

An adverse production variance may be due to several factors.

Adverse material cost variance

This could arise either from an inefficient usage of materials (i.e. a greater quantity of materials being used than was budgeted for) or because the unit price of the materials was higher than was budgeted for. If the cost variance is due to higher than expected input prices this could be due to factors such as exchange rate depreciation (if materials are imported) or general inflation.

If the cost variance is due to inefficiency in the usage of materials this could indicate wastage in production, possibly due to inferior quality materials. Alternatively, it could be the fault of workers who are demotivated, or it could be that the workers are unskilled in the usage of the materials. Action to resolve this may take the form of training for the workers, using a better quality of material, or even higher wages for staff to motivate them (although this could lead to an adverse labour cost variance).

Adverse labour cost variance

Adverse labour cost variance can either arise out of inefficiency, in terms of how much time was taken to perform the tasks planned, or because workers were paid a higher wage rate than was budgeted for. Production may have taken longer than expected due to unskilled or untrained workers. Alternatively, it could have been the result of demotivation. Again, more training may be required. The higher than planned wage rates may have occurred with general wage inflation or they could be the result of trade union pressure.

If a firm wishes to control its costs and prevent adverse variances occurring then it must analyse the variances to determine the underlying cause. Some may be due to external factors, however, those that are the result of wage rates accelerating, material wastage or workers taking too long to complete tasks may be more controllable.

PROGRESS CHECK

Discuss the possible benefits of variance analysis for a firm.

KEY POINTS

Budgets are less likely to be useful when:

- they are imposed on managers
- they are unrealistic
- they are not regularly reviewed
- they are automatically linked to last year's budget and not the objectives of the firm.

KEY POINTS

A spending budget is likely to be larger when:

- the firm has a major expansion plan
- the firm has a high level of resources
- the firm has had a high budget in the past.

KEY TERMS

Favourable variances
arise when the firm has more money than is predicted in the budget.

Adverse variances
arise when the firm has less money than is predicted in the budget.

KEY TERM

Flexible budgeting
involves reconstructing the budgeted targets for different levels of output.

Assess the view that strict budgeting is vital for a company to be successful.

(40 marks)

The main area that this question focuses on is the merits of budgeting and a careful answer would look at how budgeting can have both positive and negative implications for a firm (because we need to 'assess the view'). On the positive side, the factors to be considered might be:

- Improved control of finances.

- Less likely to experience cash flow crisis.

- Bad debts may be less likely to occur.

- More accountability of staff who are budget holders.

However, the 'strict budgeting' element indicates that there might be problems in setting tight budgets, such as:

- Demotivation of staff when faced with very tight targets for spending.

- Disagreement with staff about the size of the budget.

- If the budget is unrealistic it may mean it has to be redrafted at a later date.

The general conclusion to this sort of question would be that whilst there are advantages in setting and monitoring budgets, a tight budget may actually cause harm in terms of staff performance. It will depend on the situation in which a business finds itself if the potential harm it may cause is considered as acceptable or not. In times of recession, or changing market conditions, then strict budgeting may be the only way a firm can survive. However, if sales are rising rapidly, a strict and tight budget may prevent firms from taking opportunities that are offered from rising sales, through higher expenditure on promotion. Smaller firms may find that they need to budget quite strictly as finance is often difficult to acquire.

A good answer might highlight that effective budgeting may contribute to a firm's success but certainly does not guarantee it; success is due to a combination of factors such as effective marketing, operations and human resource management.

To what extent can a firm control its cash flow?

(11 marks)

This type of question requires you to argue for and against the view that a firm can control its cash flow. Factors in favour of the firm having cash flow under its own control would include:

- A firm can decide on the level of production and, therefore, how much it wishes to spend on production.

- Debtors can be called in if necessary.

- A firm can anticipate many problems, via cash flow forecasts, and take preventative action if necessary.

- Changes in credit policy can be used if a firm has problems with bad debts.

Even with careful planning, however, cash flow is subject to external factors that are beyond the firm's control and these could include:

- Changes in the economy (growth rates, consumer spending, exchange rates, interest rates are all relevant here) will affect sales.

- Action by competitors, especially on pricing policy, can also affect sales.

- The interrelated nature of firms that trade – one firm defaulting on debts can have a 'domino' effect on the ability of others to repay.

- Suppliers may insist on certain payment terms.

- Customers may be slow to pay, even if chased.

It is important that you consider the type of firm and the situation it is trading in when answering this kind of question. For example, if the firm is operating in a recession then it is likely to have less control over its cash flow as sales may be harder to find and customers may be unable (or unwilling) to pay. In an economic boom, overtrading may be more of a problem as sales increase quickly. In this situation, control over cash flow may be lost if the firm does not budget for this expansion carefully. Factors such as exchange rates may affect the cash flow of manufacturers who are trying to export more than firms which operate domestically; interest rate changes are likely to affect highly geared firms more than firms with low gearing.

The extent to which a firm can control its cash flow will ultimately depend on how much it plans, its power over debtors and creditors, its ability to raise finance at short notice and the extent to which external factors change cash inflows or outflows unexpectedly.

'Any adverse variance is the result of poor management.' Discuss this statement.

(11 marks)

The statement is not as clear cut as may appear and it is important that you discuss both the reasons why the statement is true and the reasons why it may not be true.

Adverse variances arise when the firm either spends more, or earns less than it budgeted for. For example, an adverse materials variance could arise from paying a higher unit price for the materials due to a fall in the exchange rate.

It could be argued that an adverse variance is due to the management of the firm in that they are responsible for controlling these budgets. There are, however, other reasons which suggest that the variance is beyond the control of the managers or that the adverse variance should not be seen in a negative manner.

Issues to be considered would include:

1. Was the budget set too tightly in the first place?
2. Have changes in the external environment meant that sales have fallen more than was predicted?
3. Is the adverse variance the result of higher production levels? If so, then perhaps flexible budgeting would be more useful?
4. Are the variances linked to other areas of poor performance?

The extent to which poor management is to blame will depend on the source of the adverse variance. Some reasons will be the fault of management; these could include a lack of control over wages and materials expenses or a failure to motivate or manage staff effectively. However, it is possible that the variance could be out of the managers' control (for example, an import tax on inputs). A trend of adverse variances is probably more worrying for a firm than a one-off, although it is likely that some action will be taken even if it is just to acknowledge that the managers are not to blame.

Student answers

'Cash is vital to a company's survival whereas profit is just a bonus.' Discuss the validity of this view.

(11 marks)

Student answer

Cash and profit are not the same thing. Cash is the most liquid of all assets and can be measured at a point in time. Profit is the outcome of trading and can only be measured over a period of time. Most firms are aiming to make a profit as their main objective but some firms are happy achieving other objectives, such as social prestige or market share maximisation.

Cash is needed by all firms in order to continue in business. If a firm runs out of cash then it may face insolvency. This would be forced on the firm by any of its creditors who it has not paid. Cash is needed to pay bills and suppliers. If these cannot be paid then a firm must find alternative sources of money in order to continue trading. Firms can use overdrafts, debt factoring, or call in their own debt. They may be able to extend the credit period if they negotiate with their own creditors.

Marker's comments

This answer began well by relating the objectives of the firm to the title and questioning the ideas that all organisations are solely there to make a profit. This could have been explored further by examining whether firms have profit as an objective all the time or if they may change their objectives at different stages of their development. For example, a small firm may be aiming to break even in the first few years as it builds up its sales base. In a recession, many firms aim for survival.

The concept of why cash is needed is stated fairly well, although the expression of ideas is rather limited. The answer needs to address the issue of profit as a bonus – in what way is it a bonus? Surely for most firms, profit over the long-term is an essential element of being in business. The significance of profit as an essential element of business performance needs to be explored further. In reality, for most private sector firms success will generally depend on maintaining an appropriate cash flow and suitable levels of profit; the two must be achieved together.

Mark: Content 2/2, Application & Analysis 2/6, Evaluation 0/3. Total = 4

'Stocks represent wasted resources. Cash is better.' To what extent is this statement true?

(11 marks)

Student answer

Stocks held by the firm could represent wasted resources as they are, in effect, money tied up in idle resources. Money has been spent on producing these stocks, which will not be released as free cash and potential profit until the stocks are sold on to a customer. This may take some time. If the firm is a retailer then the period between obtaining the stock and selling the stock may be quite short. However, a manufacturer may have to wait for some time before the goods are sold. If sales take place on credit then this period could be even longer. Stocks also cost money in terms of storage. This will depend on the type of goods that are to be stored. High bulk stocks may cost considerable amounts, especially if they are very valuable (due to security costs).

A firm will, however, want to hold stocks to meet any unexpected sales that may occur. If the firm is in a market that is growing then there are more likely to be extra sales which may be missed out on if the firm has no stocks.

Marker's comments

This answer does not really get to grips with the question. Although it deals fairly successfully with the issue of stock holding, it ignores the second half of the statement that 'cash is better'. The advantage of cash is that it is more liquid than stock. It does, however, have an opportunity cost. In comparison, the advantage of stock is that it may be sold for a profit; the disadvantage is that it is less liquid. Once again, the issue is not one or the other but an appropriate balance of the two. Cash may be required to ensure the firm is liquid; stock may be needed for the firm to trade.

Mark: Content 2/2, Application & Analysis 4/6, Evaluation 0/3. Total = 6

'A tight credit policy can only improve a firm's financial position.' Discuss this statement.

(11 marks)

Student answer

Sales made on credit mean that the firm has delivered the goods to the customers but does not receive the money from the sale until some time in the future (usually between one and three months). The firm will receive credit when buying materials from suppliers.

A tight credit policy implies that the firm will carefully assess any of its customers before deciding to grant them credit. Giving credit could be dangerous if the firm sold goods to anyone on credit. It may be the case that other firms are not reliable when repaying what they owe; they may take too long or may not pay at all. This means that the firm loses not just the profit on the sale but also the costs of production.

A tight policy should improve the firm's finances because the firm is less likely to lose money by giving credit to unreliable customers. A tight policy would involve taking measures to make sure that they will not lose money when granting credit. This could involve asking the customer for references from other firms that they have dealt with before allowing credit. It could also involve looking at the firm's finances to make sure that they are solvent (for example, the acid test ratio may show any problems with meeting day-to-day running costs). All these measures will save the firm money and therefore should be implemented.

Marker's comments

A disappointing answer despite a strong beginning. The outline of the relative advantages of adopting a tight credit policy is excellent – the style and the content are both very good, with the merits of adopting this policy well explained. The main problem is that the downside of this policy is not examined at all. If a tight credit policy is so useful, then why are all firms not adopting this approach? The answer could include the following possible reasons:

1 A tight credit policy may alienate customers.

2 Credit checks, asking for references and looking at final accounts costs money, which may be considered wasteful.

3 The firm's own suppliers may also be customers and this could result in less attractive terms being offered to them.

4 Long payment terms are often used as a promotional tool to win sales; a tight credit policy may lead to a loss in sales as consumers switch to competitors.

In any 'discussion' question, there will need to be a consideration of both sides of the argument. It is highly unlikely that a statement will be totally true or totally false and the answer should reflect that there are two sides to be discussed. It also assumes that firms do not have tight credit policies – many do. The answer will also depend on how tight the credit policy becomes and how customers react to this.

Mark: Content 2/2, Application & Analysis 4/6, Evaluation 0/3. Total = 6

Evaluate the usefulness of cash flow forecasts to sole traders.

(11 marks)

Student answer

A cash flow forecast is a very useful tool to a sole trader. Sole traders generally have the most difficulty in raising finance. A cash flow forecast will, therefore, show them when they may have trouble and need to borrow money. This degree of planning will be very useful as the more time they have to prepare the better. For example, if a shortage is predicted in a few months time then the sole trader could arrange to call in their debtors in time for the crisis or could sell off some fixed assets which would avert the problems before they happened.

A bank manager is likely to want to see a forecast before granting a loan or overdraft to a sole trader. This is because they are perceived to be a higher risk than a larger firm, such as a plc.

Marker's comments

This is not a bad answer, its main problem is that there is no real evaluation. The uses of cash flow forecasts are considered and explained fairly well. There are also some references specific to a sole trader, in that they are likely to need to produce a forecast to acquire finance.

To evaluate this question the student could have considered the fact that the cash flow forecast is only a prediction made by the sole trader. It may be the case that they cannot produce a totally objective forecast; it may be far too optimistic. The value would, therefore, depend on how accurate it proved to be.

Most cash flow crises are not predicted; they usually occur when the forecast breaks down and other factors affect the firm. For example, changing market conditions could render the forecast as useless. Also, it is important to note that the forecast in itself does not solve any problems; the sole trader would still need to take appropriate action. Even if he or she realises that more funds will be needed, this does not guarantee that they can be raised.

Mark: Content 2/2, Application & Analysis 4/6, Evaluation 0/3. Total = 6

End of section questions

1 Analyse the possible ways in which cash and profit differ.

(9 marks)

2 Evaluate the possible courses of action a firm might take to resolve a major liquidity crisis.

(11 marks)

3 Discuss the possible merits of introducing rigorous checks before allowing trade credit to customers.

(11 marks)

4 Examine the possible causes of a cash flow shortage.

(9 marks)

5 'Budgeting can both motivate and demotivate the employees of a firm.' Discuss this view.

(11 marks)

6 To what extent is a firm's cash flow dependent on the economic cycle?

(11 marks)

7 Analyse the view that firms should reduce their working capital.

(9 marks)

8 To what extent is profitability inevitably sacrificed when a firm focuses on liquidity?

(11 marks)

9 Outline the ways in which a firm might be able to prevent the occurrence of bad debts.

(9 marks)

10 'It is not the source of any variance which counts, but the size of the variance.' Discuss this view.

(11 marks)

Essays

1 'The unpredictable nature of the external environment means that any attempt to forecast cash flows is irrelevant.' To what extent do you agree with this statement?

(40 marks)

2 A small car servicing garage is facing a severe shortage of cash. Evaluate the options open to the owner.

(40 marks)

3 'The size of the budget matters less than the process of budgeting.' Discuss.

(40 marks)

4 Many new businesses fail because of liquidity problems. Should all new firms make more liquidity their priority?

(40 marks)

5 'Large public limited companies do not have to worry about cash flow.' Discuss this view.

(40 marks)

CHAPTER 5

Costing and break even analysis

Break even analysis

Break even analysis is a decision-making tool. It helps managers to estimate the costs, revenues and profits associated with any level of sales. This can help to decide whether or not to go ahead with a project. Below the break even level of output a loss will be made; above this level a profit will be made. If the break even level for a potential new product is 30,000 units but the firm estimates its sales will only be 20,000 units then, assuming it wants to make a profit, it will not go ahead with the project. If sales are estimated to be 45,000 units, it is more likely to go ahead. Break even analysis also enables managers to see the impact of changes in price, in variable and fixed costs and in sales levels on the firm's profits.

> **Break even analysis is a decision-making tool.**

To ascertain the level of sales required in order to break even, we need to look at how cost and revenues vary with changes in output.

Example of break even analysis

Rachel Hackwood operates as a sole trader. She sells sandwiches from a small shop in the centre of a busy town. The fixed costs per month, including rent of the premises and advertising total £600. The average variable cost of producing a sandwich is 50p and the average selling price of one sandwich is £1.50. The relationship between costs and revenues is as follows:

KEY TERMS

Break even output
is the level of output where total costs equals total revenue. Break even output = $\dfrac{\text{fixed costs}}{\text{contribution per unit}}$

Contribution
is 'selling price − variable cost per unit'.

Fixed costs
are those that do not change as a result of changes in output, such as rent and insurance.

Variable costs
are those that vary directly with the level of production, such as materials and packaging.

Sales revenue
is found by multiplying the sales volume (measured in units) by the selling price.

MONTHLY OUTPUT (SANDWICHES)	FIXED COSTS (£)	VARIABLE COSTS (£)	TOTAL COSTS (£ FC + VC)	TOTAL REVENUE (£)	PROFIT/ LOSS (£)
0	600	0	600	0	(600)
200	600	100	700	300	(400)
400	600	200	800	600	(200)
600	600	300	900	900	0
800	600	400	1,000	1,200	200
1,000	600	500	1,100	1,500	400

Table 5.1

As we can see, at low levels of output, Rachel makes a loss. This is due to the heavy fixed element in her costs. The loss is reduced as output rises and she breaks even at 600 sandwiches per month. Any output higher than this will generate a profit for Rachel.

To show this in a graph, plot the total costs and total revenue. It is also normal to show the fixed cost. The horizontal axis measures the level of output. At a certain level of output, the total cost and total revenue curves will intersect. This highlights the break even level of output.

The level of break even will depend on the fixed costs, the variable cost per unit and the selling price. The higher the fixed costs, the more units will have to be sold to break even. The higher the selling price, the less units need to be sold.

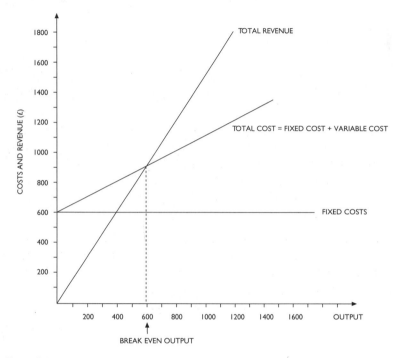

Figure 5.1 Simple break even analysis

For some industries, such as the pharmaceutical industry, break even may be at quite high levels of ouput. Once the new drug has been developed the actual production costs will be low, however, high volumes are needed to cover the high initial research and development costs. This is one reason why patents are needed in this industry. If there were no legal protection for new developments, it is unlikely that new drugs would be produced, as the high development costs might never be regained due to the competition in the market. The airline and telecommunications industries also have high fixed costs and need high volumes of customers to begin to make profits. In industries where the fixed costs are relatively small and the contribution on each unit is quite high, break even output will be much lower.

Uses and limitations of break even for decision-making

The simple break even model helps managers analyse the effects of changes in different variables (see Figures 5.2–5.4). A manager can easily identify the impact on the break even level of output and the change in profit or loss at the existing output.

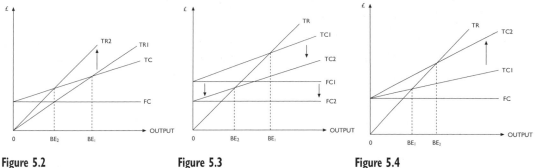

Figure 5.2
Increasing selling price

Figure 5.3
Reduction in fixed cost

Figure 5.4
Increasing variable cost

However, simple break even analysis also makes simplifying assumptions; for example, it assumes that the variable cost per unit is constant. In reality this is likely to change with changes in output. As a firm expands, for example, it may be able to buy materials in bulk and benefit from purchasing economies of scale. Conversely, as output rises a firm may have to pay higher overtime wage rates to persuade workers to work longer hours. In either case, the variable costs per unit are unlikely to stay constant.

Another simplifying assumption of the model is that fixed costs are assumed to remain fixed at all levels of output. In fact, once a certain level of output is reached, a firm will have to spend more money on expansion. More machinery will have to be purchased and larger premises may be required (either for purchase or for rent). This means that the fixed costs are likely to be stepped.

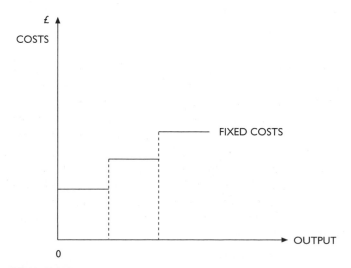

Figure 5.5 Stepped fixed costs

Firms will also incur other costs, which are partly but not directly related to the level of output. These are known as semi-variable expenses. For example, if a firm purchases more machinery, then maintenance costs will rise but possibly not in the same proportion as the increase in the capacity (capacity may double but servicing costs for the machines may only increase by 40%, for instance). These would also have to be included in a more sophisticated version of break even analysis.

Simple break even analysis also assumes that if the output is produced it will automatically sell. In reality, sales may be higher than output (if the firm is using up stock) or less than output (if the firm is building up stocks). If the sales are lower than the output produced the total revenue would be less than the break even chart suggests.

Break even charts

A break even chart enables the manager to quickly calculate the impact of changes in different variables, provided the impact on sales is estimated. However, it is a simplification and can only be as useful as the underlying information. If, for example, the items will not sell at the given price, or the cost figures are inaccurate, the decision made is less likely to be the correct one. Also, break even analysis cannot in itself make or implement a decision. Managers must be able to interpret and manipulate the chart appropriately; they must also be able to put the necessary decision into action. Using the break even chart may suggest that an increase in output and sales of 10% will be profitable, however, it is actually up to the manager to bring about the necessary increase in production, to ensure these items are sold and to keep the variable cost per unit constant.

To be effective, break even charts must be combined with the manager's own judgement. Will a particular output really be sold at this price? How will competitors react to a change in price or output levels? What is likely to happen to costs in the future? The right decision can only be made if the underlying assumptions of the model are relevant and the manager balances the numerical findings with his or her own experience.

PROGRESS CHECK

Consider the value of break even analysis in determining the price of a product.

PROGRESS CHECK

Assess the value of break even analysis as a decision-making tool.

Can a firm reduce its break even output?

Not surprisingly, firms will be eager to reduce their break even level of output, as this means they have to sell less to become profitable. To reduce the break even level of output a firm must do one or more of the following:

- Increase the selling price.
- Reduce the level of fixed costs.
- Reduce the variable unit cost.

An increase in the selling price would mean that each unit sold would generate more sales revenue and, therefore, less units would need to be sold for the firm to break even (see Figure 5.2). However, the higher price is likely to lead to a fall in sales; if this fall is relatively large this may lead to a decrease in the firm's profits. An increase in price is, therefore, most likely to be used in industries with heavily branded products, with specialised output and/or with little competition where price is a less important factor in determining demand and so demand is price inelastic. Price increases are less likely to be used when demand is highly price elastic, due to the impact on sales. Demand is likely to be price elastic when the market is highly competitive and it is easy for the consumer to swap from one product to another.

Another means of reducing the break even level of output is to cut the variable cost per unit (see Figure 5.3). This will save money for each unit produced but may have undesirable side effects. For example, cutting wage rates may save the firm money on an hourly basis but the potential drop in motivation may lead to lower productivity. This could result in higher overall labour costs per unit. Alternatively, the firm could save on material costs by using fewer inputs or finding alternative suppliers who can supply at a lower price. However, the reliability and quality of supplies must be closely monitored as this could have an adverse effect on sales.

Alternatively, a firm could reduce its fixed costs (see Figure 5.4); these could be reduced by selling off surplus capacity (machines and/or premises) or renting out part of the premises that is unused. The firm could also switch from purchasing machinery and equipment to leasing the equipment. This would shift some of the fixed cost into variable costs. However, although this saves on fixed costs, it may lead to a situation where the unit cost outweighs the selling price (due to high leasing costs) in which case the firm can never break even.

PROGRESS CHECK

Questions

1 Discuss the ways in which a firm might reduce its break even level of output.
2 Consider the possible difficulties a firm might face when trying to reduce its break even level of output.

Should a firm accept an order at below cost price?

Once a firm is producing output higher than the break even level then the firm will make a profit for that time period. Provided the output is sold at the standard selling price, then any extra units sold will add to this profit. Each additional unit sold will increase profit by an amount equal to the contribution per unit. Any extra orders in this situation might be welcomed by the firm, providing it has the necessary capacity and working capital, as those factors will increase profits.

Imagine if a customer asks to buy additional units but is only willing to pay a price below the unit cost. Intuitively we would probably reject this order on the grounds that selling output at below cost price will reduce the firm's total profits. In fact, rejecting this deal as loss-making might be a mistake, depending on the level of direct costs and indirect costs involved.

KEY POINTS

Firms are less likely to increase price when:

- the market is highly competitive
- the product or service is unbranded
- the consumer has a wide range of choice
- there are few switching costs involved for the consumer.

FACT FILE

Eurotunnel estimated the abolition of duty free shopping in 1999 cost it £100 million per year in profits. To compensate and make sure it broke even it had to increase its fares. The company hoped to regain about 80% of the shortfall from higher prices and the remaining 20% from increased sales of tax-paid goods.

FACT FILE

In the late 1990s Siemens, the German electronics and engineering giant, introduced a strict streamlining policy to cut costs. Its radical restructuring included the sale of its $10 billion components businesses, mergers to strengthen weak activities and a stronger focus on shareholder value. Cost cutting and rationalisation enabled three of its loss-making operations, Infineon, power generation and Siemens Business Services to break even by 1999.

An example of ordering below cost price

Consider the information following. A firm currently sells output at a price of £150 and is producing 2,000 units of output. The firm is presently operating at 80% capacity (i.e. further 500 units, the extra 20%, could be produced without affecting the indirect overheads). The current cost data is as follows:

	£	£
Sales revenue (2000 × £150)		300,000
Materials	80,000	
Labour	80,000	
Other direct costs	20,000	
Indirect overheads	70,000	250,000
Profit		**50,000**

Table 5.2

An order is received from a new customer who wants 300 units but would only be willing to pay £100 for each unit. From the costing data in the table above, we can calculate the average 'cost' of each unit to be £250,000/2,000 units = £125. Therefore, it would appear that accepting the order would mean selling the firm would lose £25 on each unit sold.

The order would, however, in fact add to the firm's profits. The reason for this is that the indirect costs are fixed over the range of output 0–2500 units. The only costs that would increase would be the direct cost of production, i.e. labour, materials and other direct costs. The direct cost of each unit can be found by dividing the total for direct costs by the level of output. For example, the materials cost for 2,000 units is £80,000. This means that the materials cost for each unit would be £80,000/2,000 units = £40. If we repeat this for labour and other direct costs then the cost of producing an extra unit would be as follows:

	DIRECT COST PER UNIT (£)
Materials	40
Labour	40
Other direct costs	10
Marginal cost	**90**

Table 5.3

Each extra unit sold would, therefore, generate an extra £10 contribution (selling price − direct costs). Hence, accepting the order would actually add to the overall profits for the firm by £3,000 (300 × £10 contribution). Providing the selling price exceeds the additional cost of making the product, then this contribution on each unit will add to profits.

Other issues connected with accepting the order

It will also help the firm to utilise any spare capacity that is currently lying idle. For example, if a firm is renting a factory, then this will represent an indirect cost for the firm. It does not matter how much of the factory is used, the rent will remain the same. Therefore, if a section of the factory which is presently unused could be used for further production, it might be worthwhile for the firm to make use of this. If spare capacity does not exist, however, the firm must consider the possible impact of the order, in terms of the costs of acquiring new equipment and/or premises. Taking on extra orders may lead to further extra indirect costs, which are particularly associated with this order. For example, if the customer is located some distance away then there may be delivery costs or administrative costs that are not incurred at present. This will increase the overall cost of the order.

By accepting this order the firm may also generate future sales with the new customer or, via word-of-mouth, with other customers. The firm will have to decide whether the attractions of extra orders and higher sales outweigh the fact that these sales are at a lower selling price than normal. It will want to avoid having too many of its sales at this 'discounted' price, as this lower price may start to be seen as 'normal'. Customers already paying the higher price may be unhappy and demand to be allowed to buy at this lower price.

Although the lower price is above the marginal cost of production, it may be that the firm does not cover its indirect and direct costs if too many are sold at the low price (rather than at a higher price). Though the contribution sold on these 'discounted' units is positive, sales still have to be high enough to allow for enough unit contributions to cover the indirect costs.

KEY POINTS

Accepting an extra order at below 'normal' selling price is likely to add to profits if:

- the new selling price exceeds the direct cost of production
- spare capacity exists within the organisation
- no addition to indirect costs is expected
- extra sales may be generated from accepting this order
- existing customers will not be alienated.

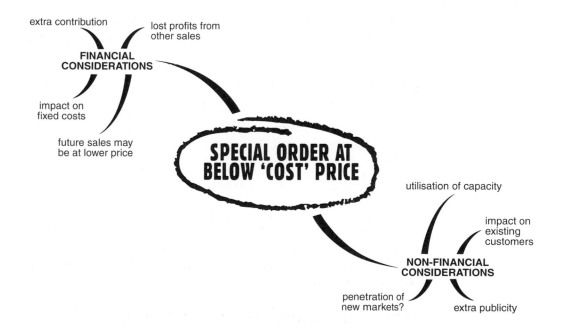

Figure 5.5

A new client has offered to buy the equivalent of 10% of your existing output at a price that is 5% less than your standard list price. Consider the factors you might take into account when deciding whether to accept the order or not.

'Buying in' products

Profits can be increased by either increasing the selling price (depending on the impact on sales) or by reducing costs. One possible way to reduce costs for a firm that uses manufactured goods would be if an alternative supplier could be found who can manufacture and sell products (or part of the products, such as components) for a lower price than the present cost of the firm producing these for itself. If this is the case then the firm will have a choice of whether to continue making the products or to buy them in from a supplier.

Considerations

KEY POINTS

Buying in components rather than manufacturing them internally is more likely to boost profits if:

- the purchase price exceeds the unit cost of production
- quality of the purchased products is not inferior
- lead times are short so that production is not delayed by late deliveries
- worker motivation is not affected significantly
- fixed costs can be saved through closing down excess capacity
- space capacity can be utilised elsewhere.

When making this decision a firm would probably consider the possible impact on its workforce. If production is being reduced then there is likely to be a reduction in the size of the workforce needed. Unless the firm can retrain the workers for other functions within the firm, such as sales, redundancies are likely to occur. This could lead to industrial action or a reduction in productivity as employees may be demotivated by seeing co-workers losing their jobs.

The firm will also have to ensure that the supplier of the product is reliable. If they are located some distance away then the lead time for delivery will become an important factor. Problems of delivery could lead to production bottlenecks, whereby overall production is halted or orders cannot be met due to unreliable suppliers. This is a particular problem if the firm is adopting just-in-time (JIT) production techniques.

The quality of the products will also have to be monitored closely. Depending on the size of the order, the firm may be able to demand their own specifications for the order. On the other hand, if the firm is only a small customer of the supplier, it may have to accept the supplier's own specifications.

If the firm does decide to buy in components or products from another supplier, it may close down all or part of the production facilities, unless alternative uses can be found, such as producing goods for other firms. If closures do take place this will save the firm fixed costs in the long-term, although the firm may be committed to paying some of these for the next few months. For example, rent or insurance may be payable annually without rebate if the service is no longer required.

In 1999 Body Shop International, the cosmetics retailer, announced it was going to shed 300 jobs as part of a restructuring plan. The company said it was making 'good progress' on the plan, and was in negotiations to sell its two manufacturing plants. The cost of the restructuring reduced profits by £16.6 million for the year up to 27 February, while store closures at the US subsidiary triggered exceptional costs of £4.5 million. That left pre-tax profits down from £38 million to £3.4 million. Job losses were expected to save £4 million in the current financial year, and £8 million in a full year. The group wanted to focus less on manufacturing and more on speeding up product development and retailing.

Question

Consider the factors Body Shop International might take into account when choosing suppliers of its products.

KEY TERMS

Cost centres are identifiable areas of the firm to which costs can be allocated or apportioned. Common examples include departments, products, branches or machines.

Profit centres can be used if the cost centres also generate revenue. For example, if a business designates branches of a firm or products as cost centre then revenue earned as well as costs incurred can be apportioned to these centres, thus giving us the profit for each centre. Some cost centres cannot be profit centres as they do not generate a revenue, e.g. the human resources department.

Costing methods

Single product

Once a firm moves away from producing a single product, it will find that costing its range of products becomes more complicated. With a single product it is relatively straightforward to 'cost' a product. One can either look at the variable cost of producing an extra unit of output or at the average total cost of each unit of output, by simply averaging the total costs of production by the number of units produced.

Multi-product

With more than one product being produced, a firm is likely to want information that shows the costs of production for each type of product. This information could be used to decide which products were worth maintaining and which ones might need to be withdrawn due to declining profitability. Costing statements can also be used to assess the efficiency of departments and when the turnover of the different business units is also taken into account, managers can be judged on the profits of their particular areas of responsibility.

The measurement of the costs and revenues of different parts of a business helps to make the people involved in each area more conscious of the financial aspects of the organisation. It also allows them to monitor their progress over time as well as enabling senior managers to set financial targets for the future.

Contribution and full costing

When costing, a firm can use either contribution (or marginal) costing, whereby the fixed costs are kept separate, or it can apportion overheads and use full costing. If

KEY TERMS

Direct costs
are clearly linked to a particular cost centre, e.g. materials and components.

Indirect costs (or overheads)
are costs that are not clearly linked to particular cost centres but are general to the business, e.g. general administration costs, corporate advertising, senior management salaries.

KEY TERMS

Contribution costing
is used when only the direct costs of production are allocated to the cost centres. To work out the firm's overall profit the total contribution of all the cost centres is calculated and the indirect costs are then deducted.

Full costing
is where not only are the direct costs allocated to cost centres but the indirect costs are also allocated to different cost centres on the basis of a pre-determined method of apportionment. If profit centres are used, the profit made by each centre can then be calculated by deducting the full cost from the sales revenue generated by each profit centre.

PROGRESS CHECK

'Few years in our long history have been as difficult as this one ... This year's results are unacceptable ... We have now reviewed every part of our operations and started a radical programme of recovery ... I am sure we will view this year as a turning point in reshaping our business for the next century.' As part of the recovery programme the company stated that: 'We must create clear profit centres with management structures, faster decision-making and distinct targets for shareholder value.'

Source: *Marks and Spencer Annual Report 1998/9*

Question

In what ways might the creation of 'clear profit centres' help to improve the company's performance?

the firm uses full costing then it has to decide how the overheads are to be apportioned or allocated to the different cost centres.

Methods of allocating indirect costs

One of the easiest ways to allocate indirect costs is to split the overheads equally between the different cost centres. However, although easier to calculate, splitting the indirect cost equally may not be as fair as it initially appears.

Allocating overheads

Example: Chase Ltd.

Chase Ltd. produces office furniture. It has decided to classify its different products as profit centres. The direct costs incurred in the production of each product are as follows:

	COMPUTER WORKSTATION	SWIVEL CHAIR	STANDARD DESK
Material costs	£20	£15	£10
Labour costs	£25	£8	£12
Packaging and finishing	£5	£7	£3
Total direct costs	**£50**	**£30**	**£25**

Table 5.4 Direct costs

Along with the direct costs of production there are also indirect costs that are not specifically related to the production procedure. These total £90,000. Further data relating to Chase Ltd. is as follows:

	COMPUTER WORKSTATION	SWIVEL CHAIR	STANDARD DESK
Annual output	5,000	3,000	4,000
Selling price	£75	£45	£35

Table 5.5 Indirect costs

We can produce a costing statement that highlights the costs and revenues that arise out of each profit centre:

	COMPUTER WORKSTATION (£)		SWIVEL CHAIR (£)		STANDARD DESK (£)
Sales revenue		375,000		135,000	140,000
Materials	100,000		45,000		40,000
Labour	125,000		24,000		48,000
Packaging and finishing	25,000		21,000		12,000
Total direct costs		**250,000**		**90,000**	**100,000**
Contribution		**125,000**		**45,000**	**40,000**

Table 5.6 Costing statement

If a firm wishes to work out the profit made by each profit centres then the overheads will have to be allocated to each one. In the example below, overheads are allocated equally:

	COMPUTER WORKSTATION (£)		SWIVEL CHAIR (£)		STANDARD DESK (£)
Sales revenue		375,000		135,000	140,000
Materials	100,000		45,000		40,000
Labour	125,000		24,000		48,000
Packaging and finishing	25,000		21,000		12,000
Indirect costs	**30,000**		**30,000**		**30,000**
Total costs		**280,000**		**120,000**	**130,000**
Profit		**95,000**		**15,000**	**10,000**

Table 5.7 Allocation of overheads

It is worth noting that the firm's overall profit should not be any different whether it uses contribution or full costing. All that changes is how it deals with the costs – either apportioning them out to the cost or profit centres for full costing or deducting them in total from the total contribution of the centres for contribution costing. If the indirect costs are allocated, the decision about how to allocate them will affect the profit or loss of each profit centre, but it will not affect the overall profit of the firm.

PROGRESS CHECK

Distinguish between full costing and contribution costing.

Allocation rules

Allocating overheads equally is the simplest and quickest means of apportioning indirect costs, but many managers do use other allocation rules. In some cases they also use different allocation rules for different types of indirect costs – this is known as absorption costing. Although these do not attempt to allocate the indirect costs accurately (in the sense that indirect costs cannot clearly be allocated to different cost centres), they do attempt to take account of relevant factors that might affect the extent to which different cost centres incur the indirect costs. For example, overall heating costs might be allocated according to the floor space of different departments.

Typical allocation rules include:

- If the indirect costs are connected with the staff of the firm, then allocating overheads on the basis of labour costs may be suitable. Examples of staff costs would include canteen expenses or the costs associated with running the human resources department.

- For manufacturing firms, the basis of allocating indirect costs may be related to the materials costs incurred by each cost centre. This will depend on the cost centres within the organisation.

- If a firm is operating in an industrial sector using expensive equipment, then the overheads may be allocated on the basis of the value of machinery in each cost centre. This is because maintenance, training and insurance costs may be related to the value of machinery in a loose way.

In some ways these rules are no more or less accurate than dividing the indirect costs equally although they may appear to be intuitively appealing and in some sense feel fairer.

Consequences of 'unfair' overhead allocation

We can rationalise over the reason chosen for the basis of overhead allocation, however, we must realise that no method is perfect. Costs being apportioned require a method to be chosen independently, precisely because there is no direct link between the cost and the cost centre. The method chosen can have unfortunate effects on the organisation as a whole. If the firm uses departments as cost centres then it is possible that using absorption costing could lead to resentment by staff. This can be illustrated through the following example.

Example: Hopkinson Ltd.

Hopkinson Ltd. has decided to allocate fixed overheads using labour costs as the basis for allocation. Fixed overheads for the organisation total £360,000 and will be allocated on the basis of labour costs (i.e. in the ratio 2:3:4) between the three branches.

	A (£)	B (£)	C (£)
Sales revenue	165,000	240,000	300,000
Labour costs	40,000	60,000	80,000
Materials costs	20,000	30,000	40,000
Other direct costs	10,000	10,000	10,000
Fixed overheads	**80,000**	**120,000**	**160,000**
Profit/loss	**15,000**	**20,000**	**10,000**

Table 5.8

Allocating overheads in this way gives the result that branch B generates the highest profit and branch C is the least profitable. The staff at branch C may be labelled as poor performers. This could lead to demotivation, rivalry between branches and lower productivity. Staff at branch C may also be worried that promotions or bonuses may not be available to them due to them rating lowest out of the three branches. However, this result is arrived at only because the high fixed overheads were allocated in these ways. If we ignored the fixed costs and considered contribution only, the following results occur:

	A (£)	B (£)	C (£)
Sales revenue	165,000	240,000	300,000
Labour costs	40,000	60,000	80,000
Materials costs	20,000	30,000	40,000
Other direct costs	**10,000**	**10,000**	**10,000**
Contribution	**95,000**	**140,000**	**170,000**

Table 5.9

Based on contribution costing, branch C provides the biggest input into earning money for the firm.

The problems that can occur when allocating overheads can lead to arguments between managers over how they should be divided up. To boost their particular division's performance, managers will be eager to change to a method that shifts some of their indirect costs onto another division.

In some ways, however, it does not matter what rules are used to allocate indirect costs. Whichever rule is used is inaccurate (by definition indirect costs cannot clearly be associated with a particular cost centre) but the actual process of allocating overheads makes everyone aware of their importance and of the need to monitor and control them. Furthermore, provided the rules are not changed over time, managers will be able to analyse the trend profit figures for different departments, products or regions. A significant increase in indirect costs will decrease the profits of all business units to some degree, regardless of how these costs are allocated. If the indirect costs continue to rise, all the managers will be able to notice this trend in their accounts.

KEY POINTS

Unfair overhead allocation is more likely to:

- lead to 'incorrect' production decisions
- demotivate workers affected by the overhead allocation
- result in rivalry between people connected with the different cost centres.

PROGRESS CHECK

Produce a costing statement for Hopkinson Ltd. as shown in Table 5.9, but with the indirect costs allocated on the basis of sales revenue. Is this a fairer method of overhead allocation?

Closing an unprofitable business

If we use the full costing method of allocating indirect overheads then we can illustrate how this information may be used to make a strategic decision in terms of closing down an unprofitable business.

In the following situation, we will look at the costing data for Beynon's Ltd., a small family chain of bakeries. The chain is owned and managed as a family concern, with the father maintaining overall control, with the three children each managing one of the three branches. Although Beynon's Ltd. is and has been profitable for a number of years, the father, James Beynon, has been convinced of the merits of segmental reporting (see Chapter Three). He is worried about the performance of the branch at Browndale, which has shown a loss for the last two years. He is particularly worried because the branch is run by his youngest son, who he considers to be inexperienced in retail management. Consider the following breakdown of costs:

	HIGHFIELDS (£)	BROWNDALE (£)	NORTON (£)
Sales revenue	22,000	17,000	26,000
Staffing costs	7,000	8,000	9,000
Supplies	5,000	4,000	6,000
Branch running costs	1,000	1,000	1,000
Marketing	2,000	2,000	2,000
Central administration	4,000	4,000	4,000
Total costs	**19,000**	**19,000**	**22,000**
Profit (loss)	**3,000**	**(2,000)**	**4,000**

Table 5.10 Beynon's Ltd.

The marketing and central administration costs incorporate many of the overall costs associated with running the bakery chain. They are indirect and not related to any one branch in particular. These have been allocated equally across all three branches, as it seemed to be the fairest method of cost allocation.

The data in Table 5.10 appears to confirm the father's belief that in the long-term interest of the firm, he may have to close down the Browndale branch and concentrate his efforts on the other two branches. If we use contribution costing, however, we see a different picture:

	HIGHFIELDS (£)	BROWNDALE (£)	NORTON (£)
Sales revenue	22,000	17,000	26,000
Staffing costs	7,000	8,000	9,000
Supplies	5,000	4,000	6,000
Branch running costs	1,000	1,000	1,000
Total direct costs	**13,000**	**13,000**	**16,000**
Contribution	**9,000**	**4,000**	**10,000**

Table 5.11

	Total (£)
Overall contribution	23,000
Indirect costs	18,000
Profit	5,000

Table 5.12

As we can see, all three branches make a positive contribution to the overall profits. The reason why the father wished to close down the branch was that it appeared to be making a loss. However, it is quite the reverse; if the branch was closed then, the positive contribution from the branch would be lost and overall profits would fall. This is because the indirect costs of production do not vary with output and, therefore, closure of a section of the firm would not lead to immediate savings. This may mean that closing the branch would be a mistake on financial grounds.

This mistake is made due to a misunderstanding of the nature of cost behaviour. If the branch is closed then the only costs that would be saved are the costs directly related to the running of the branch: the staffing costs, the supplies and the branch running costs. The costs that are indirect in nature, in this example the marketing and central administration costs, would still have to be paid as they are unaffected by output. For this decision to be made, we should use contribution as a guide for deciding whether or not to close a branch.

The Beynon's Ltd. example highlighted that contribution is a useful guide to keeping a branch open that, if we used full costing, could make a loss. This can also be applied to the production of certain product lines, or the cost effectiveness of departments. On financial grounds, contribution is, therefore, a better guide in making decisions.

PROGRESS CHECK

Consider whether full costing is a better method than contribution costing.

Continuing production even if the contribution is negative

It is possible that a section of a firm, be it a product line or a branch, is kept open even though on financial grounds that particular section is making a negative contribution to the overall profit levels of the organisation. The reason for this is that closing down a section of a business is likely to lead to a firm shedding labour that becomes surplus. The workers employed in that section may no longer be required.

If alternative employment cannot be found within the firm then these workers may be made redundant. This could impose redundancy costs upon the firm. It is likely that trade unions will be involved that may oppose any redundancies. This could lead to industrial action by workers in other sections of the firm. It may also lead to bad publicity in the media, which may affect the level of sales and profits. In this situation, a business may let natural wastage occur in the staff involved, rather than make job cuts, or it may simply decide to keep the section going. Even if there is

little industrial unrest, the effect of a closure on overall morale within the firm could be very important. It is likely that the remaining employees will be demotivated on seeing co-workers being made redundant. This could lead to unrest, and declining productivity.

In the case of a loss making product, a firm may decide to keep this in production if it has been recently launched. In the early years of the product life cycle, sales are likely to be lower than they are expected to be in later years and, as a result, the contribution may be negative. Sales will hopefully eventually rise and the costs of running this new product will eventually be outweighed by the revenues arising from sales.

Complementary products

A loss making product may also be kept in production because the firm produces complementary products. In this situation a firm may be willing to incur negative contribution in order to maintain or even boost the sales of its other products. Examples of complementary products include:

■ Pottery firms – dinner plates, saucers and cups.

■ Textiles firms – bed sheets, pillowcases and duvet covers.

Example of production of complementary products

A firm is producing garden furniture, selling parasols, tables and chairs. These form the basis of different cost centres for the firm as they are produced in different sections. The firm has produced the following contribution costing statement:

	PARASOLS (£)		TABLES (£)		CHAIRS (£)	
Sales revenue		7,000		5,000		4,000
Labour costs	2,000		1,000		1,000	
Materials costs	2,000		500		2,000	
Other direct costs	1,000	5,000	2,000	3,500	1,500	4,500
Contribution		**2,000**		**1,500**		**(500)**

Table 5.13

As you can see from the data in Table 5.13, the chairs are making a negative contribution and would appear to be lowering the overall profits for the firm. Closing down production of the chairs would appear to lead to higher profits. The profits may be boosted further if the production of the chair producing facility saved some of the indirect costs.

PROGRESS CHECK

Analyse the ways in which a firm can utilise the spare capacity that arises from a closure.

It is important to consider the impact on the sales of other products. With a firm selling garden equipment is likely that the three separate products will be purchased together as they form part of a matching set. If the production of one of these complementary products is halted, then it is likely to adversely affect the sales of the other products. This could mean that discontinuing the production of a product with a negative contribution leads to lower overall profits.

PROGRESS CHECK

Consider the factors a firm might take into account when deciding whether to keep open a loss making factory.

Why allocate overheads?

Consider the problems that occur in overhead allocation: we have to decide on a method of allocating overheads, knowing that there is no totally correct way of doing this. We also have the problem that once the overheads have been allocated they may disguise the 'true' performance of the cost centres. In the last example, we saw that a branch of a business may be closed down on financial grounds when contribution would have been more useful in making this decision.

Given these problems, one might consider why we allocate overheads in the first place? If allocation causes trouble then why make the effort? There are sound reasons why we may wish to continue allocating overheads between cost centres.

Reasons for overhead allocation

If we only allocate direct costs when costing products then we may be misled about the actual cost of a product. It may be useful for a firm to see the total costs of each cost centre so that a selling price can be set, which enables the firm to make a profit. Setting a selling price based on the direct cost only may not generate sufficient revenue to cover the indirect costs of production. An example of this would be where a firm takes on too many extra orders at a price that is below the full cost, but is higher than the direct cost of production. This may be acceptable if the firm has already passed the break even level of output. However, if the direct cost is used as a yardstick for taking on future orders, the firm may find itself in the position where it only covers the cost of production and cannot cover the overall indirect overheads of the firm.

Not allocating the indirect costs to cost centres may encourage lack of responsibility within the organisation. A firm will be trying to control the level of costs that occur in order to increase its profit margins. The allocation of direct costs to cost centres will make the managers or workers linked to that cost centre responsible for controlling these costs. The directors or senior managers will monitor the level of direct costs in each cost centre, looking at any variances that may occur and examining the reasons for these. Action can be taken if an individual or a team is continually incurring excessively high costs. However, unless the indirect costs are allocated in the same way, it is quite possible that these costs will not become the responsibility of anyone within the organisation. If this is the case, then they may become hard to control, or worse, it may be hard to prevent them from rising.

KEY POINTS

A firm is more likely to continue producing a loss-making product if:

- ceasing production would lead to a fall in sales of complementary products
- the product is a loss leader
- sales are unusually low and the products are expected to become profitable in the future
- costs associated with the products are expected to fall over time
- it is a new product that is experiencing teething problems.

KEY POINTS

Allocating overheads is more likely if:

- the firm wants to make managers more aware of overhead costs
- there is a simple, agreed and clear means of allocating them
- the firm wants to measure the profit or loss of each division or product.

Approaching exam questions: Costing and break even analysis

Evaluate the usefulness of break even analysis to a small electrical component manufacturer.

(11 marks)

The evaluation aspect of the title indicates that we have to make a judgement on whether break even analysis would be useful to the firm indicated in the title. This requires us to apply our knowledge of break even to a specific situation, in this case, a particular type of business.

In a question like this, it is common for students to list all the formulae and draw various charts connected with break even analysis. This would yield few, if any, marks as it is not answering the question. To gain marks we need to consider the uses and limitations of break even analysis, and see if these are applicable to a 'small electrical component manufacturer'. Ideas that could be included are:

1 It allows the firm to estimate the effect on profits of changes in its order levels.
2 Changes in costs and prices can be analysed, so that the effect of changes in any one of these on its profit can be examined.

However,
1 The impact of any change in price or variable costs on sales would have to be considered before the impact on profits can be calculated.
2 The model is only directly applicable for firms producing one type of product.
3 Several simplifying assumptions are made, for example, variable unit costs may not remain constant.

The value of break even will depend on the reliability of the data and the ability of the manager to analyse the information correctly. Break even can help with planning (for example, price changes) but the findings must be treated with caution, since it is based on simplifying assumptions. The value depends in part on how accurate the findings need to be; this in turn may depend on how quickly a decision has to be made.

Evaluate the benefits to the senior managers of a firm of using full costing to allocate overheads.

(11 marks)

An 'evaluate' question means that you will need to come to some conclusion, based on what you have found in your own answer. This will be unique to your own answer and will be based on how important you believed the benefits are to the senior managers. For each benefit it is important that you not only analyse the impact of that benefit but consider its relative importance. This will depend on the situation of the firm and type of firm we are dealing with. Possible benefits you may wish to include could be:

1 Encourages greater accountability amongst lower managers in being responsible for the costs.
2 No costs are left unaccounted for and, therefore, overall budgetary control and cost awareness may be improved.
3 Allows managers to see the total costs of their products.
4 May help pricing policy – especially helps avoid taking too many 'special orders'.

However, there are problems in using full costing, including:
1 The allocation method may alienate workers due to it being seen as unfair.
2 Managers may miss out on extra orders due to confusion between full and marginal cost (i.e. they may reject an extra order that does not appear to cover the costs, even though it does make a contribution to overheads).

The basis of overhead allocation will also be important. The benefits may be outweighed by the negative impact of what is perceived to be an 'unfair' allocation. Evaluation will involve exploring how the negative impact can be minimised so that the benefits clearly outweigh the costs. This will depend on the behaviour of management in matters such as overhead allocation and whether they are involved or educated in the process of allocation. It is important that you argue these points from the perspective of the senior management as this is the viewpoint set in the question title.

The manager of a small chain of grocery stores is concerned that one branch in particular has been loss-making for a number of years. Evaluate the factors involved in deciding whether to close down this branch.

(11 marks)

It is a common approach to try to encourage you to use both financial and non-financial evidence in your answer. It may be the case that the financial data will suggest one answer but the non-financial data suggests a completely different one. Here, we have a loss-making branch of an otherwise profitable organisation (we assume). The initial reaction would be that, the branch should be closed to improve the financial position of the firm. However, there are other issues to consider, both financial and non-financial, such as:

■ Would closing the branch have negative consequences for the other branches (e.g. staff morale, market share, adverse publicity)?

■ Is the branch making a positive contribution to overheads? Could this be calculated?

■ Is the loss due to internal factors, such as poor management or problems with staff? Maybe these could be rectified?

■ Does the location of the branch have any influence over its success?

■ What are the objectives for the organisation as a whole?

■ Is this loss expected to continue? How big is it?

When answering this question, it is important that you address the objectives of the whole organisation. If the firm is only interested in profit maximisation then there may be a case for closure. Even so, there will be other factors to be considered, for example, it may have guaranteed jobs or be concerned about unemployment in the area. Evaluation will tend to focus on whether the loss can be reversed. There is also the possibility that external factors may be more important in the sources of the loss, such as being located in an area with lower disposable income than the other branches. There is also the possibility that the data used to calculate the loss is based on full costing and that the cost savings from closure would not be great, or that the branch actually helps 'absorb' some of the fixed overheads of the firm.

To what extent is marginal (or contribution) costing more useful than full costing?

(11 marks)

It is important to realise that there is no definitive answer to this question. Both costing methods have uses but these would depend on the situation and the type of firm. This approach should be taken in this question. To answer the question one would not have to display financial calculations, but a thorough understanding of both methods would be needed. Possible ideas to mention in the answer would include:

- Marginal costing is more useful for special order decisions/make-or-buy decisions.

- Overhead allocation may cause morale problems if the method used is unfair or is perceived to be unfair.

- There is no 'perfect' way of allocating overheads.

- Full costing encourages greater accountability and control of costs by allocating responsibility of costs to a cost centre.

To evaluate your answer one would have to consider the relative merits of both methods. For example, marginal costing may be more useful for special order decisions. This could be followed by stating that a firm cannot use marginal costing for all pricing and order decisions as the fixed costs have to paid at some stage and only full costing would take this into account. Similarly, full costing does encourage greater accountability by making people responsible for overheads. However, if the method used for allocation is unfair then the effect on morale may lead to a decline in productivity, which may mean that the firm would have been better off not allocating the overheads.

Student answers

Analyse the possible reasons why a firm might continue the production of a loss making product.

(9 marks)

Student answer

One of the first pieces of information that we would need is to find out if the firm is producing just this one product or a range of products. If the firm is only producing one product, then they could save money by continuing to produce this product, at least in the near future. This is because the firm will still have to pay for their own fixed costs. Sales of the product may help to pay off some of these fixed costs (provided it covers the variable costs). If the firm halted production immediately, then they would still be committed to paying the fixed costs and the loss made may be worse. However, the firm should not continue to make losses continuously as they could always close down and wouldn't have to pay any costs at all.

If the firm is a multi-products organisation, it would have to look closely at its costing statements. It may be the case that the overheads of the organisation have been allocated in such a way that a product appears to make a loss. This may be due to the overheads being allocated in an unfair way. The firms should look not at profit but at the contribution each product makes. If a product makes a positive contribution, then it should be continued. If a product with a positive contribution is deleted, then the contribution will have been lost and the firm will still have to pay the same amount of fixed overheads.

However, if a product is making losses, then it may be still worth producing if it is part of a range of products that the firm sells together. Closing down production of one product may harm sales of other products and therefore harm overall profits.

Marker's comments

This is a very good answer. The student makes evaluative comments in a number of places. For example, the student immediately realises that the answer will depend on the type of firm – whether it is single or multi-product. This is very important as firms can, and in fact do, tolerate losses (consider the widespread use of 'loss leaders' by supermarkets).

The understanding of the financial workings is also impressive. One criticism was that the human side of the question was not examined. Cutting back on production will have an impact on the workforce and is likely to lead to redundancies. This may be a reason why a firm wishes to continue, at least for a while, with loss making products. However, this answer is certainly of a high standard and would, therefore, receive a mark in the top level.

Mark: Content 2/2, Application 4/4, Analysis 3/3. Total = 9

End of section questions

1 Analyse the possible value of full costing statements to managers.

(9 marks)

2 Analyse the possible use of break even analysis in decision-making.

(9 marks)

3 Examine the possible reasons why a firm might accept a special order if it means selling output at below cost price.

(9 marks)

4 Discuss the possible reasons why a firm may choose to use contribution costing rather than allocating overheads between cost centres.

(11 marks)

5 Discuss the reasons why a firm may wish to produce a component rather than purchase it from a firm at a cheaper price.

(11 marks)

6 Examine the possible implications for a firm of closing down production of a loss making product.

(9 marks)

7 Examine how marginal costing can help managers to make decisions on closing down production of loss-making products.

(9 marks)

8 Analyse the possible consequences for a firm of moving from marginal to full costing.

(9 marks)

9 Analyse the possible reasons for keeping a loss making product in production.

(9 marks)

10 To what extent does the allocation of overheads to cost centres create more problems than it solves?

(11 marks)

Essays

1 To what extent should financial data alone be used when deciding whether to discontinue product lines?

(40 marks)

2 Compare the value of financial data with other information when deciding whether or not to close down a local branch of a national supermarket.

(40 marks)

3 Consider the value of break even analysis to a firm starting up in production and design of internet web pages for other firms.

(40 marks)

4 'Many UK firms continue to produce many loss making products. This is unfair for their shareholders, and firms should take immediate action to stop production when a product is loss-making.' Discuss this statement.

(40 marks)

5 GillSwift plc receives an order from an Estonian firm for 20,000 electrical components, which would take the company up to near full capacity. However, the price offered is below the normal selling price. Discuss the factors determining whether the order is to be accepted or not.

(40 marks)

CHAPTER 6

Investment appraisal

Investment is the spending of money for future gain. A firm engages in investment if it spends money now hoping to obtain a greater return in the future. A firm may invest in a new product, a new location, machinery or an advertising campaign. Investment appraisal refers to the quantitative techniques that are used by firms to decide whether or not to go ahead with an investment. Where investment projects are mutually exclusive the techniques can be used to rank projects to select the most attractive ones.

Capital investment appraisal methods

The three main methods used for capital investment appraisal are:

■ payback

■ average rate of return (ARR)

■ net present value (NPV)

In theory, firms should use these techniques for every capital expenditure to decide on the most profitable or financially attractive option; in reality these techniques are only likely to be used for significant investments, which involve relatively large amounts of money and risk. Investment appraisal is more likely to be used when choosing a new factory location than to decide on which telephone answering machine to buy.

In larger scale investments it is very important to make the right decision and so firms will take the time to gather and analyse data. If the investment is small scale or low risk a manager may be willing to rely on intuition; if a similar decision has been made many times in the past they may rely on their experience. In many cases managers will rely on their 'gut feeling' – they may examine the quantitative data, but their interpretation of it may be influenced by their own beliefs and experience. After all, the data is based on estimates and so there must be an element of judgement throughout the process.

KEY POINTS

Intuition or experience is more likely to be used to make an investment decision when:

● the relevant data is not readily available
● the relevant data is expensive to gather
● the project is perceived to be low risk
● a decision needs to made quickly
● the manager trusts his or her own judgement
● the manager does not trust the data available.

KEY POINTS

Investment appraisal techniques are more likely to be used when:

● a large capital outlay is involved
● there is a high degree of risk if the wrong project is chosen
● the decision will be difficult to reverse
● the managers have not made a decision like this before
● the managers do not trust their intuition.

	MACHINE A	MACHINE B
Year 1	£3,000	£1,000
Year 2	£5,000	£3,000
Year 3	£3,000	£5,000
Year 4	£2,000	£4,000
Year 5	£3,000	£6,000

Table 6.1 Expected net cash inflows

Sample calculation

The different methods of investment appraisal are highlighted in the example that follows.

A firm is considering purchasing one of two machines to help improve the productivity of output. Both machines cost £10,000 and it is estimated that the machines would bring in extra cash flows illustrated in Table 6.1.

Payback

The payback period for machine A is 2 years 8 months, while for machine B it is 3 years 3 months. On this basis the firm would select project A as it has the quicker payback.

Average Rate of Return (ARR)

There are three stages used when calculating the ARR and these are as follows:

1 Calculate the overall profit for the investment: Profits of project = profits from each future year less initial costs of project.
Machine A: (£3,000 + £5,000 + £3,000 + £2,000 + £3,000 − £10,000) = £6,000.
Machine B: (£1,000 + £3,000 + £5,000 + £4,000 + £6,000 − £10,000) = £9,000.

2 Calculate the average annual profit –
Profit of machine A = £6,000; average annual profit = £6,000/5 years = £1,200.
Profit of machine B = £9,000; average annual profit = £9,000/5 years = £1,800.

3 Express the average profit as a percentage of the cost of the project –
Machine A: Average profit as a % of capital cost = £1,200/£10,000 × 100 = 12%.
Machine B: Average profit as a % of capital cost = £1,800/£10,000 × 100 = 18%.
Machine A's ARR = 12%.
Machine B's ARR = 18%.

On this basis the firm would select project B, as it has the higher ARR. [Note: the ARR method considers expected inflows and outflows of profits; the other two methods consider cash inflows and outflows. To keep our example simple we have not made a distinction between profit and cash]

Net Present Value (NPV)

The NPV method uses a discount factor to calculate the Present Value of future earnings. The reason for this is that money grows over time, and so £1 in the future is not the same as £1 today. If, for example, the discount factor for year one is

KEY TERMS

Payback method
measures the length of time taken for the income from an investment to recover the original capital costs of the project. The project with the shortest payback period would be the one selected.

Average Rate of Return (ARR)
expresses the average annual profit earned by a project as a percentage of the original capital cost of the project. This can be calculated using the following formula:
ARR = **Average profit p.a. × 100**
_____
original cost

Net Present Value (NPV)
uses discounted cash flows to produce present values for projected cash flows. These net cash flows are then totalled up and compared with the original capital cost of the project. The net present value is the cost of the project deducted from the total of these cash flows:
Net present value = total of present values − initial cost

KEY POINTS

An investment is more attractive if it has:

- a quick payback
- a high average rate of return
- a high net present value.

MACHINE A			
YEAR	NET CASH FLOW	DISCOUNT FACTOR	PRESENT VALUE (NET CASH FLOW X DISCOUNT FACTOR)
now	(10,000)	1.000	(10,000)
1	3,000	0.909	2,727
2	5,000	0.826	4,130
3	3,000	0.751	2,253
4	2,000	0.683	1,366
5	3,000	0.621	1,863

Table 6.2

MACHINE B			
YEAR	NET CASH FLOW	DISCOUNT FACTOR	PRESENT VALUE
now	(10,000)	1.000	(10,000)
1	1,000	0.909	909
2	3,000	0.826	2,478
3	5,000	0.751	3,755
4	4,000	0.683	2,732
5	6,000	0.612	3,726

Table 6.3

FACT FILE

Capital expenditure by Cadbury Schweppes was reported to be £162 million in 1998. This included projects such as construction of a bottling plant in Mexico and ongoing worldwide implementation of an integrated enterprise computer system. Marketing expenditure in this year was £726 million representing a marketing to sales ratio of 17.7%. This expenditure represented the firm's commitment to brand investment.

0.909, this means the firm believes that £1 earned by the project in one year's time is the equivalent of 90.9p today (because 90.9p could grow to £1 anyway if invested elsewhere). Similarly, if the discount factor for year two is 0.826, this means the present value of £1 in two year's time is 82.6p today (86.2p invested elsewhere would grow to £1 over two years).

Using the discount factor a firm can calculate the present value of all the expected inflows from a project. The total Present Value shows the sum that could be invested elsewhere and match the project's expected earnings. This is then compared with the cost of the project. If the Present Value is, for example, £13,600, and the cost is £10,000, the firm would invest. To generate the same earnings as the project elsewhere £13,600 would have to be invested, however, the project only costs £10,000, so it is a good deal. The Net Present Value (Present Value − initial cost) is positive (£3,600) so it is worthwhile. The bigger the Net Present Value, the better.

KEY TERM

Discounting refers to the reduction of future cash flows to take into account the opportunity cost of capital incurred when money is tied up and cannot be used at present.

The size of the discount factor depends on the interest rate – the greater the rate of return available elsewhere, the lower the sum needed to match the project's earnings, and so the greater the discount factor used.

The Net Present Value is found by totalling all the present values from each machine and deducting the initial cost. For machine A, the NPV would be £2,339 and for machine B the NPV would be £3,600. In this case we would recommend machine B as the project to go ahead with, as it has the highest NPV.

PROGRESS CHECK

Explain what is meant by Net Present Value.

Selecting the best investment appraisal method

Although the methods used to appraise capital investment are all useful, each of them has its merits as well as its problems.

Payback method

The payback method is the simplest of the three methods to understand. This could make it the preferred method for managers with limited experience. It could also be particularly useful for a firm that is interested in getting back the money invested in the investment project as quickly as possible. A firm with limited funds may wish to use the payback method, for example, because it needs to be reassured that the funds will be returned relatively quickly and may be less concerned about long-term rewards.

One problem with the payback method is that it ignores money received after the payback period has been reached. Projects with a longer payback period may therefore be financially more attractive. Firms that have adequate resources may be able to take the extra risk of waiting for the longer payback period knowing that it could lead to greater rewards. Smaller firms, however, may not be able to wait that long for the extra rewards and may opt for a quicker (and possibly safer) investment.

The appeal of a particular method of investment appraisal will also depend on an organisation's objectives and economic climate. Firms that are more concerned with survival may prefer to use payback rather than ARR and NPV methods as these look for maximum profits, but sometimes at a greater risk. This is because the returns may be higher for the project but may be spread over many years in the future.

Average rate of return method (ARR)

The ARR method has the advantage that it does compare the profitability of different investment projects and takes into account all the expected inflows of a project. This means that firms who are seeking profit maximisation can see which project brings in the highest overall return. Projects of different sizes can be compared with their returns, expressed as a simple percentage, and a manager can compare this return to alternative investment projects.

For example, a project may give an ARR of 10%; this can then be compared with the return on financial investments (ranging from high interest bank accounts to stock and share purchases). When making this comparison managers will also take account of the risk involved. Even if the returns on particular capital projects are higher than those of financial investments, the risk involved and uncertainty that may affect the return may mean that a firm chooses an alternative, with lower returns but lower risk.

Net present value method (NPV)

A failing of both the payback and ARR methods is that they do not take into account the time value of money. They do not note the fact that an expected inflow of £100 in ten years' time is less desirable than £100 in one year's time, for example. In this sense the NPV method is more accurate, as it takes account of the opportunity cost of money. However, it is quite a complex method, which can also make it difficult to use. There is also no guarantee that the manager can choose the right discount factor and the future flows are only estimates. Though there is a tendency to think this method must be technically superior because of its complexity, its findings still depend on the reliability of the data and in the suitability of the discount rate.

PROGRESS CHECK

To what extent is the NPV method better than the payback method as a means of investment appraisal?

Summary

In reality it would be appropriate for a business to use all three methods when taking any investment decision. This is because investment decisions usually relate to relatively large amounts of expenditure and the decision is not a trivial one.

Even if all three methods are used they may still be given different weighting in the decision making process; the relative importance of a particular technique is likely to depend on the priorities of the firm. If a firm wishes to avoid risk then it could assign the payback period greater importance in the decision making. This is because it will be more interested in when it regains the original investment than in the total possible returns. If the firm is solely focused on the overall profitability of a project, it is likely that the ARR or the NPV method will be favoured.

When assessing an investment, each firm is likely to have its own investment criteria. An average rate of return of 12% may be attractive to some firms but not others – it depends on what else they could be doing with the funds. Similarly, a payback of two years may be essential for some businesses (for example, if they are cash starved) but not for others. A firm will, therefore, set out its own criteria (such as a payback of three years or less and an average rate of return of 20% or more) and assess each project according to these standards.

Method (% of firms using)	Total	Rarely	Sometimes	Often	Always
Payback	86	9	14	27	36
ARR	78	16	21	21	20
NPV	80	12	23	23	34

Table 6.4
Source: Adapted from Drury, 1993

KEY POINTS

If an investment project is expected to last longer:

- Discount factors are more likely to be made on an estimate of future interest rates rather than using the current levels of interest rates.
- The less likely the cash flow estimates are going be correct.
- The discount factor selected will have a greater effect on the NPV of the investment.
- A firm will be less concerned with the payback period and more interested in the level of NPV.
- The greater the opportunity cost of money tied up in the investment.

KEY POINTS

The payback method is more likely to be used if:

- managers are more interested in liquidity than profitability
- there is a preference for using a quicker or simpler method
- the firm is not constrained by shareholders to maximise profits
- the expected profits to be earned in the future are not considered reliable.

PROGRESS CHECK

Method	Project A	Project B
Payback	2 years	3 years
ARR	18%	15%
NPV	£2.1 million	£4.3 million

Table 6.5

Based on the data above, which project would you use? Justify your answer.

Issues in investment appraisal

Investment appraisal techniques focus on quantitative data. However, investment decisions are not solely made on financial predictions. Managers will also take into account qualitative factors when deciding on whether to go ahead with the investment decisions, or deciding which project to choose from the alternatives on offer. Managers might consider:

- The impact of a project on employees

- The possible reaction of unions

- Does the project fit with the firm's objectives?

- The possible impact on the corporate image.

An expansion into armament trading, for example, may be profitable but this does not mean the firm will necessarily want to go ahead with it. Conversely, investment in new sports or canteen facilities may not be profitable but could have a significant impact on morale, productivity and absenteeism.

It is also important to remember that the data that is used in investment appraisal is largely based on projections, that is, estimates of future incomes and expenditure. If a firm is looking to automate the production line of one of its factories, it will want to know how much it can expect to save through this change and/or the expected impact on turnover. The data it uses, however, is only an estimate and may not be very reliable.

Market research

Market research would be one way of ascertaining how much the firm can expect to sell in the future, but extensive primary research is expensive and may be beyond the scope of small and medium-sized firms. This may mean that secondary research is used for the projections or that only a small investigation is undertaken to make the predictions. This could in turn render the predictions less valid. Even for larger firms the data will always be subject to fluctuations in both internal factors, such as the labour force and their wages, and the external environment, such as changes in taxation policy or economic growth (which may affect both costs and sales). In some cases, managers may estimate the figures simply by using his or her experience or intuition.

> **Investments are based on expectations not facts.**

Analyse the possible impact of changes in the economic environment on a firm's level of investment.

Investment appraisal skills

The skill of the person(s) conducting the investment appraisal will also be an issue. Many managers, especially those in firms that have recently started up, may be unfamiliar with these techniques and may fail to use them correctly. For example, the choice of discount factors can be mistaken: if the discount rate chosen is too low, the NPV of a project will be too high; if the discount rate chosen is too high then projects that are viable (i.e. with positive NPVs) may be ignored.

Costs and revenues

It is also important that only the relevant costs and revenues are included. Imagine that McDonald's decide to launch a massive advertising campaign to boost sales of all their products and, as a consequence, they also decide to expand their production of just part of their product range, for example of the Big Mac. The investment appraisal for this expansion would include the costs of the investment as well as the resulting expected sales. It would seem only fair to include part of the advertising campaign as part of the investment into the Big Mac expansion. However, this imaginary campaign was not solely promoting the Big Mac; it was promoting all of their products. This makes it hard to decide how much of the advertising campaign should be allotted to a particular product.

Sunk costs

It is also important that any sunk costs should not form part of the appraisal. For example, if a firm wishes to launch a new product, extensive research may take place before production facilities are created. The cost of the market research should not be included in the investment appraisal as it is a 'sunk' cost, i.e. it is paid regardless of whether the investment goes ahead or not.

A firm is considering investing in a new production line. Consider the factors it might take into consideration when making this decision.

Intangible investment

Certain types of investments might have no clear impact on profits and yet be intuitively desirable. Investment into training or team building could improve performance but it may be difficult to clearly identify its precise impact on a firm's profits.

The Co-Operative Bank's ethical policy includes: We will not invest in or provide financial services to any regime or organisation which oppresses the human spirit or takes away the rights of the individual manufacturers or torture equipment or other equipment that is used in the violation of human rights. We will not invest in or provide financial services to any business involved in the manufacture, sale, licensed production, brokerage of armaments to any country which has an oppressive regime … In addition, our customers' money will not be used to finance any of the following activities: we will ensure that our financial services are not exploited for the purpose of money laundering relating to the proceeds of drug trafficking, terrorism and other serious crime. We will avoid investment and currency trading in developing countries which does not support productive purposes. We will not participate in currency speculation which consciously damages the economies of sovereign states. We will not invest in or provide financial services to tobacco product manufacturers. We will encourage business customers to take a pro-active stance on the environmental impact of their own activities and will invest in companies that avoid repeated damage to the environment.

The importance of intangible investment

The importance of intangible investment is growing. The number of people employed in either service sector jobs, or firms using new technology has steadily increased in the late twentieth century. These industries rely more heavily on innovation and the skills of the individuals than traditional manufacturing industries. Trends in the organisational structures of firms and the move to flatter hierarchies have meant that more workers are required to use management skills and flexibility in the workplace. This has meant that to some extent, therefore, the role of physical investment is declining in relative importance and investment in training, in R&D and in innovation, is becoming more dominant in determining the success of firms. This makes the need to assess intangible investments accurately more pressing but no less easy.

PROGRESS CHECK

A multinational firm is considering introducing a major training programme for its employees to improve their information and communcation technology skills. Consider the factors it might take into account before investing in such a scheme.

Impact on people

New investment, particularly if it involves the expansion of production or replacement of machinery, is also likely to have an impact on the workforce of the firm. Training costs for the workforce in the use of the new machinery would be included as an extra capital cost of the investment. The firm must, however, also consider the impact on the motivation of the workforce that the new investment may have. New machinery or the automation of production may mean that the firm will no longer require the same number of employees engaged in the production process. The job losses could lead to the demotivation of the workforce, which could lower productivity. This links in with motivational theory – according to theorists such as Herzberg, Mayo and Maslow, the threat of redundancies on remaining workers is likely to lower the production rate of the firm and will usually lead to higher costs in the future.

PROGRESS CHECK

Barclaycard invested £30 million on new technology for updating its computer information systems and implementing labour saving devices in 1998. This was coupled with making 1,100 of its staff redundant.

Question

Discuss the ways in which Barclaycard may have justified this investment.

Personal values

The personal values of the managers or owners can have a significant impact on the investment opportunities it chooses. For example, a particular location may be the most financially attractive, but if the managers do not like the area they may choose somewhere else, where they would prefer to live and work. When assessing a new project, the corporate strategy team at Virgin look at the risk to the brand if it goes wrong and also whether it looks like it will be fun, as much as the overall rate of return. Their senior management team want to be involved in interesting, challenging and enjoyable projects. Other firms such as Body Shop and Ben & Jerry's have a very strong commitment to ethical issues; this means they may turn down projects that are financially attractive but which do not fit with their corporate and personal objectives.

Environmental and social issues

Environmental and social issues could also be important. If an investment is in a new plant or involves the expansion of existing facilities, there is likely to be an impact on the local environment in the form of certain external costs – the effects may include increased levels of pollution (either noise or chemical). If the firm is a retailer, for example, the external costs are likely to take the form of higher congestion around the local area. The problem facing the firm here is not extra costs – this is because external costs are paid for (or 'suffered') by the local people or area rather than the firm itself – but that the local community may protest against the spoiling of their environment, either in the form of formal complaints or pressure group action. This may result in lower sales for the firm and make an investment that appeared originally profitable, unprofitable.

Availability of funds

Whether a firm actually goes ahead with an investment will also depend on the availability of funds. It may be that there are numerous projects a firm would like to undertake but it simply cannot finance them all. A decision about which project to select would, therefore, involve an examination of the options open to the firm in terms of raising the money needed. It may be that a smaller project is chosen because this is all the firm can afford or wants to risk.

In conclusion

When looking at the factors in any investment decision, it is important that the quantitative information (gathered through investment appraisal techniques) is combined with the qualitative information (non-numerical information) that will also affect the decision. The final decision about an investment is likely to be a combination of data, experience and gut feeling.

FACT FILE

The Cowley car plant, in Oxfordshire, employed 23,000 in the 1970s. By the start of 1999 only 4,000 were employed in the car plant, in part due to the mechanisation of the production line.

FACT FILE

In 1982 British industry produced 877,000 cars. In 1998, with more robots and computers, but fewer workers, car production rose to 1,748,305.

KEY POINTS

Non-financial factors may be considered to be very important for an investment project if:

- it is public sector investment, which may be geared towards social objectives
- adverse publicity from the project may be expected (such as the Shell-Brent Spar incident)
- the firm operates in a market where public relations are of prime importance, such as one that affects developing countries
- redundancies from the workforce are likely to occur.

PROGRESS CHECK

Questions

1 Consider the possible limitations of investment appraisal techniques.
2 To what extent are non-financial factors more important than financial factors, when making an investment decision?

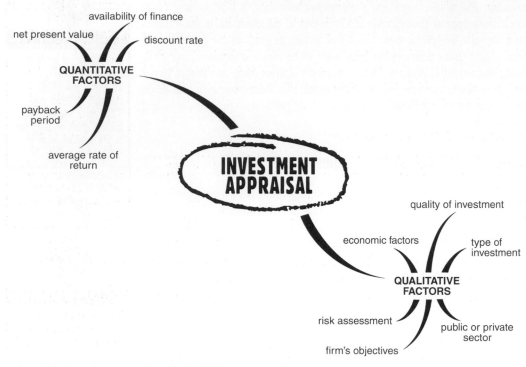

Figure 6.1 Capital investment: an overview

Investment and risk

The expected benefits of any capital project are estimates only. They may turn out to be much higher or lower than was originally predicted. For example, the financial outcome expected is subject to many external factors that could change the predicted results. Changes in competition could make sales greater or less than expected, the economy could move into a recession, the exchange rate may increase or decrease. In early 1997, the minimum wage was just a Labour Party idea; yet within two years it had been introduced and increased some firms' costs.

Forecasts over the extreme short-term (i.e. the next few days or weeks) may be made with reasonable certainty. However, this ability to forecast the future diminishes the further into the future the firm is trying to predict. A prediction a matter of months away is subject to many factors, both internal and external, that the firm cannot predict; when it comes to predicting what will happen in several years' time the uncertainty is likely to increase tremendously. This risk of getting it wrong could mean that the firm ends up with incomes or costs thousands or millions of pounds in excess of what was expected, according to the investment appraisal.

There are different ways in which a manager can handle risk. If the firm is particularly worried about the cash flow position, then one way to perhaps avoid the risk would be to place a greater emphasis on the payback period. A manager could also attempt to be deliberately prudent; overestimating costs and underestimating revenues with the forecast. This may mean that the NPV or payback may understate the benefits that the firm will actually receive. However, on many occasions people who think they are being prudent are in fact being highly optimistic – this is often the case if managers base the estimates on their own gut feeling, in a project they are particularly keen to proceed with. Alternatively, the managers of a project may wish to consider a number of possible outcomes for cash flows and potential profits. This could be based on pessimistic and optimistic scenarios. Estimates may be made not only of the expected cash flows in each scenario but also of the probabilities of each scenario occurring.

Consider the following example:

SCENARIO	PROBABILITY	FORECAST CASH FLOW	EXPECTED VALUE
Optimistic	0.2	£150,000	£30,000
Realistic	0.5	£80,000	£40,000
Pessimistic	0.3	£20,000	£6,000
	1.0		£76,000

Notice how the expected value for each scenario is found by multiplying the expected cash flow for the respective scenarios by the probability of that particular scenario occurring. This is a similar process to that used in decision trees.

The above example could be an extract from an investment appraisal for any project. It may show the predictions for the first year's cash flow. The expected value of £76,000 represents what the managers expect the investment to return to the firm in year one. If the predictions were made for the remaining years, then a full investment appraisal could be undertaken. Alternatively, a firm could conduct three separate investment appraisals based on each scenario. The end result would be that the firm had three separate forecasts for the overall return: a realistic, a pessimistic and an optimistic scenario.

Risk aversion and investment appraisal

Most people are risk averse. This does not mean that they will never take risks, but that they would prefer to avoid them. This could be said of managers making investment decisions who may opt for a project with a lower projected return, purely to minimise the risk taken. Consider the following table, which outlines the NPV for two investment projects. In each case there is an optimistic projection and a pessimistic projection.

	NET PRESENT VALUES	
	PROJECT A	PROJECT B
Optimistic projection	£650,000	£1,250,000
Pessimistic projection	£10,000	(£50,000)

Table 6.6

If there was an equal chance of the optimistic/pessimistic scenario occurring then Project B would yield a higher return on average. However, it may be the case that the manager opts for Project A despite the lower expected returns. The reason for this is that the manager may want to minimise the maximum losses that could be made – with Project B there is the danger that £50,000 could be lost. This strategy is known as a minimax strategy, whereby one is maximising one's minimum gains.

Defining the amount of risk taken

The amount of risk a manager takes is likely to depend on his or her own personality, the degree of supervision or control by senior managers or the owners and their own view of risk. If there are tight budget controls, good supervision and a clear policy of low risk investment, then a manager is less likely to undertake high risk projects. It will also depend on the potential rewards available and the extent to which this project is needed. In times of emergency, when a project is vital to the survival of a firm, managers may more willing to take risks.

Are British managers short-termist when making investment decisions?

Some analysts believe that British managers are short-termist when making investment decisions. They claim that British investment is lower than in other major industrialised economies, due to the reluctance of managers to commit themselves to long-term decisions. This short-termist approach is said to be because the major investors in the UK are institutions such as pension funds and insurance companies. The institutional investors are said to demand short-term rewards (which they need to pay out to their own investors and customers) and be reluctant to wait for long-term rewards. Managers in the UK also tend to change jobs fairly often; this may mean that when they have a new position they want to make a quick impact ready to move on again within a few years. They are therefore less likely to be interested in long-term projects if they will not be present to see the rewards and benefit from the recognition.

	No. of Shareholders	% of Total No. of Shareholders	No. of Ordinary Shares	% of Ordinary Shares
Institutional holdings	122	0.4%	154,748,912	59.6%
Directors	5	0.1%	44,218,964	17.0%
Small shareholdings	27,737	99.5%	60,8000,164	23.4%
	27,864	100%	259,768,040	100%

Table 6.7 Extract from Manchester United football club's *Annual Report 1998*

NUMERICAL INVESTIGATION

J Sainsbury Plc.: shareholders' interests at 3 April 1999
Number of shareholders: 111,403
Number of shares in issue: 1,918,215,654

RANGE OF SHAREHOLDING	SHAREHOLDERS (%)	SHARES (%)
500 and under	49.45	0.5
501 to 1,000	18.67	0.83
1,001 to 10,000	29.23	4.39
10,001 to 100,000	1.93	3.09
100,001 to 1,000,000	0.52	10.07
over 1,000,000	0.2	81.12
	100	100

Table 6.8

a Calculate the percentage of shareholders who own more than 10,000 shares.
b Calculate the percentage of shares owned by shareholders who own more than 10,000 shares.
c Comment on your findings.

KEY POINTS

Managers are more likely to take risks if:

- their own funds are not at stake (this is a problem of the divorce between ownership and control)
- the potential rewards are very high
- they are not monitored closely
- they or their bosses enjoy risk
- they will not be held responsible.

Evidence to support the view that UK companies are short-termist comes from the proportion of a nation's GDP that is taken up by investment. Britain normally figures very low down this 'league table'. This means that British industry is less likely to perform as efficiently as firms in other nations due the lack of new investment and other productivity-boosting measures. As a result, British firms may become less competitive in foreign markets, which will have an impact on the earnings of British firms. British firms also tend to spend less on R&D than firms in other countries, which may mean that there will be less new products being launched and less new innovations in the future. However, it is possible that it is not the level of investment that is important, but the quality of investment. If this is the case, then it may not be an issue that Britain spends less on investment, provided the money is spent wisely.

KEY POINTS

A firm is more likely to go ahead with an investment if:

- it has a quick payback
- it has a high average rate of return
- it has a high NPV
- the risk is low
- it fits with the firm's objectives
- it has a positive impact on the corporate image
- it is welcomed by stakeholders.

Questions

PROGRESS CHECK

1 What are the possible implications for the British economy of having a poor record of investing in R&D?
2 Consider the possible implications for a firm of the short-termist nature of many investors.

Investment appraisal in the public sector

The underlying objective of most private sector firms is usually based on increasing their ROCE. This is why techniques such as the average rate of return are

FACT FILE

Investment as a proportion of GDP (1960–93)

Japan	31.3%
France	22.4%
Germany	22.4%
USA	18.4%
Britain	18.1%

appealing, because they show the expected profits in relation to the initial investment. In the public sector, the objectives are not so straightforward.

Government considerations

Although governments do set financial targets through their annual budget, their aims are not necessarily to make a profit. In the area of health care, for example, the returns on new hospital equipment cannot easily be measured in financial terms; in education the value of a new school does not have a clear impact on the government's revenue.

If decisions about museums, art galleries, health, education, housing and so on were left totally to the private sector, it is likely that too little would be provided because so many of the benefits cannot easily be measured in monetary terms.

When undertaking a capital investment, therefore, a government will not solely focus on the financial aspects. It will wish to consider the social costs and social benefits of such an investment. These are the effects on society as a whole and cannot always be allocated monetary values.

For example, if the government decided to build a new bypass, it would not be concerned purely with the financial costs of constructing this road. It would want to consider the full social cost of building the road. This would include the private financial costs (for example, materials and labour) and the external costs to the part of society affected by the road, which could cover costs such as the noise pollution, landscape disfiguration, increase in exhaust emission and possible increases in accidents. For the road to be constructed the government would want to see that the social benefits of the road outweigh the social costs. In most cases roads are free to use and so the government will not receive any monetary revenue from this new road, but there may be real social benefits in its construction. This could include reduced congestion, cuts in costs due to journey time reductions, reductions in accidents and noise pollution in the village that was being bypassed.

Cost benefit analysis

As the objective of government is believed to be the maximisation of welfare, it is often the case that the social costs and benefit are very important in an investment project. The problem is that it can be difficult to place a monetary value on some of the costs and benefits involved. As public sector projects focus on social and not private benefits and costs, traditional investment appraisal techniques are not suitable; instead the government often uses cost benefit analysis.

Cost benefit analysis attempts to place monetary values on all the social costs and benefits associated with a project. For example, a new road may save journey time and the financial benefit of this would be estimated by comparing the actual time saved per vehicle and the wage rate of these people multiplied together. This is, of course, highly subjective, and not extremely reliable, however, any estimation is considered better than not including a value for this.

Summary chart

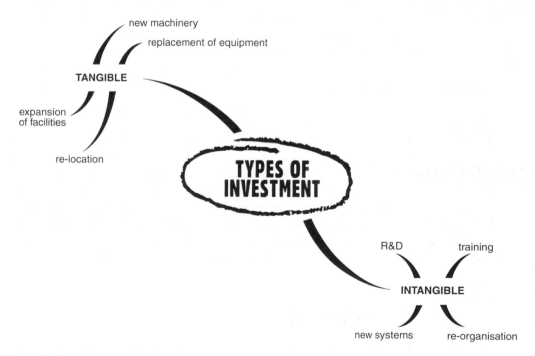

Figure 6.2 Types of investment

Approaching exam questions: Investment appraisal

Evaluate the factors that might determine the level of business investment in the private sector.

(11 marks)

All 'evaluation' questions require you to weigh up the factors in an argument. The factors that you discuss will need to be assessed for their relative importance. In this question, the reference to the private sector is designed to focus answers on firms that are more likely to aim for profits, rather than the more welfare-driven objectives of the public sector. The factors you may wish to consider could include:

1   The cost of borrowing – if interest rates are low and, more importantly, expected to remain low and/or stable, then businesses may be more willing to undertake investment financed through borrowing.
2   Investment can take many forms – this could include plant and equipment but may also take new premises or expansion. These different types of investment will be motivated by differing reasons.
3   Advances in technology may bring forward investment in new equipment or machinery – investment may also be a case of replacing worn out equipment.
4   The uses of quantitative techniques will be important for firms, so the payback period, ARR and NPV are all relevant – however, qualitative factors should not be ignored; these would depend on the projects being assessed.
5   Expectations of future rewards are crucial to investment – if firms are more optimistic about their future sales, they are more likely to invest.

To evaluate this question you would have to select the factors that you believed were the most important in determining private sector investment and justify these beliefs with appropriate knowledge or evidence. For example, if investment is sensitive to the cost of borrowing, then a change in interest rates is likely to have a larger effect. With the rapid changes in technology in some industries, firms are having to invest to maintain their competitiveness.

Expected growth in GDP may be a major factor in private sector investment; if growth is expected in the economy firms may be more willing to expand. However, not all firms will be affected by UK GDP in the same way – some may operate on an international level and global, or European income may be more important than domestic growth. Also, some firms sell products that are relatively income inelastic, in which case their investment may be affected more by changes in competition or the technology used.

Burkinshaw Travel Ltd. is a family business which provides specialist package holidays to Eastern Europe. The directors refuse to expand the business, despite the positive results from their investment appraisal if such a move went ahead. Discuss the possible reasons for the directors' decision.

(11 marks)

The obvious approach for determining investment is simply to look at the ARR and NPV and if these are positive and at a relatively high level, then the investment is likely to go ahead. However, in this question we are asked to ignore this result – the relocation is expected to be financially attractive – and consider why these results may be ignored.

This is a 'discuss' question so the factors for and against would have to be stated and developed by possibly linking factors or relating them to other external factors. The type of business is given to us and a good answer would refer to this. The factors that might have influenced the directors' decision could include:

1   The objectives of Burkinshaw Ltd. may not be focused on maximising profits. It is assumed that companies will pursue profits in the interest of the shareholders but in the case of a family firm, the directors may be more interested in other objectives, such as consolidation. They may prefer to keep the business small and manageable rather than expand and lose the family link.
2   The reliability of the data used in the investment appraisal may be questionable. It could be the case that the information used in the projection is suspect or is subject to so many factors that there is little chance of the expected profit actually occurring. The directors may not be willing to take the risk.
3   The directors may be concerned with the expected change in the market that they cater for. At present they are providing for a niche market. If they are successful, this could attract the attention of larger travel companies who might undercut Burkinshaw and steal their market.
4   The expansion may put a strain on liquidity. It could be financed externally but the interest on such a loan may outweigh any projected profit. Alternatively, the directors may anticipate higher interest charges in the future and may not wish to increase their gearing at present.

Although we cannot know for certain, the most likely reasons for the directors to ignore the data is that they are either not actively seeking extra profits at present or they do not believe that the profits will be generated.

Evaluate the possible limitations of payback when conducting investment appraisal.

(11 marks)

In this question it would be important to consider not only the weaknesses of payback but also its strengths. An evaluation question will need you to look at both sides of the argument. Although the actual question mentions only the limitations, it is important that your answer is balanced. Possible areas to focus on include:

1   Payback may be more useful for firms with limited resources, who need these resources back as soon as possible.
2   It is a simple method to use and is easy to understand – inexperienced managers may find this attractive (even experienced ones might prefer it!).
3   Payback does not take into account the opportunity cost of money – future returns are treated equally with current returns.
4   It is the most popular method of investment appraisal – is this a sign of short-termism?

A standard answer would state and explain the general disadvantages and advantages of the payback method. However, to score more highly you would need to consider the question in the context of different methods of investment appraisal.

For example, payback may not be an appropriate method for a large plc. business that is attempting to maximise profits and has no real worries over the payback period. However, a sole trader who has recently begun trading may consider payback to be the most useful method.

Placing the whole topic of investment appraisal in context will generate more marks. External influences, such as the economy, the structure and movement in the market the firm operates in will be important factors in determining whether any method of investment appraisal is useful. Also issues such as non-financial factors could be explored.

To what extent are investment decisions based on gut instinct?

(11 marks)

This is an evaluative question which requires you to examine the case for and against and reach a conclusion. The arguments for are:

■ If a decision has to be made quickly a manager may be tempted to use gut instinct.

■ If the risk is low and/or this type of decision has been made before gut instinct may be likely.

■ It depends on the perceived quality of the information – if managers are suspicious of the data or it does not fit with their experiences they may go on instinct.

■ It depends on the manager's personality and style – do they trust the numbers? Are they willing to take the risk?

Against using gut instinct are arguments such as:

■ It is a high risk strategy – in theory a scientific, rational approach to decision making should be better.

■ Why ignore the data?

■ Techniques such as payback, ARR and NPV have been designed to analyse data and turn it into useful financial information to help decision makers.

In conclusion, it depends on:

■ The nature of the decision, e.g. large scale/low scale? Routine or unfamiliar?

■ The decision taker and their decision taking style.

■ The availability and cost of data.

■ Usually a combination of the two – managers will often look at the numbers (which are projections only) and put this in the context of their experience and gut feeling.

Student answers

The directors of Yarrow Ltd., a small manufacturing firm, are considering the purchase of new machinery. Discuss the factors that might determine whether the acquisition goes ahead or not.

(11 marks)

Student answer

Yarrow Ltd. is a limited company which is owned by private shareholders. This means it is likely that the managers are aiming to maximise profits. Any investment Yarrow Ltd. undertakes should be based on the idea of increasing the overall profits of the firm. To decide if this will happen with the new machinery they will need to compare the costs of the machines with the expected extra revenues the machinery will generate. The managers of Yarrow Ltd. could use techniques such as the ARR or the NPV. These methods are useful but do have their limitations. The firm has to make estimates on expected revenues and these may not be very reliable and, therefore, the information could mislead the managers. They would also need to be sure that the machines were of high quality and were as up-to-date as possible. This will save the firm money in the long run by not having to replace machinery, as it becomes outdated.

Marker's comments

Good use is made of the information in the question – something that is often overlooked – namely, that the firm is a private limited company and that this implies that profit maximisation could be the main objective. In this case, the candidate correctly identifies appropriate methods that might be used: ARR and NPV. A good development here would have been to investigate the possibility of the divorce of ownership and control and how this may mean other objectives are being pursued by the directors, such as growth (although in a small limited company this may be less of an issue than a plc.).

Limitations of the methods are also considered but are too brief in detail and are not related to the type of firm, which would have scored more highly. Other, non-financial, factors are considered but are only just mentioned and are not developed. Also, the emphasis is on investment appraisal methods, rather than the underlying factors. This means that the answer is generally disappointing, with little development made outside of the first paragraph. Further factors were mentioned, however, the question does require 'discussion'.

Mark: Content 2/2, Application & Analysis 3/6, Evaluation 0/3. Total = 5

Analyse the possible reasons why firms use discount expected inflows when making investment decisions.

(9 marks)

Student answer

Discounting is a technique used by firms when using investment appraisal techniques. When firms make investment decisions, they will want to make as much money as possible and, therefore, an investment must generate lots of money.

Techniques are used to measure the returns on investments and one of the main ones is the NPV method. This compares future returns from an investment with the amount spent on the investment. One problem with comparing future returns is that money that is expected to be earned in the future is worth less than money earned now. For example, if the project is expected to earn £10,000 in five years' time, this is less desirable than earning £10,000 next year. Using discounted cash flow, future returns are discounted and are given a present value. This will mean that when using the NPV to make investment decisions the time value of money has been taken into account. If the discount rates are higher then less investment will be undertaken, due to the lower present value of the expected future earnings.

Marker's comments

This is a solid answer, which shows that the student has a good understanding of the use of discounting. The material is understood and clearly explained. The effect of time value of money on any investment decision is also understood well.

In terms of improving the answer, the student could have looked at why it is important that a firm would wish to take into account the time value of money and consider the impact of this on investment decisions in more detail. It could also have compared this approach to the other investment methods (such as the average rate of return) where no account of the timing of the expected returns from the project are considered. If firms are aiming to maximise profits, then they will wish to engage in investment that will make the greatest addition to profits (i.e. the highest net present value).

Mark: Content 2/2, Application 4/4, Analysis 1/3. Total = 7

Discuss whether there is any use for investment appraisal techniques when making public sector investment decisions.

(11 marks)

Student answer

Public sector investment decisions are taken by the government and will usually focus on some policy decisions that are intended to improve the social welfare of the population. This means that when the government undertakes investment, it will not use any of the techniques of investment appraisal. It will be more interested in how the investment affects the electorate. The government's main objective is to be re-elected and, therefore, any investment decision will be taken with this in mind

For example, when deciding whether or not to go ahead with the channel tunnel rail link, the government decided to move the proposed route of the link because it did not want to upset people who would have been affected by it.

Marker's comments

The student has a rather simplistic view of how the public sector operates and seems to assume all projects are judged purely on how many votes they generate. In fact, investment appraisal techniques are used by the government when making decisions. For example, the NPV technique is used for making transport decisions, such as new road construction. It is true that the government will have other objectives not centred around profit maximisation, but it is not true to say the financial impact plays no part in the decision.

A better answer would have looked at the government's objectives and the increasing trend towards greater accountability of public services, which probably means that the techniques would be used more frequently. Where there will be a difference with the private sector is that public sector firms are more likely to consider social costs and benefits.

A private sector firm is likely to ignore any of the external costs of the investment, such as pollution. However, the government has to take into account the external costs of an investment decision. To do this, it tries to allocate a financial value of some of these external costs and benefits, such as the time saved in journeys by a new bypass.

As a general rule, the student would have been better saying that the investment techniques are used but have to be modified to take into account other factors also, and that the government will not be solely concerned with profit.

Whilst it is true that the government does have to answer to the electorate and there could be some degree of electioneering when making decisions, it will also consider a wide range of factors (including revenues and costs) when making a decision.

Mark: Content 2/2, Application & Analysis 2/6, Evaluation 0/3. Total = 4

'Investment appraisal techniques rely on estimates and therefore cannot be relied upon when making investment decisions.' Evaluate this statement.

(11 marks)

Student answer

Investment appraisal techniques are used to decide whether or not to go ahead with an investment. They include payback, ARR and NPV. If they are used correctly then they can be good indicators of whether or not an investment should go ahead. However, they are based on estimates of future costs and revenues associated with the investment.

The cost of any investment should be known as that is the amount which is going to be spent now in order to generate future returns. The potential costs and revenues from the investment will not occur until some time in the future and, therefore, these will have to be estimates. It is highly unlikely that these revenues can be estimated with 100% accuracy but that does not mean that they are unreliable.

The reliability of these methods will depend on how accurate the predictions of future cost and revenues can be. For firms with plenty of money the managers can conduct extensive market research, which may make the predictions more valid. Extrapolations of back data will also help. However, firms are subject to external forces beyond their control, such as the actions of competitors, which may render the estimates useless. However, if a rival firm unexpectedly opens up in a new market then the estimates of sales may need to be recalculated. Once the investment is undertaken it cannot be undone and, therefore, the investment may cease to be profitable.

One way in which a firm can get around this is to use sensitivity analysis and make predictions for different scenarios. Having different estimates for optimistic and pessimistic situations will help avoid making incorrect investment decisions. However, it is unlikely that most managers will bother taking this into account. Small firms may not have the resources to undertake primary market research and, therefore, may use intuition instead – this will be based on subjective personal understanding, which is less likely to be correct. It is not the techniques of investment appraisal that are incorrect but the way in which they are used and the information they are using. They are tools and should be treated with care otherwise they can generate faulty information about which investment decision to take. The value of these techniques also depends on how well a manager can undertake the calculations and interpret the findings.

Marker's comments

This is a very strong answer. The student has a sound understanding about the reliability of investment appraisal techniques. Normally this sort of question would generate lots of answers based on the relative merits and problems of each technique, which is not what the question was looking for. It highlights that investment appraisal techniques are simply a management tool and rely on the underlying information and ability to interpret the data.

A suitable conclusion would also focus on the fact that investment appraisal techniques should really be used in conjunction with wide ranging information, both quantitative and qualitative. Any estimate is likely to be incorrect to some extent and, therefore, a firm should have as much information as possible before making the decision.

Other areas to explore could have been that the techniques of appraisal are only really useful if the expected revenues can actually be predicted. If the firm is engaging in new product development or investing in training for its workforce, then it will become very hard to estimate any possible return.

Mark: Content 2/2, Application & Analysis 6/6, Evaluation 3/3. Total = 11

End of section questions

1 Outline the possible merits of three techniques used for investment appraisal.

(9 marks)

2 Analyse the qualitative factors which *may* affect an investment decision.

(9 marks)

3 Evaluate the use of the net present value technique of investment appraisal to a sole trader.

(11 marks)

4 Explain the term 'discounted cash flow' and how it relates to investment appraisal.

(9 marks)

5 Analyse the possible reasons why a manager might not continue with an investment, despite a positive NPV?

(9 marks)

6 Analyse the possible reasons why public sector investment may be assessed differently than private sector investment.

(9 marks)

7 Examine the possible use to a multinational of NPV for investment decisions.

(9 marks)

8 To what extent does investment ultimately rely on a manager's personal judgement?

(11 marks)

9 Assess the possible importance of market research when making investment decisions.

(11 marks)

10 Compare and contrast the merits of payback and ARR as tools for making investment decisions.

(11 marks)

Essays

1 'The popularity of the payback method in assessing an investment project in the UK confirms the view that British managers are too short-termist.' Discuss this view.

(40 marks)

2 Consider whether quantitative techniques are more useful than intuition when making investment decisions.

(40 marks)

3 'Investment decisions are all based on expectations, so you might as well guess anyway.' Critically assess this view.

(40 marks)

4 To what extent can investment appraisal techniques help managers to decide what to do?

(40 marks)

5 A firm is considering investing in a new factory. Discuss the factors it might take into account before proceeding with this investment.

(40 marks)

Recent issues

Shareholder value

Recent measures of firms' performance, have looked at the extent to which they create value for their shareholders. The basic premise behind these measurements is that firms only create value for their shareholders if the return they generate is greater than the opportunity cost of capital. In simpler terms, if the firm generates more money than could have been earned elsewhere (by investing in financial assets) then the firm has created value. There are a number of measures of shareholder value, including Economic Value Added (EVA) and Market Value Added (MVA).

Economic Value Added (EVA)

The EVA is calculated by comparing the operating profit made by a firm with the charge for the capital that it employs. Using this method it is viewed as insufficient for a firm to simply make a profit; it should aim to make a profit that is big enough to cover the cost of its capital. If it is not covering the cost of its capital then it would have been better if investors' money had been placed elsewhere. A firm creates value if the EVA is positive and destroys value if the EVA is negative. For example, if a firm has £100 million of capital and its cost of capital is 10%, the firm, in effect, incurs an opportunity cost of capital of £10 million. If net profit was £30 million, then the firm would have created an EVA of £20 million (profit − cost of capital). If the net profit was less than £10 million then the firm would have destroyed value over that time period.

Cost of capital

The cost of capital is not simply the interest on the firm's debt. It also includes the cost of equity – including dividends and potential capital gains – as well as the risk attached to the firm's share value. A firm that is deemed to be of high risk, such as a new firm, will have a higher cost of capital because the shareholders expect a higher return for the extra risk that they take.

Market Value Added (MVA)

MVA is a further measure of shareholder value added that is now used to assess a company's performance. To calculate the MVA the money received by the firm through shares issues, borrowings and retained earnings is deducted from the current value of the firm's shares and debt. Put simply, it is the difference between what an investor can take out and what an investor has put in. A positive MVA means the company has created value for the shareholders and a negative MVA means it has destroyed value. As MVA is based on the current (or market) value of the company, it reflects the stock market's assessment of management performance.

An MVA should improve during the year if a firm has made a positive EVA. This means that if a firm has made a profit in excess of the cost of its capital, it should increase the MVA. If the EVA is persistently negative then the MVA is likely to fall.

PROGRESS CHECK

Top UK firms: MVA and EVA performance (1997)

NAME	MVA (£)	EVA (£)
1. Shell	69,507,800	− 1,506,141
2. Glaxo Wellcome	41,640,500	416,071
3. Lloyds TSB	30,559,355	803,249
4. SmithKline Beecham	29,980,390	709,623
5. Unilever	23,429,150	402,279
6. BP	18,445,365	−24,322
7. HSBC	15,303,160	1,393,622
8. Zeneca	15,303,160	231,298
9. Diageo	14,321,000	–
10. Barclays	13,533,535	97,891

Table 7.1 Source: Stern Stewart and Co.

Question

According to the report, Shell 'destroyed' value in 1997! What reasons might there be for Shell having a negative EVA?

Company reports

An annual company report is not merely a set of final accounts; it also includes the notes to the accounts, explaining the accounting policies used by the firm and the director's report, which explains strategic policy and summarises the current direction of the firm. Nevertheless, there has been increasing disillusionment with the traditional company report in recent years, and it has been alleged that the annual reports produced by many of the top UK firms often conceal as much as they reveal, concerning corporate performance. For example, between 1979 and 1990, 4 out of the 11 firms named by *Management Today* as the UK's most profitable firms, collapsed.

Company reports are too shallow and only focus on the good news of the business, which is at odds with any idea that the report should accurately and fully reflect the firm's performance to shareholders.

Explain why annual reports focus mainly on the business' good news?

FACT FILE

BT: 'Statement of Business Practice' from *Annual Report 1998* for operations within the community.
'We will:
- Contribute to the wellbeing of the societies in which we operate through our business activities and the skills of our people.
- Maintain the highest level of integrity while respecting local laws, customs and traditions.
- Work with the community and other organisations to support non-profit making activities that benefit wider society.
- Use our influence to reinforce the liberating and empowering potential of our technology.'

FACT FILE

'Among other things, we must adjust our measurements of wealth creation and profit with a charge for the natural capital employed – and, in the case of non-renewable resources, often consumed for a one-off benefit.'
Extract from: *Shell Report 1998*

Social accounting

At present there is no legal requirement made on firms to report on their contributions to society or their impact on the environment, but increasingly, firms are producing reports that attempt to show how they have taken into account their own impact on society. This could be due to any of the following reasons:

Government requirements

Governments are likely to impose a more comprehensive requirement on firms with regard to their social reporting in the future. If the inclusion of social accounting, or social and environmental auditing in annual reports were to become a legal requirement, it may make sense to begin to produce these ahead of that law being passed. This will offer firms the chance to try different approaches in their social reporting before it becomes compulsory. Also, firms may be able to influence the government in the law-making process itself. If firms have been producing audits and social accounting reports for a number of years, they may have more to offer to the process.

Environmental disasters

The introduction of social reporting may be a defensive response to recent disasters, such as the Exxon Valdez tanker, or the Brent Spar oil rig, or the Piper Alpha platform incident. These incidents will influence public opinion and may affect sales. If the firm can respond by showing that it is willing to take action to 'put something back' into society, this may ward off future criticism or at least lessen the negative impact on the firm's image and finances. It may cost the firm money but may lead to costs being minimised in the form of a drop in income.

Competitive edge

The adoption of social auditing, environmental accounting, and so on, could also be used to give the firm a competitive edge over other firms. It is clear that the Body Shop's success is at least partly due to its 'green' image and the involvement in community projects on its part has certainly not damaged sales. If other firms adopt a 'more caring' approach, this may also lead to higher sales and enable them to charge a price premium when compared with similar services offered by competitors.

Increasing staff motivation

Social reporting may also lead to higher staff motivation. For example, BT include in their social report surveys of employee satisfaction; this may lead to an improvement in morale at the workplace (similar to the 'Hawthorne Effect').

Statements of business practice

At present, the production of any of these statements is voluntary. This means that there is no external regulatory body to check that any claims made are valid. In this case, it is perfectly possible for firms to make claims that exaggerate measures taken to promote the more 'caring' side of the firm, while failing to mention any activities which may not generate positive publicity.

It appears, however, that many of the firms involved in social reporting are willing to have their social reporting either conducted independently, or at least to have the results verified and approved by an external body.

FACT FILE

Extract from the BT CARE (Communications and Attitudes Research for Employees), published in their annual report (1998): Favourable response to matters listed below (%) with BT employees compared with benchmarked data from other UK employees from other firms:

1. Leadership: BT 39%; benchmarked UK 43%.
2. People satisfaction and meaningfulness of work: BT 60%; benchmarked UK 63%.

PROGRESS CHECK

Analyse the reasons why firms may be willing to have voluntary survey results published, which do not show the firm in a favourable manner.

Risk reporting

From late 1999, businesses producing annual reports will have to include a section in which they report on their internal control systems. In mid 1999, the Turnbull Committee devised a framework in which firms are required to report on how they manage risk. Although some firms already include sections devoted to risk assessment and internal control, this will be the first time that it is compulsory for firms to include this information.

The new requirements mean that directors have to report annually on how effective the firm's internal controls are. The controls look at how the firms handle the risk that they face. The risks included focus on financial risk, such as interest rate changes, variability of economic growth or credit control. The risks also cover general business risk factors, such as competition, technological change, or changes in the regulatory framework that businesses face.

KEY POINTS

A firm that produces social reports is more likely to:

- have better public relations
- be better positioned if social reporting was made compulsory
- gain a competitive edge over rival firms that do not produce social reports.

Advantages of improved risk reporting:

- Firms may be protected from legal action when facing failure or other financial problems. If a firm has reported the potential risks that they face, it may help avoid the threat of legal action taken. For example, if a firm conceals information that it may have poor credit control, it may be liable for not taking action to resolve this earlier if investors lose money as a result.

- Smaller firms will usually have a lower profile and may have to pay more to raise capital. The reporting of risk may help to reduce the uncertainty that surrounds the firm and, therefore, they may find it easier to raise finance. This may also apply to larger firms who may be able to raise finance at lower rates.

- A firm's management may be able to respond to changes in events more rapidly. If they have planned for more unexpected outcomes, they should be prepared

FACT FILE

Extract from the *1998 Annual Report* for Orange plc. 'Financial Risk Factors: The Group is exposed to market risk, including movements in interest rates and currency exchange rates. Interest rates and foreign exchange exposures are monitored by tracking actual and projected commitments, and through the use of sensitivity analysis.'

A firm that incorporates risk management into its annual report is more likely to be able to:

- respond quicker to unforeseen changes in the external environment
- obtain finance at a lower cost
- have better informed stakeholders about the firm's policies for dealing with risk
- save money if changes have to be made.

for unwanted change. This can help save the firm money by allowing them to implement changes in policy more quickly, thus leading to less wastage of time and money.

The firms that stand to gain the most from risk reporting would be those who appear to be at greatest risk at present. If a firm operates in a highly volatile or competitive market, it is at risk from more factors than a firm operating in a stable market with fewer competitive pressures. The increased reporting of risk assessment should allow firms to face up to problems that they may or may not have to deal with. This should also allow investors to be better prepared for changes in the value of their investments within firms.

PROGRESS CHECK

Generate a list of possible business risk factors that would affect a UK firm selling package holidays to countries in Eastern Europe.

Summary chart

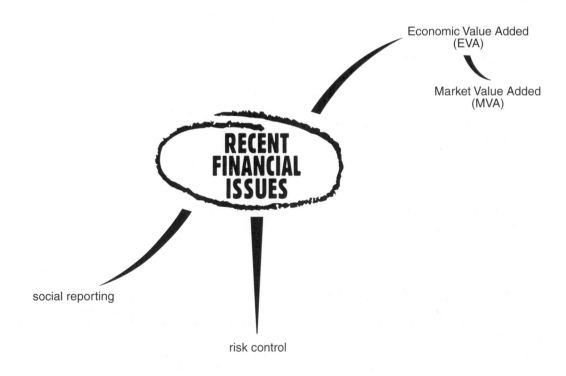

Figure 7.1 Recent issues

CHAPTER 8

Numerical data

1 Liquidity ratios and working capital management

Orange plc operate in the telecommunications sector, with focusing mainly on the provision of mobile telephones for personal use. The following table is an extract from the liquidity section of its balance sheets.

ORANGE PLC EXTRACTS FROM ANNUAL REPORT (1998)	1998 £MILLION	1997 £MILLION
Current assets:		
Stocks	29.2	17.2
Debtors	375.7	232.2
Cash at bank and in hand	39.6	13.7
Current liabilities:		
Creditors	435.4	315.7

a   Explain the term 'net current assets'.

(2 marks)

b   For 1997 and 1998 calculate the Acid Test Ratio for Orange plc.

(3 marks)

c   Based on your findings obtained in part (b) comment on the liquidity position of Orange plc.

(6 marks)

d   Analyse the ways in which a firm might improve its liquidity position.

(9 marks)

e   To what extent is profitability of more importance than liquidity for a large public limited company?

(10 marks)

2 Profit and loss accounts

TESCO PLC ANNUAL REPORT 1998	UK		IRELAND		EUROPE (*)	
	1997	1998	1997	1998	1997	1998
Sales (£ million)	13,118	14,640	–	1,028	769	784
Operating profits (£ million)	760	866	–	49	14	(3)

(*) European operations in France, Poland, Hungary, Czech Republic and Slovakia.

'… our aim is to grow the business beyond the British Isles, focusing on Central Europe, where modern retailing is relatively undeveloped. Against this, average incomes and expenditure are much lower in this area. In 1998 the opening programme starts to build up with six stores, which will have significant start-up and launch marketing costs.'

Source: *Annual Report 1998*

a (i) Calculate the profit margins for Tesco's operations in Europe in 1997 and 1998.

(2 marks)

   (ii) Comment on your findings from a(i).

(3 marks)

b Examine ways in which a firm might improve its profit margins.

(6 marks)

c Analyse the possible reasons, other than lower incomes, why Tesco might have made a loss in 1998 from its European operations.

(9 marks)

d Consider the possible benefits for the board of directors of analysing the firm's performance by region.

(10 marks)

3 Costing methods

J. Lowes Ltd. produces four separate components (AB7, ZX6, FJ32 and PL44), each of which are used in the production of home computers and related peripheral products, such as printers.

A full costing statement has been produced by the financial manager, which illustrates that two of the components are currently showing a loss. The total costs for each component are made up of 25% indirect costs and 75% direct costs.

(£000)	AB7	ZX6	FJ32	PL44	TOTAL
Sales revenue	460	400	420	300	1,580
Total cost	480	540	350	200	1,570
Profit	(20)	(140)	70	100	10

The board of directors are concerned about the loss making nature of AB7 and ZX6 and are considering whether or not to continue production of these components. There is also concern that the supplies of the imported materials may become more difficult to obtain and that the sole domestic supplier would charge at least 10% more for the materials.

a (i) Define the term 'direct cost'.

(2 marks)

   (ii) Calculate both the direct cost and the contribution made by the production of each component.

(4 marks)

b Redraft the costing statement to show the contribution made by each component, assuming that direct costs rise by 10%.

(6 marks)

c   Advise the board of directors on whether or not the production of AB7 and ZX6 should be discontinued, based on the financial grounds alone.

(10 marks)

d   If the firm decides to continue production of all four components, examine ways in which the overall profits of these products might be increased.

(8 marks)

4 Cash flows and window dressing

The following is an extract from the cash flow forecast of 'Baird's', a small shop which has been recently set up, producing and selling pottery products. In order to obtain a £5,000 loan from their bank, a cash flow forecast for the first year had to be presented.

(ALL FIGURES IN £S)	JANUARY	FEBRUARY	MARCH	APRIL	MAY	JUNE
Cash receipts						
Cash sales	400	500	400	800	1,100	1,400
Credit sales	500	900	1,000	1,100	2,000	2,800
Total	**900**	**1,400**	**1,400**	**1,900**	**3,100**	**4,200**
Cash payments						
Equipment	1,000			500		
Insurance	100	100	100	150	150	150
Rent	2,000			2,000		
Materials		300	400	600	800	850
Salaries	1,000	1,000	1,000	1,000	1,000	1,000
Miscellaneous expenses	500	600	800	900	1,000	1,500
Total	**4,600**	**2,000**	**2,300**	**?**	**2,950**	**3,500**
Net cash flow	**(3,700)**	**?**	**(1,100)**	**(3,250)**	**150**	**700**
Opening balance	**5,000**	**1,300**	**700**	**(400)**	**(3,650)**	**(3,500)**
Closing balance	**1,300**	**700**	**(400)**	**(3,650)**	**(3,500)**	**?**

The co-owner of Baird's was initially puzzled why a cash flow forecast was needed, in addition to a projected set of final accounts. However, the bank manager was adamant that one must be included as profit was 'not as certain as cash' and that it was an 'unreliable and subjective means of assessing business performance', for several reasons, including 'window dressing'.

a   Fill in the missing figures (marked by a '?') on the cash flow forecast.

(3 marks)

b   Recalculate the cash flow for May based on the assumption that credit sales fall to half the level they were originally forecasted to be.

(4 marks)

c   (i)   Explain what is meant by the term 'window dressing'.

(3 marks)

(ii) Analyse how profits might be boosted through window dressing.

(9 marks)

d   Assess the bank manager's view that profit is an 'unreliable and subjective means of assessing business performance'.

(11 marks)

Business report 1: Crumbs sandwich shop

Total for this question: 40 marks

John has run a sandwich shop, called Crumbs, for a number of years. It has been fairly successful and has built up sales over a number of years. However, in recent weeks the shop has actually become so popular that queues are a regular feature. John is concerned that the long queues in and outside the shop will put people off entering the shop, and potential sales will have been lost.

One possible solution to capture these lost sales is for John to provide a delivery service for local business. The location of the shop in the middle of the small town centre and the close proximity of several large firms means that there is a potential market for making large orders on demand delivered to the firm's own address, rather than having individuals making purchases separately from the shop. This service would require the employment of an additional part-time person and a van would also be needed. Other fixed costs would be largely unchanged as the existing premises could be utilised for preparation.

Advise John on the viability of the business proposal. Your report should consider both the financing of the new venture and the likelihood of its success. You should also state, with justification, whether or not you believe the plan should go ahead.

Appendices

Appendix A: balance sheet and selected ratios
Appendix B: investment data
Appendix C: market research
Appendix D: data on local firms
Appendix E: economic data

Appendix A: balance sheet and selected ratios

Balance sheet for Crumbs as at 30 June 1999			Selected accounting ratios for Crumbs		
	(£)	(£)		1998	1999
Fixed assets		20,000	Acid test ratio	0.95	0.59
			Net profit margin	12.5%	15.0%
Current assets	5,000		Gearing	35.0%	41.0%
Current liabilities	4,500	500			
ASSETS EMPLOYED		**20,500**	Asset turnover	1.8	2.3
Capital and reserves		12,000			
Loan		8,500			
CAPITAL EMPLOYED		**20,500**			

Appendix B: investment data

The new van is to be financed from both internal cash flow and from a loan from the bank secured on the value of the existing fixed assets. The interest charged on the loan will be set at the bank's standard variable base rate of +5%.

INVESTMENT APPRAISAL RESULTS	
Payback	2 years, 4 months
ARR	6%
NPV	£1,566

Appendix C: market research

A number of staff at nearby businesses were asked to rank the importance of several factors concerning the current provision by the sandwich shop. The purpose of the research was to see if there was a demand for the delivery service. Most important = 5, least important = 1.

BUSINESS	HIGH STREET BANK	DEPARTMENT STORE	LOCAL COLLEGE	INSURANCE COMPANY	CHEMISTS
Price	1	1	5	2	4
Size	2	4	4	3	5
Location	4	2	3	5	3
Time taken	5	3	1	4	2
Choice of fillings	3	5	2	1	1

Appendix D: employee data

BUSINESS	HIGH STREET BANK	DEPARTMENT STORE	LOCAL COLLEGE	INSURANCE COMPANY	CHEMISTS
Number of employees	66	55	37	89	18
Utilisation of staff canteen	30%	50%	60%	70%	n/a
% bringing packed lunch	30%	25%	18%	8%	66%

Appendix E: economic data

	UK	LOCAL REGION
Unemployment rate (June 1999)	6.2%	4.6%
Average GDP growth rate for 1999–2002	2.25%	3%
Annual increase in consumer spending	2.8%	3.4%

(ALL % CHANGE PER ANNUM)	1999	2000	2001
Wage inflation	4.2%	4.5%	5%
Consumer spending increase	2.8%	3.2%	1.5%
Unemployment	6.2%	6.6%	6.7%

Business report 2: Coxon Ltd.

Total for this question: 40 marks

Coxon Ltd. has been making small motors used in the production of consumer goods, such as washing machines or food processors or computing manufacture, for a number of years. It specialises in making three separate motors in three separate plants. An American firm has started producing one of these components and has significantly undercut Coxon Ltd. in terms of price. The management of Coxon have decided to cease production of this motor and to start production of a related part, used in vacuum cleaners, known as the XT56 motor.

Coxon are, however, undecided on whether to produce the XT56 themselves or whether to out-source and purchase the component from another firm. The only firm that can meet the technical specifications is a medium-sized engineering firm located in Warsaw, Poland. The advantages of using the Polish supplier is a lower price, however, this would involve closing down the section of the firm and make a section of the existing workforce redundant.

Produce a report advising the management on what you consider to be the most viable option: producing the motor themselves or purchasing the motor from the Polish manufacturer?

Appendix A: costing data
Appendix B: staff information
Appendix C: sales data
Appendix D: business surveys
Appendix E: economic forecasts

Appendix A: costing data

Breakdown of unit cost for an XT56 motor

	UK	POLAND
Materials	£5	£8*
Labour	£3	
Power	£2	

*all inclusive order price per component

Fixed costs for Coxon Ltd. are at present £200,000. This could be reduced by £50,000 if the firm out-sourced for the XT56 motor. There would also be an additional fixed cost element associated with ordering from Poland, which would cover transport, import duties, etc. This would total £40,000. This would not be paid if production were maintained at existing facilities. It is expected that the component will be sold by Coxon Ltd. for £16.

Appendix B: Staff information

	WHITELANDS	YELLOWFIELD	GREENMEADOW
Staff employed	50	80	90
Average annual labour turnover (%)	5	6	8
Trade union density (%)	50	47	66

Out-sourcing for the XT56 motor would mean Coxon Ltd. shedding staff and closure of the Greenmeadow plant. This would mean Coxon Ltd. would incur redundancy costs of £100,000, which could be reduced to £20,000 if production of the new component for vacuum cleaners was switched to the Greenmeadow plant.

Appendix C: sales data

Expected sales levels of the XT56 based on optimistic and pessimistic scenarios.

	1999	2000	2001	2002
Units (pessimistic)	30,000	50,000	70,000	65,000
Units (optimistic)	45,000	60,000	75,000	70,000

Appendix D: business surveys

Useful data based on external surveys: (10 = high incidence, 0 = low incidence).

	UK	POLAND
Degree of corruption in business/local government	1	5
Availability of government subsidies	3	7
Degree of labour market flexibility	8	4
Business stability	8	3
Other data:		
Average credit period for materials/components	43 days	25 days
Lead-time need for materials/components	22 days	34 days
Wage cost index	100	75

Appendix E: economic forecasts

	1999	2000	2001	2002
Inflation:				
Poland	6%	4%	7%	8%
UK	2%	2.5%	2.5%	2.5%
Unemployment:				
Poland	8%	9%	10%	10%
UK	6.2%	6.5%	6.6%	6.7%
Exchange rate (Zl per £)*	6.5	6.8	7.2	7.5

*Zl = abbreviation the Zloty, Polish currency

Examining tips

Interpreting financial data

Not surprisingly, an accounting and finance question will provide you with some financial data. Questions will normally focus on one particular area of the whole financial area of the syllabus, such as investment appraisal. You would usually be expected to: explain some of the key terms; make some calculations from the data; comment on your findings; suggest possible solutions to problems facing the firm.

It is important to realise that the longer questions will often expect you to not only use the financial data you have been given, but to also consider wider issues, such as the impact of the economy, the workforce or action taken by competitors. When revising, it is easy to focus too much on simply learning the equations, without thinking enough about the significance of the calculations and the limitations of the various techniques. To do well in accounting and finance questions, it is important to think about why you are using particular equations or techniques and to be aware of their limitations.

What does a particular ratio show, for example? How big should that ratio be? How will the 'ideal' ratio size vary according to the industry or the state of the economy or the market? What would make the ratio higher or lower? Common areas for questions include:

- Conducting an appraisal for alternative investment projects.

- Calculating and analysing financial ratios.

- Interpreting a cash flow forecast; suggesting and evaluating possible solutions to cash flow problems.

- Discussing the ways in which firms may window dress their accounts and how this can be achieved.

Financial data and case studies

Financial data is also common in case studies, when any recommendation about an organisation's policy usually requires reference to the firm's financial position. How will the firm raise the finance necessary to expand? Is its ROCE satisfactory? Do the expected rates of return meet its own investment criteria?

Applying business theory and knowledge

As is often the case when applying your business theory and knowledge to a specific example, it is crucial that you take into account the type of business that you are dealing with. The size of the firm will be an important issue, for example, a smaller firm may have more problems raising finance. A firm's attitude to risk may also be important – a firm that is worried about the risk of an investment is more likely to use the payback method of investment appraisal rather than net present value. Another factor is the external environment – firms may be more likely to borrow when interest rates are low than when they are high, for example.

The business sector in which the firm operates may also be relevant. Firms selling retail goods will probably be affected more immediately by changes in consumer spending than a manufacturing organisation. A producer of specialist medical equipment may be more likely to have debtors than a launderette. A firm operating in a growth market may be expected to have higher returns than one in a stagnant market.

It is also important to take account of the business objectives of the firm. An organisation that is developing a lean production policy would expect stock levels to be falling; a retailing firm that is preparing for a big increase in sales at Christmas may want stocks to increase. A firm that is concerned about the social and environmental impact of its activities may reject some projects which are profitable but socially undesirable. Firms may also sacrifice short-term profits to gain long-term market share.

In some cases you will find that the different parties involved in an organisation have conflicting objectives. For example, managers may wish to boost profits through cost-cutting exercises such as shorter breaks or the introduction of new technology. This may conflict with the views of the workforce and may lead to lower motivation levels, which could actually lead to lower overall profits and performance.

There may also be conflicting financial objectives. For example, the directors may wish to maximise profits to maximise their return to shareholders, whilst managers might be more interested in maximising sales, which might increase their personal rewards (in the form of bonuses or commission). It is important, therefore, to consider the impact of any decision on different groups and the possible reaction of different groups affected by the decision. What may be desirable for some groups might be unwelcome for others. An increase in profit margins by cutting the size of the workforce may be welcomed by the shareholders but not by the employees.

The time scale for the question may also be crucial. The short-term effect of a change in policy could be different from the long-term effect. For example, if a firm wishes to boost profits in the short-term, it could lower its selling price to boost sales volume. This would lower the profit margin, but with higher sales volume profits could increase. However, if competitors match this or even undercut the business in retaliation, the firm may lose out on profits in the long-term.

Identifying limitations of your data

Any limitations of the data that you can identify should also be included where possible. Accounting data can be equally as subjective as personal opinions. This may mean that the data is presented in such a way as to encourage you to form a certain view on the firm's performance. This may not be entirely accurate and you should try to realise and point out where distortions or misrepresentations have taken place. For example, how up-to-date is the information? Do you know how the data has been gathered, for example, what accounting policies have been used? Do you know what figures the managers were hoping to achieve? Do you know who gathered the data – some departments may be eager to push certain projects more than others.

One final point is to try and be precise when you are answering finance questions. Many answers use the terms 'profit' and 'cash' interchangeably, when in reality these have very different meanings. Similarly, people often write about 'profit' and 'profitability' as if these are the same things, when it is perfectly feasible for profit to increase and yet for profitability to decrease. Imagine that profits rise from £10 million to £12 million whilst capital employed increases from £40 million to £60 million; profit has increased £2 million but ROCE has actually fallen from 25% to 20%.

Specific advice on accounting and finance topics

Final accounts

Most final accounts questions do not involve the construction of a profit and loss account or balance sheet from scratch. The level of numerical manipulation is likely to be limited to updating or adjusting a pre-drawn set of accounts. If this is the case, then it is important that you remember the basic relationships between items in the profit and loss account and also the make-up of a balance sheet. Examples of this could involve recalculating profit based on a changed sales figure, or adjusting asset values on the balance sheet. An understanding of what the final accounts actually mean is also likely to be tested. This means that a student would have to understand the differences between a profit and loss account and a balance sheet – what can and cannot be inferred from them. Topics include how useful a profit figure is in determining performance, or how useful the balance sheet is in telling us whether the firm is in a strong financial position. This could involve considering how a firm can use window dressing techniques to boost profits or change the value of net assets, and why it may have attempted to distort their accounts.

Ratio analysis

Ratios are often seen as one of the most difficult areas on a Business Studies course. However, this concern probably arises from the need to remember the formulae ! A typical ratios question will usually require the student to calculate some ratios from accounting data. It may be the case, however, that the question presents the ratios pre-calculated. Once the ratio has been calculated, then some comment is normally required. The level of depth needed will vary, but as a general rule, the more marks allocated for a question, the more depth that will be required. The way to approach these questions is to deal with the explanation of what the ratio illustrates first of all. The result of the ratio can then be explained in terms of what the typical figure is, for example: '... it is normal for the current ratio to be between 1.5 and 2 ...'. Once you have explained the theoretical side of the ratio, you must explain the significance of the result you have calculated. Again, never forget the context – is the firm new or well-established? Is it growing? Is it managed well or badly managed? This will involve looking at the question for possible factors that may have affected the results you have. These could be both internal and external factors:

- What is the state of the economy?
- What is the nature of the market?
- What is the overall position of the firm?
- What is the nature of its product?

The return on capital employed for a well managed, established brand in a growth industry is likely to be higher than that of an unbranded product in a declining market, when the economy is in recession. In order to evaluate your ratio analysis, it may also be important to discuss what the figures do not show. For instance, if you have analysed the profitability ratios it might be worth looking at the liquidity profile of a firm to assess its overall strength. Alternatively, you may want to consider expected market trends or the firm's own plans to assess the future situation. Non-numerical factors are often extremely important – a firm may have high profits at present due to a very tough cost control policy, but at the same time, industrial relations may be poor, which could be an issue for concern.

Cash flow forecasts and working capital management

A cash flow forecast may need constructing or readjusting from previous data. This is unlikely to be designed to be overly complicated, but you will need to appreciate the differences between cash and profit (such as not including depreciation in the cash flow forecast). The layout of a cash flow forecast must be understood so that data can be read from the chart and interpreted accurately. The cash balances held by the firm at that moment in time, or, what they will be forecasted to hold in the future will need to be considered.

How a firm deals with cash flow shortages is also a common area to be tested. It is important to not only suggest solutions for improving cash flow but also to evaluate the merits for each of the possible solutions. This will depend on the type of firm, the size of the firm, or the urgency of the problem. For example, if a cash shortage has been predicted for a few months' time, the action taken may not be as drastic as for a firm that has a current ongoing cash shortage. Laying off workers, or selling fixed assets may be seen as a last resort for a firm, whereas arranging an overdraft may be the solution to a future shortage.

Budgets and budgetary control

Budgets can be tied in with cash flows but can also be examined as a separate topic. Emphasis is likely to be on the calculation of variances and the interpretation of what the variances mean. This will involve looking at sales, labour and materials variances and suggesting possible reasons for them. This could entail looking at price factors (higher wage rates, or lower materials prices) or quantity factors (less efficient labour or greater quantity of materials used). However, to score more detailed analysis marks, it would be appropriate to try and link the variances. For example, if the labour costs are higher but materials costs are lower than budgeted, it could be that the firm has given higher wage rates and staff have worked much more efficiently and have wasted fewer materials due to greater motivation.

The process of budgetary control is also likely to be tested here. The reasons for introducing a control element will be needed and the likely benefits and problems of implementing budgetary control should also be understood.

Investment appraisal

Questions on this topic will almost certainly involve calculations based on one or more of the three quantitative techniques: payback, ARR and NPV. Data will normally be presented to you in terms of capital cost and potential cash or profit flows in the future. The inflows may need some form of manipulation. The usefulness of these methods will need to be understood. More importantly, you may also need to suggest which of the methods is the most useful to the particular firm in the question, given its legal status, size and objectives.

Costing and break even

Most costing questions will start with financial calculations from given data. This could take the form of calculating contribution, break even levels of output, profit levels or costing allocation. This could be accompanied by some short definitions. For longer questions, a break even chart may be required.

You might also be asked to advise an interested party, based on the data. Common areas for advice tend to focus on deciding whether to close down an unprofitable section of the business (product or branch, etc.), or changing one of the cost or revenue variables, such as a change in the selling price. Limitations of the financial data may be considered here, such as problems with using costing methods. Accepting special orders at below cost price could be tested, to see if you understand the difference between the different costing methods and their overall effect on the financial decision.

The later parts of these questions will often focus on the wider issues involved. This may look at the negative aspects of relocation decisions, such as the effect on local communities. Alternatively, they may focus on the human aspect of a decision. It may be profitable to close a particular factory, but not necessarily desirable in terms of its impact on society or the corporate image.

Index

accounting
  financial **8**, 8, 9
  international standards 15
  management **8**, 8–9
  objectivity 17
  policy changes 12
  regulation 10–11
  subjectivity 17
accounting concepts
  business entity 11, *18*
  consistency 12, *18*
  going concerns 11, *18*
  historical costs 12, *18*
  matching concept 12, *18*
  prudence 12, *18*
Accounting Standards Board [ASB] 10, 11, 13, 49
acid test ratio 40, 76, 77, *91*
amortisation 35, 36, 39
asset structures
  balance sheets 27–8, 40–41
  external factors 29–30
  finance industry 29
  internal factors 29
  retailers 29
  service industries 28
asset turnover ratio 72, 74–75, *91*
assets
  see also fixed assets; intangible assets; stock
  current holdings 77
  debtors 34
  depreciation 34
  finite life 35
  stock valuation 33–4
auditors 8
average rate of return [ARR] 145, 146, **146**, 148, 149, *154*

balance sheets **25**
  asset structures 27–8
  borrowing 40
  business value 41–2
  capital expenditure 53, **53**
  changes to 30
  company accounts 27
  performance indicators 56–7
  retained profit reserves 40
  strong 40–42, 43
  trends 41
  working capital 40
Bank of England
  Base Rate **106**

  Monetary Policy Committee 13
bankruptcy 101, **101**, 102
book value
  assets 41
  businesses 41, **41**
  low 46
borrowing
  economies of scale 109
  gearing ratios 40, 79–80
  risks 80–81
brand names, valuation 38–9, 55
break even
  cost prices 127–8
  output **123**, 126–7
break even analysis
  charts *125*, 126
  decision-making 123, 125–6
  fixed costs 124
  simple 126
budgeting *114*
  alternatives to 111
  departmental 110
  efficiency gains 110–11
  flexible 112–13, **113**
  levels 113
  motivation by 110
  varience analysis 112–13, *114*
budgets **109**
  master 109
business entity 11, *18*
buying in 130

capital expenditure 53, **53**
  see also depreciation
  budgeting 112
  cash flow 105
cash
  balances 77, 109
  and profit 101–3
  shortages 101, 102
cash flow
  capital expenditure 105
  forecasts 104–6, *114*
  importance 101, 103
  increased output 13
  interest rates 13
  late payments 107
  management 104, *114*
  overtrading 104
  price cuts 13
  problems 106–9, *114*
  production periods 103–4

profits 47
small firms 108–9
trading on credit 104
Companies Act [1989] 25
company accounts
see also balance sheets; profit and loss accounts
availablity 8
directors' reports 26
external users 9–10, *18*, 26–7
formats 25–6
interest range 9–10
internal users 9–10, *18*
notes 26
objectivity 10
published 25–7, 56–7
regulations 10–12
subjectivity 10
'window-dressing' 11, 26, 54–6
company annual reports
see also balance sheets; profit and loss accounts
business practice 171
risk management 171–2, *172*
social accounting 170, *172*
staff motivation 171
complementary products 138–9, **138**
consistency, accounting 12, *18*
contribution **123**
negative 137–8
contribution costing 131, **132**, 136–7
cost centres **131**
costing methods
contribution 131
full 131–2, **132**
multi-product 131
single products 131
costs **46**
direct **132**, 139
fixed **123**
indirect 132–5, **132**, 139
sunk 151
variable **123**, 125, 127
credit cards 76–7
creditor days 72, 74
current ratio 40, 76, *91*

data reliability
capital investment appraisal 150
financial analysis 15
ratio analysis 88–9
debt factoring **74**, 108, *114*
debtor days 72, 73–4, *91*
debtors 34, 74, 77, 106, 107–8, *114*
debts
bad 34, 107–8, **108**, *114*
interest on 107
decision-making
break even analysis 123
capital investment 145–7
intuitive 145
performance control 45
ratio analysis 66

using accounting 8, 15, 17
depreciation
amortisation 35, 36
fixed assets 12, 34
low 35
matching 35
policies 36–7, 54, *58*
profit and loss account 35
reducing balance method 36
straight line method 36, 37
usage method 36
direct costs **132**, 139
directors' reports 26
discounting **146**, 148
dividends
cover 83
per share [DPS] 83, 84, *91*
policy 84
yield 83, 85, *91*

earnings per share [EPS] 83, 84, *91*
economic value added [EVA] 168
efficiency ratios 67, *91*
asset turnover 72, 74–75, *91*
creditor days 72, 74, *91*
debtor days 72, 73–4, *91*
stock days 72
stock turnover 72, 73, *91*
ethical policies 16, 52
examination questions, marking 2–4
examination skills 180–84
analysis 4–5
evaluation 6–7
identification 2
synthesis 5
external environments, company performance 13,
45
extraordinary items 55

financial accounting 8, **8**, 16
financial planning
cash flow forecsts 104–6
management accounting 8
Financial Reporting Standards [FRSs] 11, 38
fixed assets *159*
depreciation 12, 34
finite life of 17, 35
investment levels 30, 102
manufacturers 29
sale and leaseback 54, *58*, 106, *114*
fixed costs **123**, 124
flexible budgeting 112–13, **113**
forecasting
accuracy 154
cash flow 104–6
financial accounting 16
management accounting 16
full costing 131–2, **132**, 136

gearing ratios 40, 67, 79, *91*
high 79–80, 84

interest cover 79, *91*
   taxation 80
going concerns 11, *18*
goodwill 37–8, **37**, 55
gross profits **47**

indirect costs [overheads] **132**
   allocation 132–5, 139
insolvency 31, 101, **101**
intangible assets 12, **37**, *58, 159*
   brand names 38–9, 55
   goodwill 37–8, **37**, 55
   regulations 30
   research and development 39, 42, *159*
interest cover 79, *91*
interest rates 13, 106
investment appraisal
   average rate of return 145, 146, **146**, 148, 149,
     154
   content 151
   data reliability 150
   ethical values 152–3
   funding 153, *154*
   intangible investments 151–2, **152**
   net present value 145, 146–7, **146**, 149, *154*
   payback period 145, 146, **146**, 148, 149, *154*
   public sector 157–9
   risks 154–7
   skills 151
   social issues 153
   sunk costs 151
   workforce 150, 152

just-in-time [JIT] stock management 29, 73, 76

Late Payment of Commercial Debts [Interest] Act
   [1998] 107
liquidity 101, 103, *114*
liquidity ratios 67, *91*
   acid test ratio 76, *91*
   credit cards 76–7
   current ratio 76, *91*
   levels 78, 79
   seasonality 77
   uses of 78

management
   investment appraisal skills 151
   performance control 45
   risks 154–5
   short-termism 156–7
   value of accounting 9, 15, 17
management accounting **8**
   data reliability 15
   decision-making 8, 15
   forecasting 16
   internal usage 9
management buy–outs [MBOs] 79, 80
market research 150
market value
   businesses 41–2, **41**
   declared profits 42

increased 45
market value added [MVA] 169–70
marketing 14
master budgets 109
matching concept 12, *18*

net current assets *see* working capital
net present value [NPV] 145, 146–7, **146**, 149,
   150, *154*
net realisable values 33
non-profit organisations 103

operating profits 43–4, **47**
orders, below cost 127–30
overheads [indirect costs] **132**
   allocation 132–5, 139
overtrading 104, **104**, *114*

payback period 145, 146, **146**, 148, 149, 150,
   154
performance indicators
   balance sheets 56–7
   external factors 52
   internal factors 52
   profits 46, 51–2, 56–7
   ratio analysis 66
price elasticity 127
price/earnings ratio [P/E] 83, 85, 86, *91*
production periods, long 103–4
profit centres **131**
profit and loss accounts **25**, 43–5, 54
   ASA recommendations 49
   depreciation 35
   extraordinary items 55
   as performance indicators 56–7
   revenue expenditure 53, **53**
profit margins 70–71, *91*
   low 72
profitability **68**
   see also unprofitability
profitability ratios 67, *91*
   profit margins 70–71, 72, *91*
profits **46–7**, **68**, **102**
   after tax 44
   boosting 46–7
   cash flow 47, 101–3
   control of 45
   discontinued operations 50–51
   gross **47**
   level of 50
   operating 43–4, **47**
   as performance indicators 46, 51–2, 56–7
   relative 47
   reporting 49–52
   satisfactory 46
   segmental reporting 49
   sustaining 47
   utilisation 48, 54
prudence, anticipation 12, *18*
public sector investment
   cost-benefit analysis 158
   social benefits 158, **158**

social costs 158, **158**

Q ratio 44

ratio analysis
  decision-making 66
  performance indicator 66
ratios
  acid test 40
  controlling factors 87–9
  current 40
  efficiency 67, 72–5, *91*
  gearing 40, 67, 79–81, *91*
  liquidity 67, 75–7, *91*
  other 89
  profitability 67, 68–71, *91*
  Q 44
  return on capital employed 68–9
  shareholders' 67, 82–7, *91*
  users 67, 88, 89
research and development [R&D] 39, 42, 53
retained profit reserves 40, 48
return on capital employed [ROCE] 68–9
increasing 69
low 70, 72
measuring 68, 69
sales 71
return on equity [ROE] 83–4, *91*
revenue expenditure 53, **53**
risk assessment 80–81, 154–55

sale and leaseback 54, *58*, 106, *114*
sales
  credit 102
  forward 54, *58*
  interest rates 13
  profit margins 70–71
  revenue **123**
sales revenue, increased 48
segmental analysis 49, 54
segmental reporting 49, 52
semi-variable expenses 126
shareholder ratios 67, 82–3, *91*
  dividend cover 83
  dividend yield 83, 85, *91*
  dividends per share 83, 84, *91*
  earnings per share 83, 84, *91*
  price/earnings ratio 83, 85, 86, *91*
  return on equity 83–4, *91*
shareholder value
  economic value added 168, *172*
  market value added 169–70, *172*
small firms
  borrowing 108–9
  cash flow 108–9
social benefits 158, **158**

social costs 158, **158**
social policies 16, 52, 158, *172*
staff motivation 14, 171
stakeholders **8**, 16
Statements of Standard Accounting Practice
  [SSAPs] 11
stock
  days 72
  just-in-time 29, 73, 76
  lean production 29
  manufacturers 29
  turnover 72, 73, 74, 77, *91*
  valuation 33–4, **34**
sunk costs 151

takeovers 85
trends *see* forecasting
turnover **46**, 72, 73, 74

unprofitability 136–9

valuation
  Average Cost [AVCO] 34
  book 41, **41**
  brand names 38–9
  First In First Out [FIFO] 34
  goodwill 37–8
  Last In First Out [LIFO] 34
  market 41–2, **41**
  research and development 39, 42
variable costs **123**, 125, 127
variance analysis
  budgeting 112–13, *114*
  labour costs 113, *114*
  material costs 113, *114*
variances
  adverse **113**
  favourable **113**

'window-dressing'
  capitalising expenditure 55, *58*
  company accounts 11, 26
  depreciation policies 54, *58*
  extraordinary items 55
  forward sales 54, *58*
  intangible assets 55, *58*
  reasons for 55–6, *58*
  regulations 56
  sale and leaseback 54, *58*
working capital **31**
  acid test ratios 40
  current ratio 40
  increasing 33
  liquidity 31
  positive 40